The Ecology of Educational Systems

Data, Models, and Tools for Improvisational Leading and Learning

Bruce D. Baker
University of Kansas

Craig E. Richards
Teachers College, Columbia University

PEARSON

Merrill
Prentice Hall

Upper Saddle River, New Jersey
Columbus, Ohio

Library of Congress Cataloging-in-Publication Data

Baker, Bruce D.
   The ecology of educational systems: data, models, and tools for
improvisational leading and learning / Bruce D. Baker, Craig E.
Richards.
       p. cm.
Includes bibliographical references and index.
   ISBN 0-13-097771-3
   1. School management and organization—United States—Data processing.
2. Education—United States—Data processing—Management.   3.
Educational change—United States.   I. Richards, Craig E.   II. Title.
   LB2806.17.B35 2004
   371.2—dc22

                                                        2003021929

Vice President and Executive Publisher: Jeffery W. Johnston
Executive Editor: Debra A. Stollenwerk
Editorial Assistant: Mary Morrill
Production Editor: Mary Harlan
Production Coordination: Penny Walker, *The GTS Companies*/York, PA Campus
Design Coordinator: Diane C. Lorenzo
Cover Image: Getty
Cover Design: Bryan Huber
Text Design and Illustrations: *The GTS Companies*/York, PA Campus
Production Manager: Susan Hannahs
Director of Marketing: Ann Castel Davis
Marketing Manager: Darcy Betts Prybella
Marketing Coordinator: Tyra Poole

This book was set in Goudy by *The GTS Companies*/York, PA Campus. It was printed and bound
by R. R. Donnelley & Sons Company. The cover was printed by The Lehigh Press, Inc.

Pearson Education Ltd.   Pearson Education Australia Pty. Limited
Pearson Education Singapore Pte. Ltd.   Pearson Education North Asia Ltd.
Pearson Education Canada, Ltd.   Pearson Educación de Mexico, S.A. de C.V.
Pearson Education—Japan   Pearson Education Malaysia Pte. Ltd.

10 9 8 7 6 5 4 3 2 1
ISBN: 0-13-097771-3

Preface

ORIGINS OF THIS BOOK

We began conceptualizing this text around 1995, with the original intent of writing a follow-up to Craig Richards's 1987 book *Microcomputer Applications for Strategic Management in Education*. In the early stages, we began to realize not only how much the microcomputer tools of leadership had changed, but also the extent to which the general context for school leadership and the concept of leading complex dynamic organizations had changed.

Since 1995, an explosion of available electronic information and a proliferation of relatively inexpensive technologies for accessing, analyzing, and presenting data have occurred. Numerous books have been introduced that attempt to teach school leaders simple techniques of data analysis and presentation using available technologies such as spreadsheet, database, and statistical analysis software.

Although we believe it important that individuals have the opportunity to develop these skills, we believe it equally important to provide a *mental model* and *disciplined approach* for using such tools. The mental model we present is the Ecological Model of Leading and Learning. Our use of *ecological* is not to be confused with a literal definition of "environmental studies," but it is to be seen as a way of understanding schools and school systems as complex, interconnected ecological systems.

Our disciplined approach is *collaborative improvisation*. Whether jazz improvisation such as that performed by the small acoustic ensembles of the 1940s on 52nd Street in New York or baroque improvisation as performed by the great organ masters of the early 1700s, one element is critical to mastery of the art—practice. The great improvisers practiced for hours on end—decomposing music; learning to physically and musically perform a plethora of patterns, sequences, and tones; then recomposing and improvising with their newly expanded vocabulary.

Through the exercises in this book, we hope to provide students with comparable opportunities to practice decomposing and deconstructing data on schooling systems. Further, we hope that students may develop a sufficient analytic vocabulary to begin to recompose, reconstruct, and improvise with their new tools.

ORGANIZATION OF THE BOOK

This book is organized into six parts:

- ◆ *Part I—Setting the Stage:* Part I provides an introduction to the ecological model and the improvisational approach. In chapter 2 we provide students with a tool—the *policy options brief*—for organizing and distributing information on their organization.
- ◆ *Part II—Using Data to Describe the Schooling Context:* In Part II we introduce the student to a series of analytic tools in Microsoft Excel for organizing and presenting descriptive analyses of data. Each chapter concludes with a narrowly focused data set and a series of questions to be addressed with the data. This part concludes with a more comprehensive data set on international investment in education and student outcomes. Students are encouraged to write a policy brief on their findings from the data.
- ◆ *Part III—Searching for Relationships in Education Data:* The third part introduces the student to more advanced analytic tools in Microsoft Excel. The primary emphasis is studying relationships between variables. Tools include group comparisons, scatterplots with trend-line analysis, and bivariate and multivariate regression analysis. The end of each chapter contains a narrowly focused problem set that applies the tools presented in the chapter to data ranging from student test scores across classes to state-level data on school funding and student outcomes. At the end of part III, we provide a complex and more comprehensive data set including various school resource measures and student outcomes measures. Students are provided guidance on the process of preparing analyses for a policy brief on relationships in data.
- ◆ *Part IV—Measuring Time and Change in Schools:* This part introduces students to the analysis of change across time. Chapter 9 addresses conceptual issues involved in studying change across time; working with time-series data, including event analysis; and understanding short- and long-run cycles. Chapters 10 and 11 address more technical issues of calculating change rates and forecasting, and a special section on financial analysis, including amortization and present and future value functions. Part IV concludes with a simulation of various demographic, economic, and financial changes occurring across time in Mission Valley Springs Unified School District. Students are encouraged to write policy briefs in which they identify important changes in the district's internal and external environment, including emergent fiscal stresses.
- ◆ *Part V—System Dynamics of Schooling:* This part introduces system dynamics as an interconnected and dynamic framework for analyzing schools and school systems. Chapter 12 provides a transition from data-driven analysis to model-driven analysis. The example of student enrollment forecasting is used to show students how to transition from the spreadsheet approach of cohort survival forecasting presented in part IV to conceptualizing and eventually simulating enrollment changes across time as a series of interconnected *stocks* of students in grade levels and *flows* of students from grade to grade. Chapter 13 integrates systems modeling techniques with systems thinking concepts, including feedback loops and classic archetypes of organizational behavior such as those discussed by Senge (1990) in *The Fifth Discipline.* Downloadable system dynamic models of the archetypes are available on the book Web site.

Part V concludes with a series of more complex, comprehensive case analyses, ranging from the unintended consequences of class size reduction in California to achieving fiscal parity in New Jersey.

♦ *Part VI—Pulling It All Together:* The book provides an opportunity for synthesis with part VI. This part guides the student through a comprehensive, ecological analysis of his or her organization by using the various data and model-driven strategies presented throughout the text.

USE OF THIS BOOK IN A COURSE

For the past few years, this book has been piloted in a course titled Analysis of Administrative Problems at the University of Kansas, Lawrence and Overland Park, and in The Ecology of Data-Driven Leadership at Teachers College, Columbia University. We realize that too many data and problem sets are included in this book for you to have your students use them all for preparing full-blown policy briefs. Both of us (the authors) use chapter problem sets as lab activities to familiarize students with ways to apply the various tools to the given data and to practice going through the developmental process of preparing a data-driven policy analysis. Students then choose two of the three available part simulations (Simulations II, III, and IV), for which they prepare comprehensive policy analyses and briefs.

A note of caution: The first go-round on any such activity can be a demanding and even somewhat frustrating process because students are applying new analytic methods, sometimes using new technology and preparing documents in a novel format and writing style. However, our experience has been that, despite having initial difficulties with a steep learning curve, students rapidly grow and develop skills as they progress through the activities.

THE COMPANION WEBSITE

The Companion Website that accompanies this book is central to accomplishing your teaching objectives. In fact, think of the Companion Website as the primary instructional resource and the book as a guiding handbook. If one objective is to develop and refine analytical skills, students must practice these skills over and over. The Companion Website and book offer a practice data set and problem for each chapter of sections II through V, as well as simulations at the end of sections II, III, and IV. Students can readily access data, models, and documentation for all these chapter problem sets and section simulations on the Companion Website at http://www.prenhall.com/baker.

Diverse types of data and problems are presented. Data range from the classroom level to the international level, and from student performance data to financial, demographic, and economic data. Many of the data are derived from actual situations, including student performance and economic data on 13 countries from the Organization for Economic Cooperation and Development (OECD), and elementary and high school data published annually by the state of Vermont. Additional data sets can be downloaded from the *Data and Models Support* link on the Companion Website.

ACKNOWLEDGMENTS

I would like to thank the staff at High Performance Systems, Inc., of Lebanon, New Hampshire, for providing guidance and sample models in our early learning stages with ithink. I am also grateful to the master's degree students in Educational Administration at the University of Kansas who endured earlier drafts of this book and provided useful feedback. The faculty at the University of Kansas were also supportive, especially Jim Ellis, who made use of earlier drafts of the book and on more than one occasion gave me confidence that this project was worthwhile. I dedicate this book to Michelle, Gregory, and Ella.

B. B.

This book took more years to write than any author could imagine. It was rescued from obscurity by my colleague and coauthor Bruce Baker. To him I owe first thanks. My many other intellectual debts are too numerous to be inclusive, but several require acknowledgment by name. To Don Sweet, philosopher par excellence, who first taught me to test presuppositions; to Hank Levin, who modeled clear writing and thinking; and to John Dewey, who taught me that thinking dialectically was pragmatic, I offer my sincere thanks.

I also owe a deep debt of thanks to the individuals who have supported me emotionally and spiritually during some difficult years. I am especially indebted to David Pomerantz, who has been a living exemplar of the daily practice of compassion, wisdom, and insight and the one who taught me best to find these in silence. To my son, Michael, I owe the gift of joy, and to my wife, Elle, I owe the gift of love. Without them, I would not have had the strength or will to continue with this work.

My students at Teachers College during the past 15 years have been everything a teacher could hope for. I have learned so much from them. To each and every one, I thank you for allowing me to experiment on you with countless versions of this book. Finally, a special thanks to Kari Kaefer, my teaching assistant, who volunteered to undertake the prodigious task of editing this book. To those of you whom I have neglected to thank by name, please accept my apologies. I know full well that this vineyard was well tended by many hands, and its fruit belongs to them all.

C. R.

We both also thank the reviewers of this book: Mark Ankeny, George Fox University; R. Wilburn Clouse, Vanderbilt University; A. Reynaldo Contreras, San Francisco State University; Charles E. Kline, Purdue University; and Kathy Peca, Eastern New Mexico University.

Finally, we would like to acknowledge the superb copyediting of Kathy Riley-King. She was a great addition to the team effort required to produce this book.

Bruce Baker and Craig Richards
Lawrence, Kansas, and New York, New York

Brief Contents

Contents

Note: Every effort has been made to provide accurate and current Internet information in this book. However, the Internet and information posted on it are constantly changing, so it is inevitable that some of the Internet addresses listed in this textbook will change.

Part I
Setting the Stage

This part of the book begins with the Introduction, in which the underlying theory of ecological modeling is discussed. We then move on to an overview of the organization of the book. The Data and Models Web site that accompanies this book is also introduced, and its equal importance with the text is discussed. Finally, we describe the use of this book in a course. The topic of chapter 1 is the need for a new approach to educational leadership. First, the historical approaches are described, then the new paradigm is introduced. Three types of management perspectives and the principles of ecological systems are also covered. We end this chapter with a section on ecological thinking about leadership. The goal of chapter 2 is to show you how you can learn to write a good policy brief so that you can monitor your system and audit its ecological aspects. We begin by discussing the objectives of a policy brief, the universal rules for preparing policy briefs, and the structure and universal elements of such briefs. We then outline the specific features of the three basic types of policy briefs and end with a section on policy presentation guidelines.

Introduction

In this book, *The Ecology of Educational Systems: Data, Models, and Tools for Improvisational Leading and Learning,* we take as a given that school boards and administrators, teachers, parents, and children can all be leaders and are all lifelong learners (and should be given many opportunities to do both). The word *ecology* is an important term for us. We firmly believe that school systems at all levels are living systems, which makes them necessarily ecological systems. The world ecology movement has made us acutely aware of the many environmental crises that will confront us in the 21st century, from global warming to the mass extinction of species. Yet, what is closest to us in nature is our children. Schools can be profoundly beneficial environments within which children can develop physically, emotionally, intellectually, ethically, and spiritually. Our goal is to provide models, tools, and case studies through which you can learn and lead more effectively.

In 1987, coauthor Craig Richards wrote *Microcomputer Applications for Strategic Management in Education.* Even 10 years later, the book received acknowledgment for being ahead of its time (see Jacobson in Bromley & Jacobson, 1998). Our first intent for creating this text was to develop an update of that book, but we soon agreed that we needed to undertake a more ambitious project. Much has happened since the late 1980s in terms of the development of technology. Educational data are also much more widely available and in many cases can be directly downloaded from Web sites supported by state departments of education. Although the data explosion has opened the door to closer scrutiny from outside observers, the availability of such data can also substantially empower educational leaders.

Simultaneous to our advancement as a technology- and information-driven society has been a paradigm shift with respect to organizational leadership. With the publication of such works as *The Fifth Discipline,* by Peter Senge (1990), the way in which we view not only organizations, their complexity, and their dynamics, but also our role as organizational leaders, has changed. In a relatively short period, we have made dramatic philosophical leaps from strategic analysis and planning toward systems thinking and learning organizations, and ultimately (we hope) to ecological thinking about organizations and their environment. Information is more abundant, technology more advanced and more widely available, and our understanding of organizational dynamics more highly evolved than in the 1990s. Nevertheless, the state of data and technology use in education, as well as our approaches to management in education, still lags available data-mining technology and the modeling of organizational change in living systems used in other fields of study.

In this book, we merge new philosophies of organizational management with the development of skills for strategic analysis. Though perhaps novel in the field of education, this merger has been a part of management training at schools such as the Sloan School of Management at Massachusetts Institute of Technology (MIT) for some years under course titles such as Data, Models, and Decisions. These teachings have been brought into the realm of public policy analysis by leaders of the systems thinking movement, including George P. Richardson, winner of the 1992 Jay W. Forrester Award (for advancements in systems theory) for his 1992 book *Feedback Thought in Social Science and Systems Theory.* Richardson, a graduate of Sloan, went on to develop courses and data- and model-driven decision making for public policy makers at the Rockefeller School for Public Policy in Albany, New York.

In the majority of this book, we emphasize the development of technical and analytic skills. Yet, our desire is to develop these skills as a tool kit for use within a new mental model of school leadership, an *ecological model* of leading and learning. Our use of *ecological* is not to be confused with a literal definition of "environmental studies," but it is to be seen as a way of understanding schools and school systems as complex, interconnected ecological systems—of which water and air quality are an important aspect. In particular, we argue that the physical, emotional, intellectual, ethical, and spiritual environments are equally important to the development of the whole child. We expect at times that the blending of some of the technical tools presented and the ecological paradigm may seem to clash. Grasping how seemingly reductionist analytic methods can ultimately lead us toward a more global understanding of our ecological system can be difficult. Simultaneously acquiring analytic skills and developing new mental models is a complex task that requires substantial practice and, we expect, will come much more quickly to some individuals than to others. A useful approach may be to think of these steps as the rungs of a ladder used to get to the rooftop. Once on the roof, a person is free to let go of the ladder.

Without going into too great of detail on the underlying theory of ecological modeling, we provide you with an analogy to our goals in this book. The end goal is jazz: a collaborative improvisation, making use, through creative application, of the technical skills you develop by working through the exercises herein. The tools (computer, spreadsheet, etc.) or skills (statistical analyses, models) in isolation have little meaning. For example, consider the molded brass that composes a saxophone, and the shaved bamboo reed. Although visually appealing, even the finest saxophones produced by Henri Selmer of Paris do not, alone, produce great jazz. Aspiring jazz musicians spend a great deal of time learning patterns, scales, and phrases (applied to their particular tool) to develop an extensive vocabulary with which they may ultimately learn to improvise.

Yet, truly artistic jazz improvisation is more than just a string of these notes, patterns, or scales superimposed over a set of chord changes. The true virtuoso takes the notes and patterns and creates melodic direction—music—with them, a music that transcends the sum of its parts: the brass and bamboo (tools); the notes, phrases, and patterns (skills). However, perhaps most intriguing is what happens when a group of true jazz virtuosos come together to perform tunes that are a part of each person's standard vocabulary. In the best of situations, the music becomes entirely interactive among its participants and even their audience. Each musician plays off the ideas and actions of the others, as well as the involvement and excitement of the audience, constructing yet another level of the music that transcends the sum of its components, the individual musicians, their skills, and their tools.

Participating in *collaborative improvisation* in the context of policy analysis starts with learning the skills of data analysis and model building through *iteration*—that is, practice. Practice is the core of what we can provide you with this book. Then, you must learn to apply these skills and tools thoughtfully, and artistically, to develop a deeper understanding of your organization. Through collaborative efforts with your immediate peers and with various constituents of your organization, you may create an environment in which valuable information flows freely and feedback among the participants stimulates continued growth of the organization. Such an environment is the essence of a learning organization that is ecologically self-aware.

The Ecology of Educational Systems is both a textbook for graduate students studying educational policy and leadership and a handbook for practicing policy makers and school leaders. We believe that the philosophies espoused and the analytic skills presented in this book effectively bridge multiple levels of organizational understanding and do so in a way that, until now, has been unavailable to educational leaders.

CONTINUATION OF A NOVEL APPROACH

Many educators express the fear that use of technology isolates learners and reduces interaction (Bromley & Jacobson, 1998, p. 144), which is contrary to the modern trends of leadership through teaming and group problem solving and decision making. Richards's first book presented a novel approach to integrating data, technology, strategic analysis, and policy making. His approach was to involve students, administrators, or policy makers in teams around analyzing real policy problems. The goal was for teams to prepare and present policy options briefs based on their analysis of the given situation. Similarly, much of George Richardson and David Andersen's (1995) research promotes the value of teaming and the identification of team roles for constructing dynamic systems models of public policy problems. The activities in this book continue in this tradition and are designed for use as group problem-solving activities. The objective of many of the activities is to prepare a policy options brief (discussed in more detail in chapter 2) based on the analyses performed or models constructed.

ORGANIZATION OF THIS BOOK

Overview: General Scope and Sequence

One difficulty in designing and sequencing this book was determining where to draw the arbitrary limits on what we could and could not cover in this limited amount of space, and what might or might not be integrated into a single-semester course. What we tried to do is give you enough of a "repertoire" of the various types of tools that can be used for strategic analysis and enough practice with various approaches to problem solving to send you on your way toward further expanding your personal tool kit.

In parts II through IV of this book, we use Microsoft Excel as the central technology for strategic analysis. Many individuals may have been exposed to Excel as a tool for basic data management and for performing relatively basic mathematical functions on data—including summing, averaging, or plotting and graphing data—and we understand that many readers have gone several steps further. A typical spreadsheet activity might involve setting up a grade book, a checkbook ledger, or a budget balance sheet. We purposely bypass such endeavors in an effort to move on to more relevant analyses. However, if you are unfamiliar with Microsoft Excel, we recommend that you try these activities. You may also want to acquire a separate introductory resource such as Harvey's (2003) *Excel 2003 for Dummies* (take no offense; that is Harvey's title, not ours) to help you get started.

In education, throughout training in research methods, policy analysts are often pushed toward more costly, more complex statistical analysis software, including SPSS (Statistical Package for the Social Sciences) or SAS (Statistical Analysis System), for performing statistical analyses, such as comparing reading scores for two groups of students. Although we intend no offense to the developers of these software applications, in general, policy analysts do not need them. Most, if not all, necessary statistical analyses, including multiple linear regression, can be performed in Excel. In addition, Excel allows you to perform special financial functions and analyses (see special section in chapter 10) that are not generally available in statistical software. With Excel, you may store, organize, manipulate, and statistically analyze your data all within one setting and in one format, a format that is fully compatible across the PC and Macintosh formats. Likewise, spreadsheet software like Excel (perhaps Lotus or Quattro Pro) is usually available as a standard on any workstation in a business environment, whereas this may not be the case for specialized statistical software.

In part V, we introduce one alternative software package, ithink 6.0, for strategic analysis. We chose ithink because it allows the analyst the opportunity to study organizational processes by constructing models of the processes and running simulations. This unique software was recently adopted—through a collaborative arrangement between High Performance Systems, Inc., of Lebanon, New Hampshire, and Harvard Business School Publishing—as the primary vehicle for constructing business simulations. To use a catch-phrase of the software developer, we contend that ithink will allow us to take you to the "next step" toward actualizing the leadership philosophies of Senge and Richardson because ithink allows us to construct and "play with" dynamic systems models.

Part Synopses

Part I: Setting the Stage

In chapter 1, we attempt to develop the mind-set underlying ecological management and delineate this new approach from strategic management and its precursor, systems thinking. It is crucial that you maintain a broad, ecological perspective as you work your way through the data-driven activities of the parts that follow, such that your mind does not become too focused on the trivial. Doing so is easier than it sounds. However, if you can learn to use seemingly narrow data, as well as limited tools to monitor and characterize your exceedingly complex surroundings, you will have made substantive progress toward organizational learning. Internalizing the ecological perspective will reduce the risk of misusing data: taking a mechanical or linear view of your system and its context. Without a deep and perhaps even intuitive understanding of feedback systems, you will have difficulty applying leverage to promote positive change. We expect that these concepts will become clearer as you progress through and beyond chapter 1.

In chapter 2, we provide multiple perspectives on preparing one of the most useful documents for strategic management: the policy options brief. As policy analysts, we perform policy analyses so that we can assess the health of our system as it stands and put forth policy options as to what actions we might take in the near or distant future. In this chapter, a framework is provided for presenting these analyses and setting forth the options. Three frameworks that represent the developmental stages of the activities in this book are provided. Initial activities in parts II through IV are data driven and broad in the amount of information, but narrow in the type of information available. Thus, the first framework is for preparing the *data-driven policy brief*. This brief is primarily analytic, with limited possibilities for presenting detailed options. Second, the *model-driven policy brief* focuses on conceptual development of a model of a policy issue and the behavior of the model under varied scenarios. The objective is to test plausible policy options so that we somewhat shift the emphasis of the policy brief from analysis of symptoms represented by data to analysis of underlying processes and proposals for change.

Finally, the *ecological policy brief* is a merger of all our tools under the umbrella of ecological thinking. Unfortunately, the ecological policy brief cannot be practiced with contrived activities such as those provided herein. It requires the full contextual richness of a real-world situation. Thus, although the ecological brief cannot be prepared as a culminating activity to the simulations herein, we propose it as the primary tool for use in your real-world environment. (The final project in our classes typically requires a group policy options brief on a real school problem.)

Part II: Using Data to Describe the Schooling Context

Our objective in part II is to get you started with some basic analytic tools in Microsoft Excel. Conceptually, your goal is to find ways to use data to monitor the health of your system, to create meaningful indexes that represent features of your system, and to create descriptive profiles of your system. To some extent, this part is a random mix of examples and practice activities intended to familiarize you with the way in which data are and can be organized and analyzed in a spreadsheet. Attention is also given to what data are, where data come from, and what they mean. One aspect that makes this book distinctly different from others is that we frequently shift back and forth among, and integrate our use of, financial data, demographic data, and student performance data.

In chapter 3, we focus on data and units, with the goal of understanding how to make "apples-to-apples" comparisons. We look at the relevance of per-pupil comparisons of financial data versus total spending figures and present a cursory view of how to look at data across time. In chapter 4, we discuss the concept of efficiency indexes. Raw data can be overwhelming. An efficient way to combine numbers is by using ratios or shares (another form of ratio) to create single numbers that give you a better picture of how well the system is working. The focus of chapter 4 is on the design and development of such indexes and approaches to making indexes meaningful. In chapter 5, we introduce some basic descriptive statistical tools for profiling your system. However, we emphasize that this book by no means provides a full course on probability theory or statistics, nor do we believe that such background is necessary to accomplish the goals we have set.

Part III: Searching for Relationships in Education Data

In part III, we focus on what we refer to as *system linkages*. We could have easily chosen to title part II *Descriptive Statistics* and to title part III *Inferential Statistics*, as would be common in the pedagogy of research methods. Yet, in the practice of educational leadership, especially ecological leadership, we use these tools for different purposes. First, your objective is not to deductively test whether a given system statistically conforms to some espoused theoretical construct, but to use a variety of data-analytic frameworks to inductively study the features of the system. Your goal is simply to better understand how the system is working by assessing symptoms and underlying processes. Second, we are constantly "messing" with the system: We are less interested in proving a theory than in improving the school.

What, then, do we mean by *system linkages? System linkages* are measured by the relationships among data—the various measures and various types—that are produced by the underlying processes of a system.

These relationships can be as simple as differences in group mean scores resulting from different instructional practices, as addressed in chapter 6, or can be as complex as studying the various correlations among socioeconomic variables, access to resources, and student performance across many schools, as discussed in chapters 7 and 8. Causal inference from relationship, or linkage, analysis can be a sensitive, and even dangerous, subject. We address relevant cautions and appropriate use of causal inference in chapter 8. We also introduce the idea that perhaps not all linkages in a system conform to the usual expectation promoted in traditional statistical analysis. That is, many educational variables neither are independent nor follow a linear relationship.

Part IV: Measuring Time and Change in Schools

System dynamics continue to be overlooked in educational research and in educational management. Although we have become adept at determining how one school differs from another, our skills and tools for understanding how organizations change with time have lagged. In general, our primary objective in policy analysis is to seek options to promote change. Although understanding differences across organizations is valuable, doing so provides us little direct knowledge of how to effect change. In addition, such analyses often mislead: We presume that the current conditions, the indicator readings at the present moment, are stable. This assumption can be ill founded during strategic planning. Conditions are as often getting better or getting worse as they are staying the same.

In chapter 9, we present a broad, conceptual overview of methods for studying data across time and using these data to tell a story of the behavior of the system producing the data across time. In chapter 10, we delve into some basic mathematical methods for studying change across time. The critical issue we explore is that change is synonymous with *time*, the denominator of all basic kinematics equations but so often ignored in analysis of educational data. At the end of chapter 10, we also include a special section on financial tools available in Excel for projecting future costs and values. In chapter 11, we present a few basic approaches to extrapolation, or forecasting, in an effort to extend your skill base from strategic analysis to the use of strategic planning tools.

Part V: System Dynamics of Schooling

In part V, we take the "next step." By this point, we have spent a great deal of time assessing the data generated by the underlying processes that compose the complex system in which we work. The objective of this part is to introduce the tools for constructing both theoretical and practical models of the most critical processes. The tool kit we use, as previously mentioned, is ithink 6.0, developed by High Performance Systems, Inc., of Lebanon, New Hampshire.

In chapter 12, we make the transition from data and matrices to process models by deconstructing and reconstructing a common educational management problem—analyzing the interaction among enrollment, staffing, and instructional costs with time. Although the matrix method of enrollment forecasting is presented in part IV, in chapter 12 we sequentially build the process model, subsequently linking the process model of enrollment flow to personnel demands and ultimately to costs. In chapter 13, we begin to integrate our process-modeling skills with systems thinking and systems theory. We present an overview of the concepts of balancing and reinforcing feedback by using school-based examples and ithink models. In chapter 14, we expand our models beyond simple, single feedback loops into more complex theoretical and practical models of educational problems. In chapter 14, we present relatively complex cases that range from The Simultaneity of Language and Knowledge Acquisition of LEP Students in New York City Schools to Converging Toward Compliance: *Abbott v. Burke* and New Jersey School Finance.

Part VI: Pulling It All Together

In chapter 15, we take the final leap toward applying the various analytic tools and frameworks in ecological analysis of real-world situations. No contrived cases are used in this part. The objective of chapter 15 is by no means to provide a rigid framework for performing ecological analysis or preparing the ecological brief. Instead, the objective is to provide one example of how ecological analyses can be performed and to provide a guided process for you to use to practice structured improvisation on your institution.

DATA AND MODELS WEB SITE

Rationale

Our material can be considered either a book with a Web site or a Web site with a book. Too often, materials that accompany textbooks are seen as merely peripheral or supplementary activity. In contrast, the Web site that accompanies this book is central to accomplishing the objectives of this book. If the goal is to develop and refine analytic skills, you must practice these skills repeatedly to prepare for your real-life situation. Some of the analyses you perform with the data or models on the Web site may turn out poorly, whereas others may be impressive. You may struggle to find the best ways to explain difficult mathematical concepts that reflect the future of your organization. Now, on the practice field, is the time to go through such struggles. The development and refinement of your skills in strategic analysis is a continuous process. This process, under the best of conditions, involves embedded reinforcing feedback loops among you, the book and the Web site, and external reviewers of your policy briefs. Ideally, this feedback loop will continue well after you work your way through this product. We hope that both the book and the Web site will be of reference to you in the future.

Web Site Contents

You will encounter a diversity of data and problems in this book. Data range from the classroom level to the international level and bridge student performance data to financial, demographic, and economic data. The emphasis is that simple, commonsense standards and universal tools can be used to analyze any type of data. Many of the data are derived from actual situations, including student performance and economic data on 16 countries from the Organization for Economic Cooperation and Development (OECD), and elementary and high school data published annually by the state of Vermont. By the time you complete the activities in this book, you will never again be intimidated by data, technology, or a combination of the two.

Data, models, and documentation for all chapter problem sets and part simulations are included on the Web site. Again, please consider the Web site to be the primary instructional resource and this book a guiding handbook. The Web site and book contain a practice data set and problem respective to each chapter of parts II through V, and part simulations at the end of parts II, III, and IV. The Data and Models Support link will enable you to download additional data sets.

Use of the Web Site

When you click on a data file, your browser should ask you whether you want to open the file in place or download it to your hard drive. You may choose either option. If you choose to open the file in place, your next steps will depend on which browser you are using. If you are using Microsoft Internet Explorer, the browser should automatically recognize that the Excel spreadsheets (.xls files) should be opened with Excel. If you are using Netscape Navigator, your browser may ask you to select which program to use to open an Excel file. In this case, locate Excel on your hard drive (or C:\ drive) and select it as the appropriate application.

Given the preceding discussion, you will need to have some basic hardware and software to make use of the Web site. The system and software requirements are as follows:

- ◆ Macintosh (system 7.0 or higher) or Windows ('95 or higher) platform
- ◆ Microsoft Internet Explorer or Netscape Navigator (any recent Web browser will do)
- ◆ Microsoft Excel (provided by the user [version 5.0 or higher for Macintosh or Windows (as in Office '95 through Office XP)]).

In addition, you must download or have already installed the following:

- ◆ Adobe Acrobat Reader (to read .pdf documentation files)
- ◆ ithink save-disabled demo (for models in parts IV and V)

Although we attempt to provide substantial step-by-step explanations for addressing the problem sets in this book, we do not assume the book to be a comprehensive guide to using any of the software discussed. Students less familiar with spreadsheet software, or computing in general, may need to seek additional resources.

To take full advantage of this text, you need not purchase ithink, which is a relatively expensive software package. Rather, a free save-disabled demo is available at http://www.hps-inc.com. The free demo will allow you to run and modify models available for download on the Web site for this book. However, you will not be able to save your models or changes to your models in this version. Although we use ithink in this book, similar software packages are available, including Vensim (Ventana Systems, Inc., Harvard, MA) and Powersim (Powersim Software AS, Bergen, Norway). A fully functional version of Vensim—the Vensim Personal Learning Edition (PLE)—is available for downloading at http://www.vensim.com. In part V, we provide some examples of translations of our ithink models to Vensim. We also provide Vensim versions of our models on the book Web site, as well as other updated information as we learn more about additional resources of use to students and teachers.

1

Toward an Ecology
of Leadership

The truth of the matter is that "Other men have laboured and ye are entered into their labours" (John I:38), and this text is not only a reminder of the need for humility, it is also an epitome of the vast evolutionary process into which we organisms are willy-nilly entered.

Bateson (1991, p. 12)

Another approach to educational leadership might seem to be the last thing required in a time of eroding public confidence in which schools appear to be unable to repair the damage to their legitimacy. Yet, after conducting a study of educational administration programs in the United States, the National Policy Board for Educational Administration (hereafter called *the Policy Board*) reported widespread dissatisfaction with both the content and the pedagogy of educational administration degree programs. Specifically, the Policy Board (1993) reported that most educational administration programs "reflect a shopworn theoretical base and fail to recognize changing job requirements. These programs need a serious overhaul" (p. xii).

Among the Policy Board's recommendations were that member institutions should implement changes in their curriculum that would emphasize knowledge and skills in the following four types of major domains:

1. The *functional domains* of leadership, information management, problem analysis, judgment, organizational oversight, implementation, and delegation
2. The *programmatic domains* of the instruction and learning environment, curriculum design, student guidance and development, staff development, measurement and evaluation, and resource allocation
3. The *interpersonal domains* of motivation of others, interpersonal sensitivity, oral and nonoral expression, and written expression
4. The *contextual domains* of philosophical and cultural values, legal and regulatory applications, policy and political influences, and public relations

Many of the recent policy prescriptions for educational reform have indicated that structural change is necessary for any significant improvement. At the same time, the research on the results of educational reform is persistently cautionary (see, for example, Cuban & Tyack, 1993, and Sarason, 1996). If change were easy or even necessarily better than what went before, educational improvement would be trivial to manage. However, one conclusion that has emerged from the literature on reform is that incremental reforms are unlikely to produce solutions to systemic problems and deep structural reforms are exceedingly difficult to implement for political and economic reasons. In this text, we propose a new way of thinking about schools and school leadership because we are convinced that a new way of thinking is required for us to escape the horns of the incremental–restructural dilemma.

The failure of educational theory to meet managers' needs has its parallel in the business sector, where leadership theory has followed the old paradigm with even more rigor. Makridakis (1990) summarized more than 30 management theories since the 1960s that have risen and fallen from favor in business management circles. The most "scientific" of these attempted to predict future organizational outcomes. Predictive power is the de facto norm for the validity of the theory under the old paradigm. However, just because a model of organizational behavior predicts, we are not entitled to conclude that the views we hold about the world correspond to reality. In technical terms, using prediction and control as criteria for verifying belief is an instance of affirming the consequent, a procedure that is not logically justified (Eisner, 1991; Popper, 1959). We like to use the notion of "a useful fiction" to avoid this problem.

Some historical perspective is helpful. Beginning in the 1960s, the discipline of educational administration arose from a strong reaction against an anecdotal approach to leadership development. Prominent scholars in the field at the time argued that only through "management science" could we hope to improve educational institutions (Culbertson, 1988; Griffiths, 1988). This effort to increase the rigor and credibility of leadership studies borrowed heavily from other social science disciplines like sociology, economics, and organizational psychology. Along with the borrowed theory came borrowed methods of research that social scientists adapted from the old scientific paradigm. Its main characteristics were rooted in the work of three giants of early science: Descartes, Newton, and Bacon. Such adaptation led to a misplaced effort to establish predictive validity as the test of leadership effectiveness. The quest for predictive validity in the field of educational leadership has largely failed. No empirical model of leadership has been developed that says that if an educational leader will do things in sequence, he or she will have a successful organization.

We have responded to the Policy Board's recommendations by proposing a model of leadership that is ecological in perspective and derives its theoretical roots from the emerging literature on complex adaptive systems (Holland, 1995; Lewin, 1992; Zohar & Marshall, 1994). As we articulate our perspective, we also explain some of the practical reasons why the old paradigm fails and why the ecological perspective can help us to better understand and lead educating institutions.

The new paradigm in science is often referred to as *systemic*, or *ecological*. Throughout the text, we use the term *complex adaptive system* for the generic case of any system that has the properties we describe subsequently, including ecological systems that are limited to the class of complex adaptive systems that are living systems. The new paradigm is not in opposition to the old but a model of a higher order, much as a three-dimensional world is of a higher order than that of a two-dimensional world. The rules of the three-dimensional world are different from those of the two-dimensional world, as is our perceptual capabilities within it. Understanding the new paradigm is not simply a matter of academic learning. It requires the experience of *metanoia*—a shift of mind and a subsequent shift in perception. Nothing we write will give you this experience, just as nothing a jazz instructor writes will give you the experience of playing jazz. Rather, such a shift results from practice and experience—and ultimately insight. Like our predecessors, we are still borrowing theory and method from science, but in this case we are also borrowing an emerging paradigm.

At least five basic differences distinguish the old paradigm from the new. First, the essential strategy of the old paradigm was reductionist: By analyzing the parts, a person could better understand the whole. Proponents of the new paradigm argue that when the whole is a complex system that is open and adaptive, it is more than the sum of its parts. Complex adaptive systems have emergent properties that create new complex adaptive systems even more complex than themselves. The evolution of species is one biological example of the property of emergence in complex adaptive systems. The evolution of educational systems is another.

Second, the old paradigm was essentially structuralist. Advocates of the Cartesian paradigm hold that structures give rise to forces and mechanisms, which, when they interact, create processes. Proponents of the new paradigm hold that structure is the manifestation of complex process—and, furthermore, structure itself is process. The web or network of relationships in complex adaptive systems gives rise to apparent structures, but even the structures are ever changing. In fact, structure and process are distinguished mostly by their relative rates of change. Our bodies are relatively more solid than water, but 1 billion neutrinos have passed through us unnoticed in the time it takes to read this sentence.

Third, in the old paradigm, scientific description was held to be independent of the observer and the process of knowing. It was objective. In the new paradigm, we argue that a person's *epistemology*—understanding of the process of knowledge—is to be included explicitly in the description of natural phenomena. Without a consensus about which epistemology is correct, an individual has a special obligation to make it explicit. For example, some theoretical physicists are arguing that the mind is the root substance of the phenomenal world—in large part because in the quantum world the experimenter's mind affects the results of the experiment.[1]

Fourth, in the old paradigm, the metaphor of knowledge as building—fundamental laws, principles, blocks, and so forth—has been a constant of Western philosophy for thousands of years. The new paradigm replaces building blocks with networks. Its proponents argue that even our descriptions of phenomena are constructed of information networks. Unlike the old metaphors, networks are nonlinear, nonhierarchical, and without a foundation. The results of some research suggest that both animals and humans can share a mental space that allows for coordination beyond that explainable by individual linear reactions.

For example, slow-motion films of bird flocks have revealed that a flock of 50,000 birds can turn in complete synchrony in less than one 70th of a second. Such synchrony is not a question of following the leader; the flock functions as one integrated unit. Cambridge biologist Rupert Sheldrake (1995) explained this phenomenon as a self-organizing morphic field. Similar inexplicable phenomena occur with insect societies. From 1911 to about 1950, beehives and ant colonies were studied as organisms—or, rather, as superorganisms. The famous sociobiologist Edward O. Wilson began his work as a student of social insects. He wrote the following:

> This concept was a dominant theme in the literature on social insects. Then, at the seeming peak of its maturity, it faded, and today it is seldom explicitly discussed. Its decline exemplifies the way inspirational, holistic ideas in biology often give rise to experimental, reductionist approaches which supplant them. For the present generation, which is so devoted to the reductionist philosophy, the super-organism concept provided a very appealing mirage. It drew us to a point on the horizon. But, as we worked closer, the mirage dissolved—for the moment at least—leaving us in the midst of unfamiliar terrain, the exploration of which came to demand our undivided attention. (1971, pp. 317–319)

---

[1]Peter Russell, in *The Global Brain Awakens*, argues that the next step in the evolution is the development of a global consciousness: "We could therefore hypothesize that the integration of society into a super organism would occur through the evolution of consciousness rather than through the physical or biological evolution" (1995, p. 148). Roger Penrose, Professor of Mathematics at the University of Oxford, argues in *Shadows of the Mind* (1994) that important aspects of the brain are noncomputational. Penrose draws on the laws of quantum physics to explain nonlocal characteristics of the brain and proposes that the global nature of consciousness can be explained only within the rules of quantum mechanics.

However devoted Wilson was to reductionism, he readily acknowledged, "The total simulation of construction of complex nests from a knowledge of the summed behaviors of the individual insects has not been accomplished and stands as a challenge to both biologists and mathematicians" (p. 271). Wilson said, in Lewin (1992), "Its time to look at the whole once again, and, yes, I think we can begin talking about insect colonies as super organisms, but without the mysticism" (p. 117).

Professor Brian Goodwin, a developmental biologist at Open University in England, made the same observation about the development of organs within organisms and concluded that the challenge cannot be met by reductionism. He argued that it is incorrect to conclude that the set of instructions in the chromosomes of a fertilized egg provides the complete instructions for determining the timing and details of the formation of the heart, the central nervous system, the immune system, and every other organ and tissue required for life. Goodwin (1994) believes that we need to know the principles of organization that are involved in the system to explain what forms it can take. He concluded that the morphology of organisms is not explicable solely by the action of their genes.

Sheldrake (1995) argued that the notion of morphogenic fields is widely used by developmental biologists like Goodwin to explain how, for example, your arms and legs have different shapes even though they contain the same genes and proteins. He called this same capacity among bees, termites, and homing pigeons a *morphic field*. He stated,

> I suggest that the holistic, self-organizing properties of systems at all levels of complexity, from molecules to societies, depend on such fields. Morphic fields are not fixed but evolve. They have a kind of inbuilt memory. This memory depends on the process of morphic resonance, the influence of like upon like through space and time. (p. 82)

Sheldrake made a wry observation about computer simulations of complex adaptive systems, asking, What is it in the physical world that corresponds to the program in the computer that sets the conditions for emergence and keeps track of all the individual actions of the simulated "cellular automata"? He concluded that the most promising approach would be to think of the holistic organization of emergent activity like termite colonies in terms of morphic fields.

Fifth, and finally, the old paradigm held that knowledge could be fixed, absolute, and certain. The new paradigm acknowledges that no system of thought, not even mathematical proofs, is both closed and self-consistent. This paradigm holds that the human capacity for truth is partial and limited; therefore, so must be any description of reality we construct. Next, we discuss some of the formal characteristics of ecological systems.

PERSPECTIVES ON MANAGEMENT

At least part of the problem was identified by the Policy Board. To the extent that graduate schools of education fail to aggressively seek out alternative theoretical models and to test them, we will continue to train school leaders in the mechanistic paradigm of the 19th and early 20th century. For example, both school leadership texts and management texts reflect the wider society's emphasis on conceptual knowledge, and the better texts incorporate analytic- and critical-thinking exercises to the relative neglect of holistic and synergistic thinking.

In addition, many educational management textbooks are derivative of research in the business world that also functions in this mode. With the professionalization of educational administration that coincided with an effort to make it scientific, the business of managing schools has become divorced from the unique mission of schools to educate and nurture children. We must wonder, for example, why, as professors of educational management, we prefer business metaphors over pedagogical metaphors to explain the school as an organization. Is it because of the status of business—the proximity to power and wealth so valued in our society? the reluctance of male-dominated departments of educational administration to look to a pedagogical field of study dominated by women for insight into school management? or simply the poverty of educational leadership theory?

Whatever the reasons, we are now convinced that an ecological model of schooling should reflect the best pedagogical principles and practices in all aspects of organizational life. For example, if schools were conceived of as complex adaptive systems, in which any subgroup of the system has many redundant features, what are the implications for school leadership? Consider this illustration: Learning theory tells us that only a small percentage of lectured material transfers to the student. Yet, school administrators are dismayed when school-board members cannot recall the major points of their presentations on the budget and often attribute such failure to recall to the "absence of professionalism on the board." If such administrators modeled good pedagogy, board members would be learning twice.

Much of the work of administrators is teaching and learning about the life of schools and school districts as organizations. We have a considerable amount of research in education about effective adult education strategies that would be useful to administrators attempting to communicate to school boards, teachers, or parents their rationale for building a new school or closing an old school. A cursory review of educational administration programs leads to the conclusion that they do not promote adult pedagogical expertise as part of the core learning experiences of school leaders any more than the pedagogy of children.

To better understand the progression from old paradigm to new, we tagged the aggregate network of organizational behavior along three progressive dimensions. For the purposes of the current discussion, we distinguish among managing for compliance (Type I), managing for performance (Type II), and leading for a dynamic and sustainable organizational ecology (Type III).

The implicit domains of knowledge and approaches to teaching and learning change as the paradigm moves from Type I to Type III (see Figure 1–1). Type I is typically characterized by both a management style and a learning behavior focused on compliance with received knowledge (usually in the form of rules and regulations) about how the organization must conduct itself. Learning is in the form of compliance or noncompliance with the rules and regulations along the lines of the classic Weberian bureaucracy. With Type II (performance management), the balance of control shifts from the external environment to the internal environment by increasingly relying on skill-based knowledge. More concretely, it shifts from external control by professional organizations and regulatory agencies to internal and local professional autonomy. This shift has occurred precisely because external regulators have concluded that performance and excellence cannot be attained by regulatory compliance with standards for inputs and processes, or because the organization

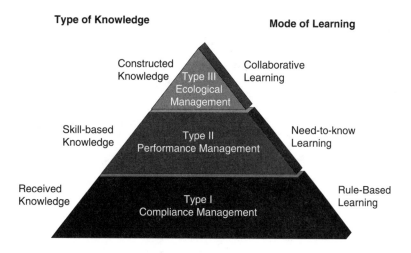

FIGURE 1–1
Hierarchy of Management Frameworks

has escaped from the bureaucratic model by establishing itself as an independent or for-profit organization. One by-product of this approach is a shift from a linear and mechanical response to oversight to a narrowly but more creatively focused effort to improve outcomes in a less regulated environment.

Each solution creates a new set of challenges. One unintended consequence of the narrowly defined emphasis on limited outcomes (e.g., mathematics and reading test scores) is an instrumentalist orientation that encourages expertise in a narrow set of skills directly related to boosting test scores. Another consequence is that independent schools, religious schools, and for-profit schools often select or screen students who conform to the goals of such schools' narrower educational vision. Within the public school system, we see counterproductive efforts to restrict the curriculum to basic skills instruction, with its consequence of radically reducing or eliminating altogether the fine arts curriculum.

Type III management admits that knowledge is constructed not only for children in the classroom, but also for adults in organizations—that organizational learning is reciprocal and collaborative (Marsick & Watkins, 1999). It begins with a set of assumptions about complex adaptive systems—of which schools are but one example—and proceeds to engage in a set of learning strategies whose outcomes are transformational and ecologically healthy for all members of the organization. We summarize the goals, foci, and analytic and evaluative frameworks representative of compliance, performance, and ecological types of management in Table 1–1.

A regulatory approach to management (Type I) describes the strategies of most school managers. It is true that organizations must have rules and regulations to provide for a safe environment and the smooth functioning of routine tasks. For most school systems, an overlapping grid of local, state, and federal regulations can virtually define the goals, focus, analysis, and evaluation. Especially for urban schools that face rigorous state monitoring standards, as in Connecticut, New Jersey, and New York, accountability becomes synonymous with meeting state standards.

TABLE 1–1
Managerial Frameworks

Framework feature	Management type		
	I	*II*	*III*
Goal	Compliance	Performance	Ecological health
Focus	Regulations and standards	Inputs	Sustainable growth, emergence, and transformation
Analysis	Comparative (with standard)	Resource mix, technology of production	Relationships, significant differences, and trends
Evaluation	Accountability measures	Cost-effectiveness	Synergistic learning through experience and introspection

Unfortunately, leaders in many school systems fail to reach beyond responding to the standards of state and federal officials to formulating proactive strategies for school improvement. The production-oriented models, including those of the effective schools movement, attempt to shift the focus from state mandates to identifying and focusing on the inputs that are most highly correlated with desired student outcomes. At its most sophisticated level, the model attempts to determine which resource combinations deliver the desired outcomes most cost-effectively (Levin & McEwan, 2001). A review of the effective schools research shows that the model has shifted from an exclusive reliance on the five or six key predictors of student achievement to far more complex models with intermediate goals related to school processes as well as alternative methods of assessing outcomes (Bliss, Firestone, & Richards, 1991). However, this methodological drift has also undermined the original model substantially.

PRINCIPLES OF ECOLOGICAL SYSTEMS

Until now, our comparison of the ecological paradigm with the classic paradigm has used reasonably comfortable metaphors. Is there a more rigorous set of first principles for ecological organizations? A first sketch of some core features of organizational ecology follows.

Emergence

Ecological systems are both a product of and a producer of other ecological systems. One thing that emerges from ecological systems is ecological *sub*systems. We can see many examples of evolutionary emergence in the natural world, from beehives to rain forests. In human society, we can see a parallel evolutionary emergence from tribalism to political parties, superstition to religion, hunting and gathering to workplaces, and informal apprenticeship to schools and universities. We might say that emergence occurs when organization gains an ecological niche within chaos.

Complexity is unpredictable. Some educational leadership theories—for example, those of effective schools and outcome-based education—argue that if the school pays attention to a few select variables, predicting and controlling student achievement will become possible. Yet, research on complex adaptive systems tells us this is not the case. All complex adaptive systems generate a local ecology.

Those that are dynamically stable and self-regenerative cannot be re-created by extracting the critical factors at some end state. Mathematical models of ecosystems repeatedly demonstrate that a sustainable, dynamic equilibrium is the product of unique developmental contingencies. In repeated trials, the critical species of the ecosystem are not the same (Holland, 1995). What features and processes do these diverse ecological systems share?

Each ecological system is a network of many "agents" that act simultaneously. In the hive, the agents are bees; in a rain forest, the agents are species; in an institution, workers and clients. At the level of a system of higher education, the agents might be campuses. Thus, the exchange network changes as the level of analysis shifts from microcosm to macrocosm. However defined, each agent finds itself in an environment produced by its interactions with other agents in the system. Each agent is constantly acting and reacting: Nothing in the environment is fixed, yet each agent has an identity that simultaneously contributes to a larger identity. In the context of U.S. society, people have particular difficulty internalizing that our individuality is only one aspect of our identity and our relatedness and shared aspects are another.

Adaptive Decentralization

Another feature of ecological systems is that their control is decentralized. The brain does not have a master neuron, nor does a master cell exist for the developing embryo. In a marketplace, hundreds and thousands of independent decisions about price, quantity, and quality are interacting to create and re-create supply-and-demand relationships. Although these complex relationships are regulated, they defy control by a central authority. In fact, many economists argue that regulation by central authorities often creates market distortions that are worse than the unregulated side effects of the raw market (recall price controls).

Coherent systems arise from the cooperation and competition of the agents. The rules of baseball arose from many local agreements by competing teams and were gradually generalized and formalized. The competitors agreed to cooperate in structuring their competition so that the purpose of the game—a test of team skill against team skill—could be realized. Teams cannot prove their skill without a tough competitor. Nor can a team rise to the "zone" of peak experience if every move is regulated. Successful games are complex, are competitive, and provide just enough structure to foster the emergence of peak performance—and, at their best, the outcome is unpredictable. Successful proliferation of games like baseball also requires leagues (niches) based on developmental ability (e.g., Little Leagues, college leagues, farm teams, and professional teams).

Redundancy

Ecologies are redundant. They have many levels of organization, with one level serving as building blocks for the next level. Groups of proteins, lipids, and nucleic acids form cells; groups of cells form tissues; the tissues form organs; the organs link in a symbiotic system. Further, and extremely important, complex adaptive systems are constantly rearranging the building blocks of the system, learning, adapting, and evolving. Multiple and overlapping levels of organization are characteristic of an ecology. The current trend to flatten the organization, replacing older hierarchical structures through reengineering and restructuring, has fostered the development of many informal and project-focused organizational niches in their place. One advantage of the new forms of organization is that they are highly adaptable and responsive. One disadvantage is that unless the central administration replaces the management control paradigm with a paradigm consistent with ecological sustainability, the culture at the bottom and the culture at the top will be at odds.

Anticipation

All complex adaptive systems anticipate the future. Prediction goes beyond simple foresight, or even consciousness. From bacteria up, every living creature has an implicit prediction encoded in its genes: "In x specified environment, agent y is likely to do well." More generally, every complex adaptive system is constantly making predictions based on its various internal models of the world—its assumptions about the way things work. More important, these models are active; they are like subroutines in the computer. When xyz conditions hold, implement strategy abc. In short, internal models are the building blocks of organizational behavior, and they are constantly being tested, refined, and rearranged as the organization gains experience. When the boundary conditions for adaptation are exceeded, the organism often keeps repeating the strategies that were successful under the old conditions rather than conducting the organizational learning necessary to find the new leverage points of change. This behavior leads to organizational failure, which in turn creates an opening in the ecosystem for new models to compete.

Distinctions

Another key feature of ecological systems is the universal use of *distinctions* as a mechanism for the formation of aggregates. We use markers to note distinctions. Imagine playing chess with all white pieces. Simply by coloring one team black and the other white we increase our ability to observe and act on properties previously obscured by symmetry. Markers also facilitate selective action in complex systems, allowing filtering, specialization, and cooperation. Marking facilitates complexity. Complexity in turn fosters the emergence of meta-agents (higher order agents). One example of a meta-agent is the brain; another is the modern educational organization. During a lifetime, every cell in our brain is replaced many times, yet our sense of self remains unaffected. Organizational identity persists even though the members and even the mission may change many times. Schools and colleges are a classic example of how meta-agents sustain identity as students and faculty flow into and out of the organization. As Holland (1995) said, "Ultimately, tags [markers] are the mechanism behind hierarchical organization—the agent/meta-agent/meta-meta-agent/. . . organization so common in *cas* [complex adaptive systems]" (p. 15). However, when we believe that the markers are the "thing itself," terrible consequences can ensue: The behavior becomes the child; the failing grade becomes a failure; the delinquency becomes a delinquent.

Complex adaptive organizations usually have many niches, each providing a special environment for its various agents. Moreover, when the niches are filled, the system creates new niches and new opportunities and challenges. Thus, complex adaptive systems are never in absolute equilibrium. They are more often characterized by cycles of punctuated equilibrium. However, even complex adaptive systems can entropy to extinction. Although homo sapiens may be nature's best attempt to understand itself at this stage of evolution, that we will succeed is not a foregone conclusion. It is equally possible that if we fail, we could be replaced by another effort—homo pacifist?

When we exploit nonrenewable resources without consideration for the future, we make avoiding entropy much more difficult. The negative impact (high costs) associated with depletion of natural resources is a case in point. Some countries are sustained in part by the export of nonrenewable materials such as oil, coal, iron ore, copper, aluminum, and scrap metal. As Deming (1993) observed,

> These are temporary blessings; they can not last forever because the cost of production rises as the supplies are exhausted. To live on gifts, credit, or borrowed money is not a long-term solution, either. . . . We ship out, for dollars, iron ore, partially refined aluminum, nickel, copper, coal, all nonrenewable. The Japanese paid us about 18 cents for the metal in the microphone that I use in lectures. We buy the metal back from them in the form of a microphone for $2,000, possibly $1,800—value added! (pp. 3–4)

It is not too far-fetched to view the enthusiasm for learning and teaching of students and teachers as nonrenewable resources, that once they are squandered we can retrieve them only at a high price. Sometimes educational organizations indulge in chronic overspending without sensitivity to the public's limits for taxation. However, the capacity to tax is a natural resource for educating institutions that can also be easily depleted and difficult to replenish.

Holism

Werner Heisenberg, a Nobel Prize–winning physicist, demonstrated that the mere act of observing a particle affects the outcome of the observation. It is not possible to determine the position of a particle accurately if we observe its momentum, or its momentum if we observe its position. The same phenomenon applies to most leadership theories. In our slavery to experimental design, we have labored so rigorously to remove the effect of observation on the outcome that we have denatured the ecology of leadership and learning and in the process produced theory of little value to leaders on the job and hence to learners.

We recall an apocryphal story about the early research on behaviorism. Behaviorists would attempt to make pigeons run through mazes for a reward of corn. Desperate to get free, the pigeon would exhaust itself by beating its wings against the cage in which the maze was located. For researchers to make behaviorism work, they first had to starve the pigeon to one third of its body weight. Now we have several generations of laboratory pigeons and rats raised in captivity who no longer have a lust for freedom coded into their genes. The restrictions necessary to create reliable observation frequently are so intrusive to the learning environment that the researcher is no longer testing in situ but rather testing whether the intervention works in the restrictive conditions of a laboratory. Some analogous examples are (a) high-stakes test indicators that get manipulated by teachers and students and distort curriculum, and (b) evaluation systems designed to test for implementation of unpopular curriculum reforms that lead teachers to tell their students things such as, "O.K., kids, the supervisor is coming now. You know he likes cooperative learning, so we're going to work in groups today." In addition, when teachers know that the average job tenure of a school superintendent in any given district is less than 3 years, they quickly learn to respond to the new reforms with symbolic rather than substantive behavior. Long-term loyalty to the children and their needs is, systemically, impossible. After all, the next superintendent will have a new reform.

ECOLOGICAL THINKING ABOUT LEADERSHIP

In the preceding discussions, we sought to briefly represent the need for a new paradigm in leadership theory by making the bridge between pure theory and what an ecological perspective might yield in an effort to improve schools. Some key constructs such as (a) emergence, (b) adaptive decentralization, (c) redundancy, (d) anticipation, (e) niches, and (f) holism are fundamental to learning how organizations in general and schools in particular might be understood ecologically.

However, how do practice and thought differ in the new paradigm? The same distinction that natural ecologists make between ecological conservation and transformational ecology applies. The conservation approach simply suggests that the environment exists for humankind and humankind should wisely manage the scarce resources of the environment in its self-interest. The transformational approach takes the position that human beings are not merely custodians of nature but a part of nature: The evolution of humanity is nature's attempting to understand itself through the human mind.

We cannot manage the environment because the part cannot manage the whole and we cannot remove ourselves from the whole to make the whole other (Naess, 1989). Leakey and Lewin (1995) argued with conviction in their alarming book, *The Sixth Extinction*, that human society is so much in denial about its natural origins and dependency on nature that we are well on our way—at the rate of 30,000 extinct species per year—to literally paving the way for the next massive extinction of flora and fauna on earth.

In an educational context, an ecological approach to the learning environment of children takes the position that children are not merely a vital resource that must be protected, nurtured, educated, and socialized for us to preserve and advance human society but that children are also ourselves. We can no more divorce ourselves from our codependence on children than we can on the need for water and air. At the species level, without children we are, by definition, extinct. Thus, only by a collective act of pathology do we permit the neglect, abuse, and miseducation of children and the destruction of the air, water, and earth they need—not only to survive but to prosper. A self-regulatory model of educational ecology will not solve the educational problems of the 21st century. A transformational ecology would be much less worried about public or private, teacher or mentor, phonics or whole language, or constructivist or behaviorist than it would be about a healthy diversity of approaches.

We cannot imagine the educational systems of children or adults apart from what we express in our own modes of thinking, feeling, and acting. It is not that we must transform ourselves before we can transform our schools, but rather that schools reflect who we are. Changing schools into the kind of nurturing environments in which children thrive means that we already envision the competencies and behaviors and leadership needed to create them. As we self-actualize and create ever more sophisticated and thoughtful versions of school, doing so will transform us as a species. Ultimately, we will reach the point of conscious coevolution rather than the blind and indifferent evolution of natural selection. However, we will not accompish this *over nature*. We will accomplish it only *as nature*.

Educational institutions are learning environments from which we cannot extricate ourselves any more than we can extricate ourselves from the physical environment. From the viewpoint of transformational ecology, the nature of self-understanding is neither subjective nor objective: It is transactive. Eisner (1991, p. 52), referring to John Dewey, described this transactive view as the locus of human experience. Whatever we know is the result of experience, and experience is the result of an interaction between a postulated subject and a postulated object.

However, we would take Dewey's philosophy one step further, asking, "Where does experience lie?" If we say, "In the brain," we are subscribing to dualism. If we say, "In the environment," we are subscribing to behaviorism. Instead, we argue that experience occurs in the mind—which includes all of nature.

Thus, we must lead as members. Managing from within acknowledges that decisions made by members change the decision maker as well as the other members of the organization. Educational leaders do not have a place outside the system whereupon they can stand to evaluate it without affecting the results of the evaluation. In fact, the very act of evaluation changes the behavior of both evaluators and the subject of the evaluation (Cronbach, 1982).

However, we do not reject subjectivism or empiricism as irrelevant, but rather treat methodological perspectives as useful fictions. It is useful to empathize with the confusion or pain of a child having difficulty in school from the child's view. It is also useful to look at the problem as objectively and dispassionately as possible. (No one wants a teary-eyed surgeon in the operating room.) However, we would argue that both the empathic and the dispassionate perspectives lie on a continuum that is essentially relational. In the one case, we are attempting to arrive at understanding by minimizing the distance; in the other case, by increasing the distance.

If the history of school reform has been about finding the best means to accomplish agreed upon ends, the future will be built on the realization that we and our children may be nature's best effort to understand itself. As adults, we are largely responsible for facilitating this effort by providing a nurturing, reflective learning environment for children.

Schools are just one of the ways that we transfer knowledge and build ecological capacity. We are not proposing a new model of social Darwinism. The issue is not a question of survival of the most fit. If this were so, cockroaches would rule the world. According to Lewin (1992),

> The pure Spencerian view of the world, therefore, is that increased complexity is an inevitable manifestation of the system and is driven by the internal dynamics of complex systems: heterogeneity from homogeneity, order out of chaos. The pure Darwinian view is that complexity is built solely by natural selection, a blind, non-directional force; and there is no inevitable rise in complexity. [Frank Ryan, in *Darwin's Blind Spot* (2002), makes a compelling case that *symbiosis*, the blending of separate life-forms, accounts for many gigantic leaps in evolution.] The new science of Complexity combines elements of both; internal and external forces apply, and increased complexity is to be expected as a fundamental property of complex dynamical systems.
>
> Such systems may bring themselves to the edge of chaos, a constant process of co-evolution, a constant adaptation. Part of the lure of the edge of chaos is an optimization of information, whether the system is a cellular automaton or a biological species evolving with others as part of a complex ecological community. At the edge of chaos, bigger brains are built. (p. 149)

Thus, the human species—as suggested previously—is nature's best attempt thus far to understand itself. In this sense, we stand on the backs of all other life-forms, including cockroaches, so that the natural world can better know itself. Unhappily, this global evolutionary effort currently has more possibility and potentiality than it does lived experience. Humanity, as we know it, could be a natural experiment gone awry.

Is ecological thinking a panacea for education? Not in the short run. The crisis is likely to continue for the foreseeable future, but an ecological approach to education will not begin to solve the crisis until school leaders, teachers, children, the public, and other governmental and civic leaders begin to think and act ecologically.

So why study a new approach to leadership when it is unlikely to provide us with immediate advantages? If educating institutions are places where new knowledge is born and tested, then testing a new approach to the leadership of learning institutions seems to appropriately "model the model." This redundancy is an exemplar of complex and emergent activity. If we could create sufficiently diverse school settings, processes, and pedagogy, schools could become seeds of adaptation and emergence. However, centralization and bureaucratization currently have a death grip, reproducing extinction.

Nor are we appealing for a romantic return to the instinctive and intuitive participation in nature experienced by native and aboriginal peoples. Our task is much more difficult: We must overcome the burden of our alienation from nature and with it our atomistic illusion of self apart from all else and emerge self-consciously aware. We must overcome what Albert Einstein called "the optical delusion of consciousness" that we are somehow separate from the whole of creation.

2

Writing Policy Briefs

Writing a policy brief is both a craft and an art. The subject of this chapter is the craft of writing policy briefs. The craft of writing a good policy brief is a didactic and iterative enterprise: Expertise is acquired through the practice of analysis and synthesis and the exercise of judicial temperament. Such skills are taught or learned only with considerable effort on the part of teacher and student. The art of writing a good policy brief is intuitive and creative: It cannot be taught, but it can be learned.

OBJECTIVES OF THE POLICY BRIEF

For-profit businesses issue quarterly reports. Analysts of the for-profit sector regularly prepare detailed reports of the organizational and financial health of various businesses. Educational leaders (by law in most cases) publish annual budget documents and financial reports according to state formats and guidelines and with greater frequency are participating in preparing annual performance reports and objectives. Typically, the ideal underlying such activities—organizational learning and strategic management—is lost to the cumbersome and restrictive nature of the paperwork involved. The activity becomes one of basal compliance with the externally imposed guidelines. As a result, educational leaders rarely take or have the opportunity to perform comprehensive, ongoing analyses for the specific purpose of organizational improvement or internal organizational learning.

When analyses are performed for the purpose of making policy decisions, they are too often reactionary, perhaps addressing the issue that received the most attention at a recent board meeting, such as "That new attendance policy" or "Do we really need metal detectors?" Often, issues emerging from the special interests of a particular constituent serve as diversions from understanding the bigger picture of how and how well the system is working. We do not mean to suggest that you simply allow all such "diversions" to fall on deaf ears, but that each issue that is raised is simply one small indicator of the overall health of your system. Many significant issues may never even rise to the surface through these venues. You have to find them yourself.

For this reason, we recommend what we refer to as *system monitoring and ecological auditing*—the ongoing task of tracking indicators of the educational, economic, financial, and political health of your organization. We propose the policy brief as a format for reporting on system monitoring and ecological auditing. Creating a policy brief requires use of the analytic tools presented in the following parts of this book. Although a policy brief might be used to respond to an issue of contention, our ideal is that participants in the learning organization, not exclusively the formal leader, will continually perform audits of their context and share the results of these audits with their peers, their superiors, and the community when relevant. In this chapter, we present three types of policy briefs: (a) the data-driven brief, (b) the model-driven brief, and (c) the ecological policy options brief. Each style of policy brief has different goals, but the three styles are not mutually exclusive. In fact, as you proceed in this textbook, you will find that the data-driven brief provides a stepping stone to the model-driven brief, and the model-driven brief to the ecological brief.

UNIVERSAL RULES FOR PREPARING POLICY BRIEFS

Before we delve into the details of each type of policy brief, three universal rules for the preparation of any policy document should be considered.

Rule #1: Keep It Short

These days, given the mandated paperwork in school systems, educational leaders and other constituents will not take the time to read a lengthy analytic document (30–40 pages with multiple charts and tables). Most simple analytic policy briefs can be kept to about 5 pages of text with two or three accompanying tables. An ecological, more comprehensive policy brief may range from 10 to 15 pages. In either case, a key component of the brief is the first page, the *executive summary*. The executive summary is a 1-page snapshot of everything that is covered in the brief, the most important portions being the major findings and the policy recommendations. Often, the person reading a policy brief will not read past the executive summary.

Rule #2: Keep It Simple

By the time you complete the tasks laid out for you in this book and develop your analytic tool kit, we expect you to have acquired considerable skill in manipulating data. Typically, when preparing a brief, you will perform a variety of relatively complex analyses or construct some intricate models. Ultimately, however, any analyses you perform and findings you want to present must make sense.

Explain your findings in intuitive, not statistical, terms. As we see it, there are only two times and places when you would want to use formal statistical language to convey a message. One is when you are talking to other statisticians, which we expect to be a rare occurrence. The other is when you do not want your audience to understand a word you are trying to say, but you want to sound like you know what you are talking about. We do not mention ethics that much in this textbook, but the idea that ethical leadership is paramount is implicit in our theory of a healthy educational ecosystem. Your central objective for preparing these briefs should not be to "look good" or "sound smart" but to inform yourself and inform the organization with the goal of improving the learning environment of children and teachers. We assure you that the other outcomes will emerge as a secondary effect, given that you perform the central mission effectively. Your goal in writing about your "numbers" and models is to seek their intuitive meaning, perhaps through analogies that convey what you, the data, and the models actually mean.

Like your language, your data, charts, tables, models, and so forth are most effective if kept simple. To some extent, *simple* means limited—no more than two to three tables and charts in a 3- to 5-page brief; no more than three to five in a 10- to 15-page brief. After you have run 50 analyses, or constructed seven alternative model structures, reducing your information to such a small space may seem daunting. This activity will require some practice and some creativity. Let one guideline stand, however; that is, each chart or table should be clear enough to stand alone, plainly conveying its message to the uninformed reader. Consequently, we recommend giving your analyses a pilot run with your peers.

Rule #3: Keep It Logical

Logic and organization are crucial to the preparation of a high-quality policy brief. Subtlety is not a virtue in this case. Subheadings are key. One approach to developing a logically flowing policy brief is to encapsulate your analyses and findings into two or three major categories. Doing so will allow you, from the outset of the brief, to set forth Goal 1, Goal 2, Goal 3, and so forth. In general, following more than three goals through a brief becomes confusing. We realize that these issues may not fully emerge or classify themselves to you until after you perform your analyses or construct and run your models. Hence, reframing your brief is an ongoing process.

As you work toward the final draft of any brief, we suggest that you try to maintain a parallel structure to your analyses and findings when possible. That is, if you set forth three goals as the centerpiece of your brief in the introduction, as you begin your analyses, stick to the same goals in the same sequence, and do the same as you present your major findings. This approach makes more sense when you are building your brief backward from the goals that emerge, a process noted in the preceding paragraph as *reframing*. Conversely, policy recommendations and evaluation of these recommendations should involve substantial interconnectedness of the goals at hand; thus, we do not expect your policy recommendations to be delineated in the same manner or bound to the same sequence.

Maintaining clarity in the logic of your brief requires that you establish some arbitrary limits on what you include out of the plethora of exploratory analyses that you performed. In the end, in an effort to construct a coherent, logical, digestible policy brief, you may find that you have to file the majority of the analyses you performed and concisely summarize the rest. Nevertheless, the additional analyses may come in handy for future briefs. The key is that the brief at hand conveys a clear, logical, and compelling image of the current condition of your organization as it relates to the goals you envision accomplishing.

STRUCTURE AND UNIVERSAL ELEMENTS OF POLICY BRIEFS

Each of the three types of policy briefs we discuss has a few universal elements. The basic structure of each of the three types of policy briefs is shown in Figure 2–1. The major contrast among the three types of briefs is that the ecological policy options brief is a far more comprehensive approach than either of the other two. In addition to involving more in-depth analysis of both quantifiable and nonquantifiable attributes of both the internal and the external environment, the ecological brief places far more emphasis on the design and evaluation of potential policy options. Data-driven briefs are primarily analytic, addressing and characterizing system attributes through data but falling well short of providing detailed, comprehensive descriptions of policy options. Similarly, model-driven briefs emphasize the analysis of the systems problem more than the potential solutions.

The common features among the three briefs are discussed first, in this section. Then, in the following sections, we explore the elements that distinguish the three policy options briefs.

Executive Summary

As noted previously, the executive summary is a one-page snapshot of your entire brief (without charts or tables, but you may refer to particularly informative numbers). Your

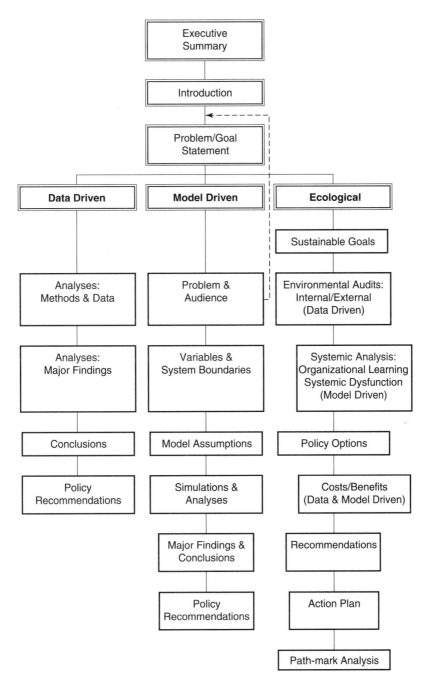

FIGURE 2–1
Basic Structure of the Three Types of Policy Options Briefs

executive summary is most effective if it has subheadings according to the structure provided in this chapter, excluding the executive summary itself. (You have no need to summarize the summary.) Emphasis should be placed on the major findings and policy recommendations. Bulleted points and other methods of emphasis, used sparingly but appropriately, are recommended.

Introduction

The introduction to a policy brief is a crucial element in the successful presentation of the brief. The first paragraph should have a thesis statement, such as the following:

> *This policy brief addresses the issue of inadequate classroom space at Excelsior Academy.*

Furthermore, an excellent introduction tells the reader what is coming next and in what order. For example,

> *In the following pages, we discuss the key elements of a policy options brief.*

Key terms are also defined in the introduction. For instance, in our current discussion, *organization* is defined as the skeleton of a structurally sound policy options brief, whereas *content* is the substance of the brief, and *style*, the type of language used to communicate the content of the brief. As you are aware, each part of a skeleton is anatomically functional. Imagining ourselves with either fewer or more bones is difficult. So it is with a good outline. Within each anatomical category, you are provided with examples of efficient and functional content. Finally, style is a crucial element in any persuasive essay, and the policy options brief is the ultimate persuasive essay.

Problem or Goal Statement

An excellent problem or goal statement isolates, by category, the nature of the problems or goals presented in a policy brief. The categories we believe most useful to organizing our thinking about policy options have us focus first on resource flows from the external environment to the internal environment. We then focus more holistically on organizational learning goals and patterns of dysfunction created by inappropriate habits of response to environmental challenges and opportunities. In the following sections, we illustrate in italics and discuss the general principles in the text immediately following the italics. A by-no-means exhaustive subset begins with a statement of the organizational vision that is at the heart of our concern. For example,

> *Excelsior Academy has made a commitment to provide a safe, nurturing, and educationally appropriate classroom facility.*

THE DATA-DRIVEN ANALYTIC BRIEF

Conceptual Overview

Data, as we discuss in more detail in part II, provide us with snapshots of the various symptoms of our organization. Exploring the data generated by our organization allows us to develop our perceptions about the performance and overall health of our organization. Exploring data is one step toward organizational learning. Organizational learning through data analysis is primarily an inductive activity. In discussing computer programs that search for patterns in data (neural networks), Frank Lemke coined the phrase *knowledge extraction from data*. Although we do the same work manually rather than by neural network, we are also seeking to extract knowledge when we explore the data generated by our organization to prepare a data-driven analysis.

This approach can be difficult to grasp by individuals trained in more traditional educational research methods, in which the emphasis is on deductive hypothesis testing. The rationale for the different approach stems from the different goals of traditional research methods and organizational learning. In traditional research methods, our objective is to test the extent to which educational data conform to, or "fit," some generalizable and theoretically grounded model so that we can further our understanding of educational systems in general. Organizational learning, although still requiring a broad perspective, is *case specific*. Your objective is to get to know your organization and its context. In many cases, you are better served by bringing with you not a single theory or hypothesis to test on your institution, but rather some loosely formulated "notions" about what might be important to know.

Preparation of the Brief

One approach to preparing the data-driven brief is to work your way through the variety of data analysis tools at your disposal so that you get to know your data. Once you perform a series of analyses, consider them to be like a potential storyboard, or a series of frames in a film. Iteratively resequencing the analyses may reveal to you an interesting story line or the potential story line to pursue. At this point, you will likely need to go back and perform additional analyses in an effort to "plug holes" or find the "missing link" in your story line. In a sense, a theory has emerged for you in the form of a story line, and now some more traditional deductive testing is necessary.

Structure of the Brief

When you are writing the analyses of a data-driven brief, we recommend the following structure:

- ◆ *Executive summary*
- ◆ *Introduction*
- ◆ *Goal statement.* For a typical data-driven brief, you should have a limited number of goals. State them clearly and concisely. In general, your objective is to characterize the current condition of your organization (through data). However, this statement is perhaps too broad to use in the brief itself. It is not only possible but also likely that the objectives will become clearer after you perform some analysis, which will allow you to narrow the scope of your discussion. Typically, two to three broad goals are sufficient for a three- to five-page brief.
- ◆ *Analyses (methods, data, and major findings).* This section of the brief is where intuitive explanation is the key to your success. In the clearest possible language, you must explain the analyses you performed and the meaning of your findings. Use

numbers. Refer to them in your discussion, and refer to your tables and charts. However, be sure to emphasize what you learned—the findings:

Our enrollment forecast shows a 3% increase in enrollment per year (see Table 1).

One basic rule of thumb is to never refer to a table or a chart you have not included (makes sense) and to never include a table or a chart you do not refer to (more often a problem). If it is in the brief, it should be connected to the central goals. It should convey an important message, and it should convey this message clearly and efficiently.

♦ *Conclusions.* The conclusions are just a brief opportunity to encapsulate your major findings. You may even find this brief section to be unnecessary or redundant when the findings are vivid and self-explanatory.

♦ *Policy recommendations.* Unfortunately, the pure data-analytic model of organizational analyses is somewhat static. Although we can paint a vivid picture of where our organization is, and perhaps in data terms where it has been and where it is headed, the data-analytic perspective does not generally provide us with opportunities to make explicit recommendations for reform strategies. What the data-analytic approach does do for us, in terms of policy recommendations, is to identify emergent symptoms—potential problems in our performance indicators—that need to be further explored and continually tracked as we attempt changes in strategy. Changes in strategy are changes in process, and to this point, with our data-analytic framework, we are maximally informed on the condition of outcomes but minimally informed on the nature of processes.

THE MODEL-DRIVEN POLICY BRIEF

Conceptual Overview

If computer modeling were fulfilling its promise, this would (also) be a golden age for policy analysis, with the computational power of computer models supporting significantly better decision making than was possible thirty years ago. However, the principal result of the increasing use of computer models seems to be not a marked improvement in the quality of decision making, but rather a growing sensitivity to the shortcomings of models. (Bankes, 1993, p. 435)

Bankes's concern stemmed from what he characterized as a "fundamental confusion between two very different uses for computer models" (p. 435). Bankes referred to these fundamental uses as *consolidative* and *exploratory* modeling.

In *consolidative modeling*, we have an abundance of information on our system, such that we can intricately model the system as it actually exists, with minimal ambiguity and uncertainty. Consolidative models are an exceptional tool for developing our understanding of "how our system works" when we have the necessary information and when uncertainty or chaos is not a large organizational factor. For most organizations, meeting both conditions is difficult. However, this fact does not, as some individuals argue, negate the utility of modeling strategies for policy analysis.

Exploratory modeling involves developing a broader conceptual framework of "how the system would behave if certain assumptions were correct." One method of exploratory modeling that we study in this text involves running a series of computational experiments to explore the implications of varying assumptions about resource inputs and flows on outcomes. Although exploratory, this process is deductive, applying scientific methodologies to testing a variety of plausible, yet uncertain, scenarios. The data-analytic framework previously presented is less effective (as was noted) for determining strategy than is exploratory modeling because the data-analytic framework encourages a false sense of certainty defined by the data at any given point in time.

Bankes (1993) presented a useful framework for delineating approaches to exploratory modeling:

Data-driven exploratory modeling. This type of exploratory modeling "starts with a data set, and attempts to derive insight from it by searching over an ensemble of models to find those that are consistent with the available data set" (p. 443). Data-driven exploratory modeling may become a useful way for you to blend the data exploration methods promoted in this book with the modeling approaches.

Question-driven exploratory modeling. This type of exploratory modeling "searches over an ensemble of models believed to be plausible ways to answer the question of interest" (p. 443). When less is known, or available in terms of data, question-driven modeling allows us to explore a multitude of possible ways in which the system might work. This approach can be particularly useful to educators, for whom data continue to be sparse.

Model-driven exploratory modeling. This type of exploratory modeling "involves neither a fixed data set nor a particular question or policy choice, but rather is a theoretical investigation into the properties of a class of models" (p. 443). Somewhat more conceptually elusive, model-driven approaches, as described by Bankes (not to be confused with our use of the phrase), refer to mathematical experiments with newly proposed model structures. The objective is to determine the relationships of the new models to existing models and to validate the behavior of the new models.

With Bankes's framework in mind, our objective in education policy analysis and in education strategic management is to find ways to constructively use both consolidative and exploratory models to address real situations that face us—in our school, district, state, or nation, and in our broader context. At any level of the system, uncertainty is involved, and this uncertainty must be recognized, not ignored or assumed away. When we are applying or testing our models, the simple question "What if?" should pass through our minds frequently.

Ecological thinking requires us to keep in mind that the model that we construct and test today to assess the potential scenarios of tomorrow and beyond is based on a system that is continuing to evolve—just as we are as participants in the ecosystem. Thus, our answer to the question "What if?" when it is asked tomorrow, given a new set of conditions, may be quite different from our answer to the question when it is asked today. Therefore, we borrow yet another concept from Bankes and colleagues (Lempert, Schlesinger, & Bankes, 1996)—*adaptive strategies*: That is, the strategy, or plan, keeps changing as conditions change, and the conceptual model and hence the computational model evolve, which yields new certainties and new sets of uncertainties.

Construction of the Brief

Construction of the model-driven brief is the easy part; developing and constructing the model or models is a far more complex task that is not addressed until part V. For the most part, the model-driven policy brief is about reporting on the model(s).

Because the model-driven brief requires testing of alternative scenarios or assumptions (e.g., low inflation–high inflation, declining enrollments–growing enrollments), you must exercise great skill in cooking down the many possibilities into the few that are most relevant to the goals of the brief. It is important to resist the temptation to show your audience all the ways in which the model behaves. If you do not, the audience will suffer from information overload. So, once again, your goal is to "keep it simple" and carefully select the two or three scenarios you believe to be most probable or most informative to the audience. One method of framing scenarios is to present low-, moderate-, and high-probability events. For example, for a nuclear power plant, these events might be a complete meltdown (low probability), a shutdown (moderate probability), and a minor leak (high probability).

Structure of the Brief

A basic structural outline of the model-driven brief is as follows:

- ◆ Executive summary
- ◆ Introduction
  - • Problem and audience
  - • Goal statement
- ◆ Model conceptual overview
  - • Variables and system boundaries
  - • Model assumptions
- ◆ Simulations and analyses
- ◆ Major findings and conclusions
- ◆ Policy recommendations

As you can see, the model-driven brief and the data-driven brief have substantial similarities in structure. Thus, we next discuss only the differences in detail.

Audience. Typically, in a model-building activity, multiple constituencies or representatives of multiple constituencies are involved. You should identify the constituencies represented in the model-building process because their roles and special interests play a substantial role in shaping the theoretical structure of the model.

Variables and system boundaries, and model assumptions. Whether derived from patterns identified in data on the organization, from philosophical ideals of constituents, or from existing literature (such as Senge's archetypes of organizational behavior), some theoretical basis will exist for the way you chose to structure your model(s). This theoretical basis, and the assumptions that accompany it, should be explained as simply as possible. In general, this section of the brief is where pictorial representations of the model are presented. Key mathematical relationships underlying the model should also be defined at this point.

Simulations and analyses. Again, you should exercise caution in this portion of the brief, trying not to overwhelm your audience. Little real difference exists between the structure of your presentation and that of a data-driven brief. The key difference is to clarify the conditions of uncertainty underlying the various scenarios you choose to present.

Major findings and conclusions, and policy recommendations. The findings and recommendations have one major difference from those in the data-driven brief. In a model driven policy options brief, both the findings and the recommendations are focused on gap analysis and the alternatives available to close the gap. By *gap analysis*, we mean the identification of a current level of performance and a specific desired future level of performance. Often, the recommendations specify the most cost-effective means of closing the gap.

THE ECOLOGICAL POLICY OPTIONS BRIEF

The ecological policy options brief combines the use of data-driven methods and model-driven methods, but you apply them much more broadly to your organization and its context. You simply cannot perform true ecological analyses and prepare ecological policy options briefs by using the contrived case studies presented in this book. Thus, we expect that during your time with this book, you will make more frequent use of our two previous frameworks. In fact, the data- and model-driven frameworks are useful in practice as well. However, we believe it important to provide a detailed description of the ecological method as a way not only to bring together all the tools and skills you develop by using this book, but also to apply these tools toward assessing the full richness of the ecology of your organization. We guide you through this application in chapter 15.

Policy analysis is necessarily derivative of social theory. Our guide to constructing an ecological policy brief in this book borrows heavily from the literature on systems theory, organizational learning, and ecological modeling (see Holland, 1995; Scott, 1981; Senge, 1990; and Simon, 1957). Rather than digress into a review of this important literature, we refer you to the previous chapters and the References section at the end of the book.

The skeletal structure we propose is based on an ecological, or dynamic, system. It has numerous advantages over other frameworks. Policy analysts can build into the model whatever psychological, sociological, political, or economic constructs (or biases) they deem appropriate. Only four rules pertain:

1. A social system can vary in scope from the microlevel (e.g., the family) to the macrolevel (e.g., the nation).
2. Social systems comprise individuals, groups, institutions, and organizations.
3. An infinite universe guarantees that whatever the level of analysis, factors external to the system are likely to have a profound influence on what occurs within it: Only the universe is fully specified.
4. Each level of a system is of necessity connected to all other levels of the system, either directly or indirectly. The notion of reciprocity and feedback are core concepts in an open system.

The final point is as much a caution as it is an axiom. Whatever our level of analysis—micro, modal, or macro—it is only a partial rendering of a complex picture. Figure 2–2 is a schematic depiction of an ecological model of policy analysis (and a preview of what is to follow).

Elements of the Brief

The following discussion is intended to provide a summary of the salient elements you are expected to include in an ecological policy brief. The discussion follows the flow of Figure 2–2. Both its content and its structure are intended as a guide to the novice policy analyst. We already covered the importance of the executive summary and the introduction. In this section, we focus on the following:

- ◆ Sustainable goals
- ◆ Environmental audits: external and internal
  - • Systemic analysis
- ◆ Policy options
  - • Costs and benefits
- ◆ Recommendations
- ◆ Action plan
- ◆ Path-mark analysis

Sustainable Goals

Sustainable goals already presume a knowledge of ecological systems and their principles. We cannot overcontrol such systems. Rather, our purpose is to provide the proper structural conditions, flow of resources, and critical mass of creative, ethical, and intellectual

FIGURE 2–2
Ecological Model of Policy Analysis:
Network Structure

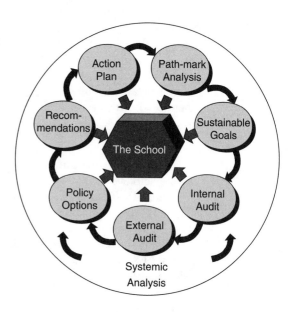

talent to pursue our educational goals successfully. Ecological goals are sensitive to the proper developmental needs of children and the resource constraints of the community. Whenever possible, the educational system is seeking synergistic linkages with other services and agencies to accomplish its mission. Doing so might mean working with family and youth services, religious institutions, municipal parks and recreation, and the juvenile justice system, among others. The goals should be described not in an end state but as a progressive path. For example,

> During the next 5 years, Excelsior Academy seeks to increase the participation of female students in high-level mathematics and science programs with the goal of interesting more young women in careers in science. One set of indicators of this goal might be (a) the percentage of females participating in such classes, (b) their academic performance in the classes compared with that of males, and (c) the percentage indicating a college preference for science and mathematics majors.

External Environmental Audits

The purpose of external audits is to anticipate and understand the major trends in economic, political, environmental, and social forces that may influence the organization positively or negatively. The purpose of auditing is not to protect the status quo. These environmental pressures might be not only necessary but also productive. For example, desegregating public schools took initiative and courage on the part of some academic leaders, and many of them suffered for their convictions. Where we have failed, such failure has occurred because government was unwilling to address residential segregation and its role in segregating students by social class. The following scenario might be illustrative of another example at the school level:

> The competitive position of Excelsior Academy has been weakened by aggressive marketing by regional competitors. Distance learning and nontraditional programs are also reducing the former effectiveness of a strong regional barrier to competition. Furthermore, Excelsior Academy has raised its per-pupil spending to levels that are dangerously high and likely to create some market backlash in the near future from irate parents. On the positive side, Excelsior Academy basks in the glow of its status as a market leader among academic institutions.

Traditionally, external environmental audits of educational institutions have been built around a few key factors. These institutions are often sensitive to changes in demographic trends, economic conditions, teacher quality, and market competition. For example, in the K–12 system, rapidly growing student enrollments can quickly exacerbate staffing, facility, and workload ratios. Rapidly declining enrollments can be equally traumatic for colleges, leading to faculty layoffs, closed programs, and reduced support services. To this list of traditional external environmental challenges we can add weather disasters, racial conflicts, drugs and violence, and political instability.

External environmental problems are outside the immediate organizational system. For example, the state department of education may require compliance with new and more demanding high school graduation requirements while failing to address the resource problems that attend meeting these standards. The school may need additional funding or a national shortage of faculty in critical fields of expertise might exist. These problems of the political and economic environment frequently define the constraints within which policy options must be addressed. One policy option is to change the external environment.

Internal Environmental Audits

In internal environmental audits, you simply apply the same careful analysis of financial, organizational, demographic, and curricular factors inside the organization as you did outside it. Needless to say, the notions of internal and external are subjective and another of the "useful fictions" we use to provide a structure to our auditing of the environment. Let us continue with our example of Excelsior Academy:

> *The budget and planning offices of the Academy are currently understaffed as the result of an unanticipated retirement and a second staff member's following a spouse out of state. This has resulted in poor planning data and a budget shortfall for the current year. A prompt response to personnel and information management system deficiencies has been undermined by instability on the Board of Trustees and the central administration. A crisis mentality prevails in the decision-making structure, and many important but routine management functions have been delayed or ignored.*

Internal environmental audits are designed to identify fundamental structural or functional strengths and weaknesses within the institution or organization. From an ecological perspective, dysfunctional organizations have resource allocation and consumption patterns that are debilitating to organizational health. We use the term *resource* in this instance to connote both human resources and financial resources. Perhaps, for example, the entire faculty of Excelsior Academy is aging, which is driving average labor costs well above the norms of competitors and leaving students with the perception that the curriculum is not current or relevant.

Systemic analysis. Although delineating the external from the internal and dissecting the various social, economic, and political attributes of a system is a vital process, it can at times obscure for us the global behavior of the system that is revealed by the collective internal and external attributes and their interconnectedness. After performing a detailed internal and external audit, you should step back from the system to seek potential systemic issues that may fall into either of two major categories: organizational learning problems or systemic dysfunction.

Organizational Learning Problems.

> *The staffing difficulties in the budget office were not recognized in a timely fashion because the district does not maintain a staffing profile with anticipated turnovers and contingency staffing plans. Furthermore, the information management system of the district does not include a list of intelligence reports critical to informed decision making.*

Communication problems are fundamentally organizational learning problems. Both within the organization and to the larger community, they can express themselves as (a) inadequate organizational or environmental intelligence, (b) information overload, (c) poor dissemination of information—either up and down or laterally—in the organization,

(d) conflicting valuation or interpretation of intelligence, or (e) flawed causal models held by members about the relationship between information and outcomes. If I believe Scholastic Aptitude Test (SAT) scores are an inappropriate measure of the quality of my students, I will not necessarily view the students' declining performance on the SAT at Excelsior Academy as relevant or interesting.

Organizational learning problems often present themselves through symptomatic behavior. Some examples are as follows: (a) Members feed on rumors because the formal leadership of the organization does not effectively communicate its intentions or positions on controversial matters. (b) Organizational power is defined by access to corporate intelligence. (c) It is organizationally taboo to speak about certain chronic organizational dysfunction (Argyris, 1990).

Another kind of organizational learning problem has to do with communication across organizational boundaries. For example, school boards, parents, students, teachers, and administrators may each have sharply divergent views of the goals of the district or its problems. These political problems directly affect the feasibility and support for various policy options.

The solution to many kinds of organizational learning problems is to change organizational structure and practices. However, research shows that changing the structure (e.g., reducing classes) does not automatically change the process (teacher-centric instruction). Thus, dysfunctional organizational learning strategies impede effective policy making at the system level and is not simply a by-product of poor organizational structure.

Systemic Dysfunction. In one approach to systems analysis, which we find helpful, several basic patterns, or archetypes, of systemic dysfunction often appear in complex organizations (Senge, 1990). Some of the more important archetypes for educational systems include the following:

- Fixes that fail
- Success to the successful
- Shifting the burden
- Eroding goals
- Tragedy of the commons
- Limits to growth

Each archetype, as well as others, is described in detail in Senge's book *The Fifth Discipline.* They are also given more attention in part V of this book. What is important to understand about systems archetypes at this point is that they share certain features. First, each archetype functions across time as a series of cycles. As the cycles progress, the problem snowballs. Thus, early recognition and intervention in a systems cycle pays a premium. Second, each cycle contains, somewhere within it, an implicit set of perverse incentives. Some group of actors benefits by continuing in the dysfunctional behavior. Finding the perverse incentive structure (and removing it) will usually lead to positive options for leveraging the pattern in an ecologically beneficial direction. Failed attempts to alter the cycle usually fail because they do not successfully offset or neutralize the perverse incentives. Third, without a systems perspective, educational leaders will be unable to identify or rectify systems cycles that undermine a healthy organizational ecology.

Once you identify the major drivers in a system cycle, it is helpful to document them with examples, statistical evidence, inference, or perhaps even pure speculation, if necessary. For example, an audit of the external environment might point out special political problems (e.g., voter apathy) that constrain the feasibility of recommendations that are otherwise reasonable if you assume healthy voting patterns. As an illustration, a large budgetary increase may not be feasible when your state does not fully fund its school finance formula and the district has failed to get a majority vote for the past 10 years on incremental increases in the budget. One section of the policy brief should attend to sources of evidence, however formal or informal, that the policy options under discussion are viable. For example, if clients or colleagues were surveyed, indicate how representative you believe your data to be and why.

Finally, you should explain why a problem is a problem and for whom it is a problem. Parents from affluent communities whose children are highly successful in school will often be less concerned about the dropout rate and more concerned about the availability of advanced placement courses for college-bound students. You may safely assume that what is defined as a problem is itself a highly political issue. Conversely, some problems are difficult to get on the public agenda because they will divert resources from the dominant interest groups. An example of systemic dysfunction in the context of Excelsior Academy might be as follows:

> *Five years ago, in response to state and federal mandates and financial incentives, Excelsior Academy allocated a significant sum of funding to remedial education programming with 8 to 12 students per class and specially trained remedial teachers. At that time, about 7% of all students were identified as remedial. Students with weak academic skills learned about the support systems at Excelsior and applied in increasing numbers to attend. Today, more than 20% of all students are in remedial classes, and the average cost of educating a remedial student is nearly twice the cost of regular instruction. Furthermore, remedial students are 50% less likely to graduate. In short, nearly 40% of the instructional budget is devoted to 20% of the students. Regular instruction has been cut to accommodate the increased demands of remedial students. A program for gifted students has been cut altogether.*

Policy Options

Policy options can be organized most efficiently when they respond to the subcategories of problems identified in the previous step. Thus, for example, when Excelsior Academy is confronted with rapidly increasing enrollments, the option "Building a new wing to the Academy" can be systematically analyzed by using the basic concepts just introduced. When we are investigating the organizational feasibility of an addition, immediate questions come to mind, such as Should the addition be built to reduce class size as well as overcrowding?

Communication factors also raise additional questions: Will the addition serve the educational needs of Excelsior Academy? Are the requirements to implement the construction within an appropriate time frame? Is funding the addition politically feasible? Has the board effectively communicated the need for an addition to its constituents and clients?

Similarly, a number of environmental issues may need to be addressed. For example, will the state department of education support the addition politically or financially? Is the site appropriate environmentally—will the district be building on a floodplain or an earthquake fault?

Finally, are the costs in line with the benefits? Are alternative methods of addressing the overcrowding available that are more cost-effective? For example, has the district conducted an enrollment forecast that demonstrates a long-term need? Would portable units be a reasonable short-run alternative? Is leasing an option? Will busing students from one attendance zone to another solve the overcrowding?

An excellent discussion of options includes at least the following: (a) doing nothing, (b) compiling a list of alternatives, (c) estimating expected benefits for each alternative, (d) estimating costs, and (e) estimating the organizational capacity to implement the option. Other dimensions to the problem may present themselves (e.g., combinations of solutions), but (a) through (e) seem to be the minimal subset of possibilities.

Selecting among alternatives can be most efficiently accomplished by studying the particular issues raised in the problem statement. Then, each alternative should be carefully evaluated in terms of whether or not it satisfies the economic, political, technical, and cost criteria of a sound educational solution. A well-organized evaluation of alternatives might be summarized in tabular form, as in Table 2–1.

Costs and benefits. Addressing the costs and benefits associated with each policy option is critical to any meaningful policy options brief. In economics, we use the term *costs and benefits* when both sides of the equation can be quantified in dollars. Every policy has trade-offs: The key policy issue is to identify these trade-offs. From a programmatic

TABLE 2–1

Examples of Methods for Summarizing Policy Options Costs and Benefits

Example 1: SWOT (Strengths, Weaknesses, Opportunities, and Threats) Analysis[a]

	Strengths	Weaknesses	Opportunities	Threats
Option 1				
Option 2				
Option 3				

Example 2: Cost Analysis[b]

Policy option	Costs	Utility	Benefits	Effectiveness	Feasibility

Example 3: Audit Framework

	Internal			External		
Policy option	Economic feasibility	Political support	Technical capacity	Economic feasibility	Political support	Technical capacity

[a]For a thorough discussion of SWOT analysis, see Goldberg and Sifonis (1994).

[b]For a more specific definition of cost analysis methods, see Levin (1983).

perspective, we are interested in two kinds of costs and benefits: private costs and benefits and social costs and benefits. Perhaps a given policy option—for example, an expanded summer school program for students in the lowest achievement quartile—has modest individual benefits to the one quarter of students who benefit from the program—perhaps slightly higher average lifetime earnings profiles. When the benefits cannot be reasonably assigned in dollars (e.g., reduced dropout rates, teenage pregnancy, and juvenile justice contacts), we evaluate in terms of *cost-effectiveness*. Most educational programs are measured in this way, for example, 500 dollars of tutoring for each 10 points of increase in test score performance.

Of course, as is often the case with redistributive programming, who pays for the cost of the summer school program may not be who benefits. Thus, the community's sense of enlightened self-interest can significantly affect the feasibility, support, and scope of redistributive programs. It may also be the case that a project has external costs that are absorbed by a group other than the beneficiary. One illustration, frequently in the news, is the placement of facilities to serve at-risk populations—such as halfway houses for juveniles, the homeless, drug addicts, or unwed mothers—in residential neighborhoods. Residents often oppose such programs because the residents bear new risks for which they are not compensated, such as reduced property values and perceived threats to their families, whereas the benefits to society are diffuse. Implementing policy options with diffuse social benefits and concentrated risks is difficult when political support is required.

Table 2–1 provides examples of convenient methods for summarizing costs and benefits or strengths and weaknesses of policy options. Such tables should be accompanied by a discussion of the assumptions underlying each evaluative summary. For example, you should define how the benefits of a particular option are measured and what costs are included in making the cost–benefit judgment. Some judgments will be more arbitrary than others. Clarity in underlying assumptions is critical to the usefulness of the evaluation.

Recommendations

In each case, the policy analyst's recommendations should be contingent on the goals of his or her organization. Will a quick fix suffice, or is the organization willing to bear the costs involved in a structural solution? The analyst must be sufficiently objective and flexible to recommend a range of solutions. We all think we know what should be done, but is the policy option feasible? Does it have the necessary political and economic support? Does the organization have the capacity to implement the policy? Most important, a recommendation needs to be embedded in a plan of action. If you cannot provide a fairly detailed list of steps that need to be taken to implement the recommendation, it is unlikely to be implemented.

It is helpful to identify the types of problems that are likely to remain at each range of solution. You might want to recommend short-range and long-range solutions to increase the likelihood that your organization will initiate some range of solutions. (*Remember:* One axiom of policy studies is that incremental reforms are more likely to be implemented than are substantive reforms. Incremental reforms are also less likely to solve serious problems. Our strategy for escaping the horns of the incremental–restructural dilemma is to use ecological knowledge to leverage reforms that can have both a low cost and a high impact.) Finally, the analyst's recommendations should include a strategy and a timetable for implementation.

Action Plan

The action plan describes how the recommended option should be implemented. The principal elements of an action plan are as follows:

◆ Leadership (who is responsible)
◆ Time line (major implementation benchmarks)
◆ Budget requirements
◆ Staff requirements
◆ Facilities requirements
◆ Support services required
◆ Publicity or community coordination

A detailed description of each of these elements would take many pages. In the brief, you should instead devote a few sentences to each, providing specific estimates in the appropriate denomination (e.g., months, dollars, personnel, square feet, etc.). For the purposes of the brief, a thumbnail sketch of the action plan is sufficient. Once the recommended policy is approved, more detailed information—including full budget sheets, line allocations, personnel commitments, and PERT (program evaluation review technique) charts—might be required for full implementation.

Path-mark Analysis

In subsequent chapters, we spend a great deal of time developing the data-gathering and analyzing tools for path marking. We define *path marking* as benchmarking across time. We reiterate that in dynamic systems it is even more important to know what path your organization is following than to know precisely where it is at any moment on the path. Of course, points in time establish the basis of trend data. For each policy goal you identify in your brief, you should think about how you plan to measure the progress of the organization in accomplishing and sustaining the goal with time. We strongly urge you to think of multiple possible indicators for each major goal. Doing so mitigates against the natural organizational tendency to manipulate the indicator (which is often easier) than to accomplish the difficult work of attaining the goal.

POLICY PRESENTATIONS

We highly recommend practicing policy presentations along with writing policy options briefs as a way to enhance the experience of students using this book in a semester course. In general, the same outline structure for the three types of briefs will make for a sound organizational structure for a presentation. Some differences exist between preparation of the written document and preparation of slides in software such as Powerpoint. Although we already emphasized the rule "keep it simple" when we were talking about briefs, when you create computerized slides, this message is all the more important. Following are six guidelines for preparing policy presentations:

1. *Use no more than 1 slide per minute* (i.e., for the typical 15-minute presentation, 15 slides).

2. *Everything on your slides should be large enough, bold enough, and clean and clear enough to be seen easily from the back of the room.* This means you should do the following:
   a. Stick to a 28-point font or larger for text (24 point at minimum for data labels).
   b. Use block, not rounded or stylized, fonts. They are boring but vivid.
   c. Stick with simple color contrast schemes such as white on a black or blue background, or yellow on blue (a white background can be too bright). Avoid background graphics, especially those that run behind text. New standard templates in Powerpoint are particularly poor in this regard.
3. *Simplify your charts and tables.* Unfortunately, you may not simply cut and paste the tables and charts you made for your brief from Word into Powerpoint. Document tables and charts are generally too complex for presentations. You will need to simplify and clarify.
4. *Avoid the three-dimensional (3-D) temptation.* Do not use 3-D in any graph unless the data have a third dimension ($x - y - z$). Using 3-D makes aligning your data with your axes difficult for the viewer.
5. *Avoid too much animation.* Slick transitions between slides are generally acceptable, and a chart or table that fades in or out can be a nice touch. Text building can also be effective when you want to sequentially build an argument or a point. However, too much animation is at first distracting (Slides 2 and 3) and then grows old and becomes annoying by Slide 6 or 7 (if not before). Also, avoid sound effects simply intended to accompany a flying graphic.
6. *Practice, practice, practice.* Do not wait until you are in front of your audience to practice.

Using Data to Describe the Schooling Context

The first step as a school leader seeking to solve administrative problems is to know your school or school district's environmental context. In fact, any ongoing description of environmental context will inevitably reveal organizational challenges. The tools in this part are intended to be used for proactive rather than reactive analyses, and for deepening your understanding of your organization as characteristics are revealed, inductively, through data. To achieve an ecological perspective, you must continually seek systemic insights. Because organizations are fluid, dynamic, and ecological, they are intelligible: They have deep patterns of organization that can be discovered and worked with to leverage school improvement. An ongoing quest for insight is not the same as pressure-driven assessment requested by a third party or a special interest group. Issues that emerge in the latter way frequently lead to the mere management of symptoms rather than to alteration of dysfunctional processes. Symptomatic reform buries the real cause of the dysfunction even deeper and eventually provokes a deeper crisis.

Continual "context setting" in an organization is also referred to as *systems monitoring*. Consider the analogy of a frog in a pot of water over a low fire. As the temperature of the water increases, so does the temperature of the frog, an amphibian. Because the change in temperature is occurring slowly, the frog will cook without attempting to escape from the pot.[1]

Now imagine that the frog is you, seated at a desk, with a telephone. All the while, you are forced to deflect a number of random telephone calls, which distract you from noticing changes in your wider environment. What do you need in order to understand the situation and prevent burnout? One strategy is an ongoing monitoring system. In the former case, monitoring water temperature would be a key component of the monitoring system. However, the frog could not have known this ahead of time. Similarly, he cannot possibly monitor everything. Thus, the frog needs to design and track a series of efficient indicators.

An *efficient indicator* conveys a system characteristic with a single piece of information, such as a number. A good set of efficient indicators provides substantial information about the condition of an entire system. Much remains to be done regarding efficient indicator design. Many school leaders are inhibited by the fear of combining financial data and student performance data; they are afraid to discover that the status quo in leadership is not working and that change is necessary. You will learn to overcome this inhibition in this part.

School analyses too often focus on single-year collections of data across institutions, especially student performance data. These analyses are called *cross-sectional studies*. Although they provide useful comparisons from one student, school, or district to the next, they fail to capture the dynamics of an educational system. Recall, in the case of the boiling frog, that the vital information was not the current temperature, or a particular past temperature, but where the temperature was headed—the general trend and the rate of acceleration toward the critical or boiling point. It is of the utmost importance to look both ways when you are assessing schools and school systems (Figure II–1). You must know both the position and the trajectory of the indicator relative to the goal. To paraphrase an Indian wisdom story, we do not want to be like the mouse confidently walking south on the back of an elephant while the elephant is walking north.

In chapter 3, we present methods for organizing and summarizing data and making "apples-to-apples" comparisons. In chapter 4, we explain the development of efficient indicators and demonstrate ways to creatively combine financial and performance data by using methods such as ratio analysis. Also in chapter 4, we discuss the importance of using value-added measures when we assess student, school, or district performance and how to integrate these measures into more complex indicator systems. In chapter 5, we review the statistical methods and terminology necessary for practicing school leaders.

FIGURE II–1
An Added Dimension: Time

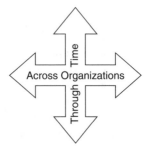

---

[1]The "Parable of the Boiled Frog" is also discussed in Senge's (1990) *The Fifth Discipline* (p. 22).

3

Organizing and Manipulating Data

TYPES OF DATA

What are the basic types of data that are available or accessible in schools? What is the organizational structure of these data, and what are some simple methods for presenting and comparing data? Figure 3–1 shows a broad classification of the types of data required for comprehensive ecological analysis of your organization.

Typically, school systems measure student performance, demographic characteristics of student and staff populations, and revenues and expenditures. Inextricably linked to these measures are various additional demographic and economic indicators. Our examples emphasize internal financial and performance data because these data are often more readily available. However, you will notice that these data are continually interwoven with broader economic and demographic measures in the problem sets and part simulations at the end of this chapter and the following chapters.

Teacher-generated assessments of students, such as grades or grade point averages, national standardized test scores, and state-sponsored or -mandated performance assessments all fall under the category of student performance data. The proliferation of school data has increased the pressure that leaders feel to prepare reports and make sense of the information.

QUANTIFICATION OF INFORMATION

Different types of data must be measured in different ways. Financial, student performance, and other survey data can be quantified in three basic ways (Table 3–1):

1. *Nominal or categorical data.* Such data have a name or category descriptor such as m = male or f = female. Letter labels might also be replaced with a number code such that 0 = male and 1 = female. These numbers lack hierarchy or order. That is, a 1 is not necessarily higher than a 0 in this case.

FIGURE 3–1
Data for Ecological Analysis

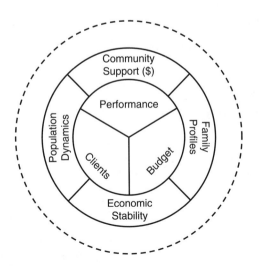

TABLE 3–1
Data Quantification Examples

Student (Nominal)	Gender (Nominal; 0 = m, 1 = f)	Class Rank (Ordinal)	ITBS Score (Interval)
001	0	23	78
002	1	10	83
003	0	7	93
004	1	2	99

Note: ITBS = Iowa Test of Basic Skills.

2. *Ordinal data.* Ordinal data are a set of numbers that represent a rank order, such as team standings in sports or opinions on a 5- or 10-point scale. With ordinal data, you can assume, for example, that the team rated 1 is better than the team rated 2 or 3, but you cannot assume that the distance between 1 and 2 is the same as the distance between 2 and 3.

3. *Interval data.* Interval data are a set of numerical data that have both an order and a defined distance between units. The measure of distance in inches or centimeters, the measure of time, and the measure of money are all examples of interval data.

SAMPLING

As noted previously, data collection and data analysis provide snapshots of an institution. You must continually remind yourself that you are viewing not the system, but limited pieces of information extracted from the system. In the end, this information may or may not provide you with a useful system representation. Testing its utility, or monitoring the ecology of your organization, is what establishes its validity. The more frequently you sample data from your system or school, the greater your ability will be to represent the system precisely. However, in doing so, you must be careful to maintain a grasp of the big picture. Consider the four graphs in Figure 3–2.

In Sample 1, only four points represent system behavior. The four points paint a crude picture of a system. Increasing the number of points measured, in Sample 2, results in a clearer, more precise, smoother picture of the system. However, what if all our new measures do not fall into a neat, clean, precise pattern? Would the overall picture truly be like the dot-to-dot graph in Sample 3? Could you predict with any confidence where the next data point will lie?

Economists make a helpful distinction between data collected (or sampled) and the *processes* that generate the data: the underlying dynamic features of the system. Data points are simply measures taken at various places through various points in time, with instruments of varying precision and accuracy. Thus, data may be "noisy," scattered, and not perfectly representative of the underlying process. Perhaps this is the case in Sample 3, and Sample 4 better represents the general pattern emerging from the underlying process.

FIGURE 3–2
Sampling Data

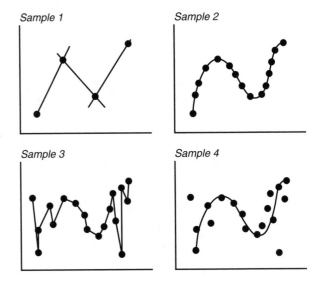

Sometimes, you must step back from noisy, oversampled data, and *fuzzify*,[1] so to speak, the picture of the data to see an emergent pattern. This technique is similar to the softening of eye focus used to get three-dimensional images to arise from two-dimensional color patterns.

BASIC STRUCTURE AND ANALYSIS OF FINANCIAL DATA

Let us begin with a relatively small and simple data set: budget and enrollment data for seven city elementary schools. Beginners should work through each of the early examples by entering the data into an Excel spreadsheet in the cell locations indicated in Table 3–2. Please note that, in general, data are organized such that fields or variables are the headings of columns, and cases (e.g., schools) run down the side. This is similar, for example, to the layout of a grade book.

Following are the instructions for graphing the total budgets of the schools (see Figure 3–3):

1. Highlight the data and labels from cell A1 to cell B8 (see Table 3–2). If you include the labels in your highlighting, Excel will automatically label your graph.
2. Click the Chart Wizard toolbar. The icon is a small red, yellow, and blue bar graph.
3. Select "bar graph" and follow the Chart Wizard steps.

You can also try preparing graphs of the data in the other columns. Once you have highlighted the column of school names, to highlight a nonadjacent column, hold down the

---

[1]We use this awkward word because it represents a specific technique used by artificially intelligent computer algorithms that seek general patterns in noisy data.

TABLE 3–2
Budgetary Data for City Schools

	A	B	C
1	**School**	**Total Budget**	**FTE Pupils**
2	Liberty	$ 2,513,061	601
3	Cecil	$ 2,459,967	632
4	Madison	$ 2,007,184	477
5	Washington	$ 1,917,220	386
6	Brent	$ 1,908,424	491
7	Park Heights	$ 1,530,635	361
8	Lakewood	$ 1,122,006	195

Note: FTE = full-time-enrolled.

control key (PC) or the apple key (Macintosh) and then highlight. Also, try changing features of your graphs (adding labels, changing colors, etc.). You can change most features by double clicking the object of interest. Another option is to select Chart Options from the Chart menu.

Now consider what Table 3–2 and Figure 3–3 indicate about the spending habits of these schools. Liberty spends the most and Lakewood spends the least. Unfortunately, this fact does not mean much. One reason that Liberty spends more is that it is one of the larger schools and Lakewood is one of the smaller schools. For this reason, a much more appropriate approach is to compare schools by per-pupil expenditure (PPE) rather than by total budgets. Even so, consider the several causes of variations in PPE among schools. Special education funding, percentage of teachers with advanced degrees or seniority, and small class sizes all contribute to higher PPE. Only the first possibility is educationally defensible; the others may have positive or negative consequences for the children in these schools. Always try to relate your knowledge of school systems and spending to your work with numbers to ground abstract exercises in reality.

The PPE can easily be calculated by adding one column to your table (number of pupils) and dividing numbers in the Total Budget column by the numbers of pupils (see syntax

FIGURE 3–3
Comparison of Site-Based Budget Totals

Note: You can add the data labels shown by selecting Chart Options from the Chart menu and going to the Data Labels file tab.

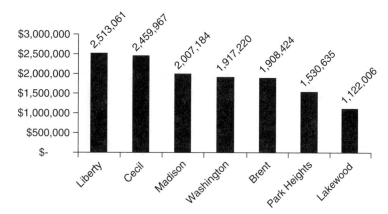

TABLE 3–3
Syntax for Excel Calculations

Cell Label	A	B	C	D
1	School	Total Budget	FTE Pupils	PPE
2	Liberty	2513061	601	=B2/C2
3	Cecil	2459967	632	=B3/C3
4	Madison	2007184	477	=B4/C4
5	Washington	1917220	386	=B5/C5
6	Brent	1908424	491	=B6/C6
7	Park Heights	1530635	361	=B7/C7
8	Lakewood	1122006	195	=B8/C8

Note: FTE = full-time-enrolled; PPE = per-pupil expenditure.

[formulas] displayed in Table 3–3). Figure 3–4 indicates that Lakewood, the school with the smallest total budget, has the highest PPE.

As suggested previously, you must consider both *cross-sectional comparisons* of students, schools, or districts, and *trends and patterns of change through time*. In addition, appropriate use of units can have a significant effect on the picture you are trying to paint. Table 3–4 displays expenditure and pupil data for a school district through time. At a glance, you can easily see that both the number of pupils and the total budget for the district are increasing. One way to gain a better understanding of trends is to look at the percent change from year to year. The basic calculation for percent change, if we use data from Table 3–4, is as follows:

[1986 Expenditures ($152 million) − 1985 Expenditures ($150 million)]
÷ 1985 Expenditures ($150 million) = 1.33%

The common denominator allows us to ask another question. Why do PPEs for these seven elementary schools vary by almost 2,000 (see Figure 3–4)? (Lakewood PPE − Brent PPE = $1,867.)

The Excel syntax for this particular worksheet is also displayed in Table 3–4.

FIGURE 3–4
Comparison of Site-Based Per-Pupil Expenditures

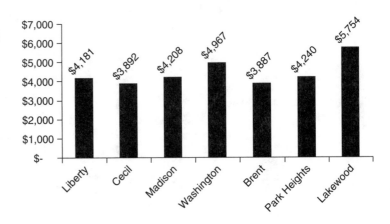

TABLE 3–4

Syntax for Calculating Percent Change

	A	B	C	D	E	F	G
1	**Year**	**Total Expenditures**	**Percent Change**	**Total Pupils**	**Percent Change**	**PPE**	**Percent Change**
2	1985	150000000		25000		=B2/D2	
3	1986	152000000	=(B3-B2)/B2	26000	=(D3-D2)/D2	=B3/D3	=(F3-F2)/F2
4	1987	154000000	=(B4-B3)/B3	27000	=(D4-D3)/D3	=B4/D4	=(F4-F3)/F3
5	1988	156000000	=(B5-B4)/B4	28000	=(D5-D4)/D4	=B5/D5	=(F5-F4)/F4
6	1989	158000000	=(B6-B5)/B5	29000	=(D6-D5)/D5	=B6/D6	=(F6-F5)/F5
7	1990	160000000	=(B7-B6)/B6	30000	=(D7-D6)/D6	=B7/D7	=(F7-F6)/F6
8	1991	162000000	=(B8-B7)/B7	31000	=(D8-D7)/D7	=B8/D8	=(F8-F7)/F7
9	1992	164000000	=(B9-B8)/B8	32000	=(D9-D8)/D8	=B9/D9	=(F9-F8)/F8
18		**Average %Change**	**=AVERAGE (C3:C17)**		**=AVERAGE (E3:E17)**		**=AVERAGE (G3:G17)**

Note: PPE = per-pupil expenditure.

A few features are worth noting on the final worksheet (Table 3–5). (For a more thorough discussion of time and change, please see part IV.) First, although the incremental change in total expenditures remains constant, the percent change decreases with time. Remember that the constant $2 million increment is divided by successively larger

TABLE 3–5

Expenditures and Enrollment From 1991 to 2000

Year	Total Expenditures($)	Percent Change	Total Pupils	Percent Change	PPE($)	Percent Change
1991	162,000,000	1.25	31,000	3.33	5,226	−2.02
1992	164,000,000	1.23	32,000	3.23	5,125	−1.93
1993	166,000,000	1.22	33,000	3.13	5,030	−1.85
1994	168,000,000	1.20	34,000	3.03	4,941	−1.77
1995	170,000,000	1.19	35,000	2.94	4,857	−1.70
1996	172,000,000	1.18	36,000	2.86	4,778	−1.63
1997	174,000,000	1.16	37,000	2.78	4,703	−1.57
1998	176,000,000	1.15	38,000	2.70	4,632	−1.51
1999	178,000,000	1.14	39,000	2.63	4,564	−1.46
2000	180,000,000	1.12	40,000	2.56	4,500	−1.40
	Average percent change	1.22		3.18		−1.90

Note: PPE = per-pupil expenditure.

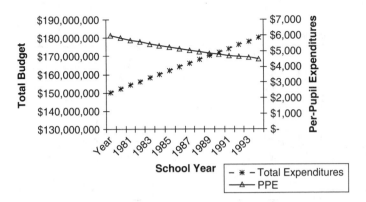

FIGURE 3–5
Total Expenditures Versus Per-Pupil Expenditures Across Time

denominators. Second, the average percent change in number of pupils is not the same as the percent change in the total budget. The average percent change for the total budget is 1.22%, whereas the average percent change for pupils is 3.18%. Therefore, the school district in question is facing a substantial decline in per-pupil spending.

Graphically, the contrast between total budget growth and change in per-pupil spending can be seen in Figure 3–5. This particular chart is a combination chart with two y axes. The two axes are needed because of the different scales of the variables. To construct this graph, follow these instructions:

1. Highlight the Year, Total Expenditures, and PPE columns.
2. Click the Chart Wizard tool.
3. Select "combination chart," choosing the option with two lines.
4. Continue the labeling steps.

MATRICES AND MATRIX OPERATIONS

You have already organized data in rows and columns. You can also refer to each value that appears in a database as a *data element*. These elements, when placed in a column, make up a *vector*. Multiple vectors combine to form a *matrix*, or grid, of data. Organizing data into matrices becomes particularly useful when you encounter large amounts of data and when you perform repeated functions on each element in the matrix. Consider Table 3–6, which represents a sample salary step scale for a school district. In this table, the various steps from 1 to 15 are listed as cases, and their relative pay levels are the data elements. Different fields are provided for various levels of educational attainment.

When you plan school budgets or salary schedule negotiations, you must be able to determine the total cost of implementing such a scale. This matrix of salary levels applies to yet another matrix: the number of faculty members at each salary level (Table 3–7).

To calculate total costs for the salary schedule, we must multiply each of the full-time-employee numbers by their respective salary levels; that is, multiply the second matrix by the first matrix. The grid structure of the spreadsheet simplifies this task.

TABLE 3–6
Sample Salary Schedule

Step	BS	BS+16	MA	MA+16	MA+32
1	$24,500	$25,000	$25,500	$26,000	$26,500
2	$26,000	$26,500	$27,000	$27,500	$28,000
3	$27,500	$28,000	$28,500	$29,000	$29,500
4	$29,000	$29,500	$30,000	$30,500	$31,000
5	$30,500	$31,000	$31,500	$32,000	$32,500
6	$32,000	$32,500	$33,000	$33,500	$34,000
7	$33,500	$34,000	$34,500	$35,000	$35,500
8	$35,000	$35,500	$36,000	$36,500	$37,000
9	$36,500	$37,000	$37,500	$38,000	$38,500
10	$38,000	$38,500	$39,000	$39,500	$40,000
11	$39,500	$40,000	$40,500	$41,000	$41,500
12	$41,000	$41,500	$42,000	$42,500	$43,000
13	$42,500	$43,000	$43,500	$44,000	$44,500
14	$44,000	$44,500	$45,000	$45,500	$46,000
15	$45,500	$46,000	$46,500	$47,000	$47,500

Note: BS = bachelor of science (degree); MA = master of arts (degree); +16 and +32 = additional 16 and 32 graduate credit hours, respectively.

TABLE 3–7
Distribution of Teaching Staff

Step	BS	BS+16	MA	MA+16	MA+32
1	2	1	0	0	0
2	14	2	2	0	1
3	23	0	1	0	0
4	24	3	6	0	0
5	13	5	12	0	0
6	13	7	15	0	0
7	10	5	7	1	0
8	9	7	9	0	1
9	12	3	8	3	1
10	9	3	8	1	1
11	5	1	12	0	1
12	12	3	10	1	1
13	6	2	9	1	2
14	4	1	22	3	6
15	50	3	30	6	2

Note: BS = bachelor of science (degree); MA = master of arts (degree); +16 and +32 = additional 16 and 32 graduate credit hours, respectively.

TABLE 3–8
Salary Schedule × Distribution of Teaching Staff = Cost

Step	$BS	$BS+16	$MA	$MA+16	$MA+32
1	49,000	25,000	0	0	0
2	364,000	53,000	54,000	0	28,000
3	632,500	0	28,500	0	0
4	696,000	88,500	180,000	0	0
5	396,500	155,000	378,000	0	0
6	416,000	227,500	495,000	0	0
7	335,000	170,000	241,500	35,000	0
8	315,000	248,500	324,000	0	37,000
9	438,000	111,000	300,000	114,000	38,500
10	342,000	115,500	312,000	39,500	40,000
11	197,500	40,000	486,000	0	41,500
12	492,000	124,500	420,000	42,500	43,000
13	255,000	86,000	391,500	44,000	89,000
14	176,000	44,500	990,000	136,500	276,000
15	2,275,000	138,000	1,395,000	282,000	95,000
Totals	7,379,500	1,627,000	5,995,500	693,500	688,000
				Grand total	16,383,500

Note: BS = bachelor of science (degree); MA = master of arts (degree); +16 and +32 = additional 16 and 32 graduate credit hours, respectively.

Table 3–8 shows a new matrix of values generated by multiplying the first matrix by the second matrix. Table 3–9 displays the formulas for generating these values. Once the first formula has been entered into cell B39, the Autofill function can be used to copy the function down the column and across the row.

Take a close look at the formulas. Each formula is systematically adjusted by column, from B21*B3 to B22*B4, and by row, from B21*B3 to C21*C3. (To use the Autofill function, place the cursor on the lower right-hand corner of a cell such that the cursor turns into a dark plus sign: **+.** Then, hold down the left mouse button and drag the formula.)

Suggested Activity

Your district has a teacher shortage. The administration's goal is to increase beginning teachers' salaries to attract beginning teachers to the district while holding senior teachers' salaries down. Divide the class into an even number of groups of three or four students. Pair the groups so that one group represents administration and the other represents teachers. In the teacher group, some students should represent seasoned teachers with advanced degrees; others should represent new teachers. Ask the teacher and administrator groups to prepare new step scales for negotiation that result in 3, 5, and 7% increases in the total budget.

TABLE 3–9

Syntax for Matrix Calculations

	A	B	C	D	F
1					
2	Step	BS	BS+16	MA	MA+32
3	1	21500	25000	25500	26500
4	2	26000	26500	27000	28000
5	3	27500	28000	28500	29500
6	4	29000	29500	30000	31000
18					
19					
20	Step	BS	BS+16	MA	MA+32
21	1	2	1	0	0
22	2	14	2	2	1
23	3	23	0	1	0
24	4	24	3	6	0
25	5	13	5	12	0
26	6	13	7	15	0
36					
37					
38	Step	$BS	$BS+16	$MA	$MA+32
39	1	=B21*B3	=C21*C3	=D21*D3	=F21*F3
40	2	=B22*B4	=C22*C4	=D22*D4	=F22*F4
41	3	=B23*B5	=C23*C5	=D23*D5	=F23*F5
42	4	=B24*B6	=C24*C6	=D24*D6	=F24*F6
43	5	=B25*B7	=C25*C7	=D25*D7	=F25*F7
44	6	=B26*B8	=C26*C8	=D26*D8	=F26*F8
54	Totals	=SUM (B39:B53)	=SUM (C39:C53)	=SUM (D39:D53)	=SUM (F39:F53)
55					=SUM (B54:F54)

Note: BS = bachelor of science (degree); MA = master of arts degree; +16 and +32 = additional 16 and 32 graduate credit hours, respectively.

STRUCTURE AND PECULIARITIES OF STUDENT PERFORMANCE DATA

Because of the way in which schools are structured, the organization and analysis of student performance data can become complicated. In recent years, statisticians and educational researchers have designed special statistical methods for education. Perhaps the

FIGURE 3–6
Hierarchy of Schooling

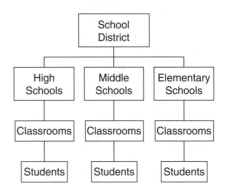

most common discussions revolve around the idea that when we "randomly" select students from schools or districts to assess the performance of the school or district, these students are anything but random representations of the school or district. The bottom line? Although school districts are organized into many levels, in the end learning occurs in the classroom. Despite continued efforts to equalize educational opportunity, no single classroom is like the one immediately adjacent to it.

A typical view of school district organization is shown in Figure 3–6. This figure represents a data-generating process; however, the data generated by a given pool of students depends on their particular classroom and school. We refer to this dependence as *nesting*. This means that students are not randomly distributed throughout the system, nor are they randomly affected by the system—which creates a host of problems for data analysts.[2] Subsequently in this chapter, you learn simple methods for resolving nesting problems.

Student performance data are found in Table 3–10. Note that individual students are assigned a code, or student identification number, and represent individual cases in the database. Each student is also assigned to a particular school in the district with a nominal

TABLE 3–10
Tabular Layout of Hierarchical Data

	A	B	C	D
1	**Student ID**	**School #**	**Math Class ID**	**Math Score**
2	001	1	001	92
3	002	1	001	85
4	003	1	002	73
5	004	1	002	85
6	005	2	001	98
7	006	2	001	87
8	007	2	002	89
9	008	2	002	94

[2]For more information on this topic, see Bryk and Raudenbush (1992).

or categorical code and is assigned to a particular math class with a nominal or categorical code. Providing coding layers allows the opportunity to glean much more information from data than student numbers and math scores alone. We can now determine performance differences by school, by classroom, and by type of student, all the while "controlling" for classroom and school environment. Structuring performance data in this way may require additional effort at the school or district level because testing agencies will not typically have this information.

(RE)ORGANIZATION AND MANIPULATION OF DATA SETS

Ranking, Sorting, and Filtering Data

Another function that can be performed in Excel is ranking and sorting data. This feature can help you to compare students, schools, or countries with one another with regard to a particular index. For example, Table 3–11 shows that the United States spends more per pupil than other countries on the list. When graphed, sorted data make a more vivid impression than do unsorted data.

IMPORTANT: WHENEVER YOU SORT DATA, YOU MUST REMEMBER TO HIGHLIGHT ALL THE COLUMNS IN THE DATA SET AND SORT THE ENTIRE DATA SET TOGETHER, EVEN IF YOU WANT ONLY TO SEE HOW THE CASES RANK ON A GIVEN VARIABLE. IF YOU REORDER ONLY ONE SECTION OF YOUR DATA, YOUR DATA ELEMENTS WILL NO LONGER BE ALIGNED WITH THE APPROPRIATE CASES. THIS CREATES A SCRAMBLED DATA SET.

TABLE 3–11
OECD International Comparisons

Country	Average Spending per Pupil (U.S. $)
Belgium	4,660
Denmark	4,660
Finland	4,350
France	4,600
Germany (FTFR)	3,860
Ireland	2,240
Italy	4,470
Netherlands	2,290
New Zealand	2,340
Norway	5,420
Spain	2,840
Sweden	5,450
United States	6,010

Note: Data from *Education at a Glance*, by Organization for Economic Cooperation and Development, 1999, Paris: Author.

To sort data in Excel, do the following:

1. Highlight the data and the labels.
2. Select Sort from the Data menu.
3. From the pop-up window, select which column to "Sort by." (If you highlighted labels at the top of your rows, the labels should appear on your selection list. If they do not, check to see that the Header Row circle is marked.)
4. Click OK.

When you are working with very large data sets, you may want to isolate and study subsets of data. For example, from a large data set of all students in a school, you might want to extract students by gender, race, or ethnicity. In the following example, we extract schools by the grade levels that they serve. It is extremely important to make appropriate comparisons by identifying and extracting the best possible comparison group.

Current versions of Excel contain a simple, elegant data-extraction feature. Use the Sort function (discussed previously) and highlight the data subset. Copy and paste it to a new sheet, or use the Autofilter feature. Try this with Table 3–12:

1. Highlight the data and labels (as with the Sort function, highlight the entire block, not just the data of interest).
2. Select Filter–Autofilter from the Data menu. Small downward arrows should appear at the top of each column.
3. Click on one of the arrows. You should see a list of all the different elements that appear in that column. For example, if it is a gender column, you should see "M" and "F." The list will also include "blanks" if blank fields exist in your data.

TABLE 3–12
Public Schools Database

	A	B	C	D	E
1	**PSID**	**LEAID**	**GRADES**	**ENROLL98**	**LSY98**
2	PS002	T001	K-6	148	177
3	PS007	T002	PK-8	102	175
4	PS008	T238	K-6	77	175
5	PS010	T003	K-8	209	181
6	PS015	T007	K-8	195	175
7	PS017	T009	PK-6	84	175
8	PS018	T010	K-8	261	175
9	PS381	T011	PK-8	950	180
10	PS020	T012	PK-8	1084	175
11	PS021	J048	K-8	303	180
12	PS022	T013	K-8	214	175
13	PS023	T138	K-6	165	175

Note: State level; unit = school; PSID = public school ID; LEAID = local education agency (district) ID; LSY = length of school year (days).

TABLE 3–13
Filtered Data: K–6 Schools Only

	A	B	C	D	E
1	**PSID**	**LEAID**	**GRADES**	**ENROLL98**	**LSY98**
2	PS002	T001	K-6	148	177
4	PS008	T238	K-6	77	175
13	PS023	T138	K-6	165	175

Note: PSID = public school ID; LEAID = local education agency (district) ID; LSY = length of school year (days).

4. Select a parameter from the list. Once you have done this, all fields not containing this parameter will be hidden and the arrow will appear blue, which indicates that the field is filtered. You can unhide the cases by clicking on the blue arrow and selecting "all."

In Table 3–13, we filtered according to the grade levels of the school, selecting K–6 as our parameter. Thus, the list is reduced to only K–6 schools. This data set contains schools in rows 2, 4, and 13. To work further with this data, copy (ctrl-c) the block of K–6-only schools and paste (ctrl-v) it onto a separate spreadsheet, then rename the new sheet appropriately. In general, you should not "mess with" the integrity of your main database. Similar cautions are pertinent regarding sorting features.

This tool is also particularly useful for removing blank or bad data from your data set. For example, if a number of schools failed to report their enrollments in the preceding data set, we could remove them from the data set by selecting the "blank" parameter on the ENROLL list to show only the schools not reporting enrollments. Then, we could highlight and delete these rows from the database. Again, sorting and deleting should not be done with the main database, but with a copy in which you intend to specifically analyze enrollment data.

Subtotaling

For a subtotaling example, see Table 3–14. With these data (assuming that they extend beyond the given parameters to a larger data set), you might want to show average scores by gender, by program, or both. If the data in Table 3–14 were financial data, you might want to sum expenditure categories.

TABLE 3–14
Sample Student Database

Student #	Gender	Program	4th Grade	8th Grade
1	m	1	33	55
2	f	7	32	75
3	f	1	35	52
4	m	8	45	81
5	m	4	26	74
6	f	3	25	65

Note: School level; unit = pupil.

FIGURE 3–7
Excel Subtotaling Dialog Box

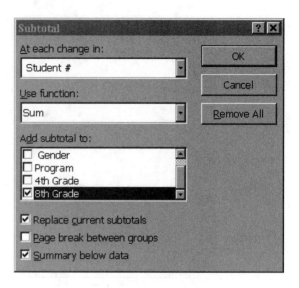

If you select Subtotal from the Data menu, you will see the screen shown in Figure 3–7. The "At each change in" drop-down menu allows you to select which categories you want to subtotal.

NOTE: FIRST YOU NEED TO SORT THE DATA BY GENDER, FOR EXAMPLE, SO THAT ALL FEMALE STUDENTS ARE TOGETHER AND ALL MALE STUDENTS ARE TOGETHER. OTHERWISE, THE PROGRAM WILL GENERATE SUBTOTALS FOR EACH CLUSTERED SEQUENCE OF MALES AND FEMALES SEPARATELY. THE RESULT OF SORTING BY CLASS, THEN GENDER, IS TWO LAYERS OF SUBTOTALING.

The "Use function" drop-down menu allows you to select the value you want to report: Sum, Average, Standard Deviation, and so forth. The "Add subtotal to" toggle boxes allow you to indicate which values you want to subtotal. Depending on your selections, your output may appear as shown in Figure 3–8.

Clicking on the "−" symbols in the left margin allows you to display either all data, select groups, or subtotals. These tabs are similar to the Autofilter function.

PivotTable

Another useful automated feature is the PivotTable feature. This feature, as with the Subtotal function, presents summary analyses of subgroups within a larger data set. Using the same data as used previously, you can produce Table 3–15.

Steps for constructing a PivotTable are as follows:

1. Highlight the data you want to analyze and select PivotTable from the Data Menu. A PivotTable Wizard will appear and walk you through the construction of the table:
   a. *Question 1:* What are the data you want to analyze? (should be highlighted)
   b. *Question 2:* What kind of report do you want to make? (table and/or chart)

1 2 3		A	B	C	D	E
	1	Student #	Gender	Program	4th Grade	8th Grade
	2	3	f	1	35	52
	3	16	f	1	32	75
	4	18	f	1	25	65
	5			1 Average	30.66667	64
	6	23	f	2	33	65
	7	32	f	2	36	65
	8			2 Average	34.5	65
	9	6	f	3	25	65
	10	13	f	3	32	75
	11	44	f	3	33	55
	12			3 Average	30	65
	13	8	f	4	45	81
	14			4 Average	45	81

FIGURE 3–8
Excel Subtotaling Output

2. Click Next, and the highlighted data range should be shown.
3. Click Next, and you are given the option to put your table on the same or a different worksheet than the worksheet with the data.
4. At this point, you may click either Finish or Layout. Layout will allow you to set up your PivotTable and select the variables and the values (mean, sum) you want in your table.
5. Click Layout and the screen shown in Figure 3–9 appears.
6. Select the categories that you want to cross-reference. For example, select "by gender and program," as shown in Figure 3–10.

TABLE 3–15
Summary of Test Scores by Program and Gender

Gender	Data	Program 1	Program 2	Total
Female	Average 4th Grade	30.67	34.50	33.92
	Average 8th Grade	64.00	65.00	65.81
Male	Average 4th Grade	34.50	33.33	32.67
	Average 8th Grade	68.50	76.67	70.96
Total Average of 4th Grade		32.20	33.80	33.32
Total Average of 8th Grade		65.80	72.00	68.28

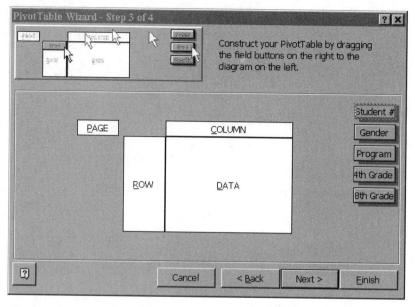

FIGURE 3–9
Excel PivotTable Dialog Box

7. You may present sums, averages, or any variety of statistics in your table, just as with the Subtotal function. To do so, double click the value (fourth-grade scores) you want to move into the Data area. This will bring up a menu of statistical options. After selecting the values you want to report, drag the field into the Data area.
8. Click OK.

One particularly useful characteristic of both the Subtotal function and the PivotTable tool is that the output tables are "actively" linked to your data. This feature may prove useful for demonstrations. For example, if you double click on the average score of females in Program 1 in the PivotTable, Excel will generate a report of female student scores in Program 1.

FIGURE 3–10
Example of PivotTable Preparation

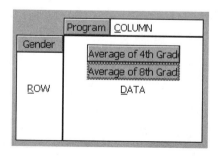

SUMMARY

In this chapter, you learned basic methods of organizing, presenting, and analyzing data. You also learned a number of basic spreadsheet skills. Please understand that this book does not discuss all the relevant possibilities for data analysis. The intent of this chapter is to stimulate thought about approaching data in a spreadsheet format. We encourage you to consider additional possibilities.

ADDITIONAL RESOURCES

Berk, K. N., & Carey, P. M. (2004). *Data analysis with Microsoft Excel: Updated for Office XP* (2nd ed.). Belmont, CA: Brooks/Cole.

Harvey, G. (2003). *Excel 2003 for Dummies*. New York: Wiley.

PROBLEM A

Introduction to Data Manipulation and Graphing

Background: For the past 5 years, your school district has implemented a series of 10 reading instruction strategies for its elementary and middle schools. The same groups of students participate in the programs each year. The district has collected data on the programs, including costs, student participation, and student performance, and has organized the data as follows:

Program Cost Data: This worksheet consists of the total cost of each program and the numbers of pupils served (annual average).

Student Performance Data: This worksheet consists of the average performance levels for students participating in the program for each year of participation from Grade 4 through Grade 8.

Individual Student Data: This worksheet consists of data for randomly extracted sets of five students from each program, including their gender and scores in both fourth grade and eighth grade.

Your Mission: Prepare a summary report of the programs for presentation to the school board next week. The superintendent of the district has provided you with the following guidelines:

Task 1: Graph and compare the cost attributes of the reading programs. Construct appropriate units (cost per pupil) for comparison when necessary. Use the Program Cost Data worksheet. Provide a brief narrative of your major findings.

Task 2: Analyze the student achievement characteristics across time. Determine the individual and average rates of gain. Use the Student Performance Data worksheet. Provide a brief narrative of your major findings.

Task 3: Compare the performance of male and female students. Extract the two groups. Rank and sort the groups. Use the Individual Student Data worksheet. Provide a brief narrative of your major findings.

Sample Figure and Table Using Problem A Data

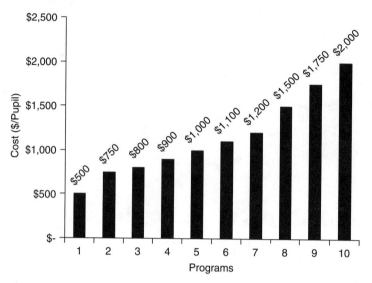

FIGURE 3–A–1
Program Costs Per Pupil

TABLE 3–A–1
Average Performance Change (%)
for Five Reading Programs

		Program			
Grade	1	2	3	4	5
4–5	5.7	24.3	18.2	7.9	30.8
5–6	10.8	19.6	33.3	4.9	21.6
6–7	9.8	14.5	17.3	11.6	17.7
7–8	15.6	14.3	16.4	8.3	9.6

4

Developing Indicator Systems

Ratio, percent, and share analyses provide other ways of making "apples-to-apples" comparisons. Using the pupil as the denominator in the beginning of chapter 3 is a form of ratio analysis, in which the number of pupils is used to adjust the scale of comparison. In the following example, the relative proportions of spending help us to compare budget categories from year to year. This analysis could similarly be performed when we are comparing school with school. In Table 4–1, we present an overview of the role of shares and ratios as indexes.

Table 4–2 lists the city schools budget summary for all funds for 2000–2002. Instructional spending and the total budget appear to be climbing from year to year. You could apply the methods described in chapter 3 to determine which is growing faster and make assumptions from your findings. However, in this case, let us try a different approach.

Remember that each category, or line item, represents a share of a whole. Try to determine whether the share of spending allocated to General Instruction (line 743) is constant or not. You may look at shares in terms of either "total instructional allocations" or "total budget."

Table 4–3 displays instructional spending as a share of total instructional spending, and each support service category as a share of total support services. The shares are simply percentages of the whole, taken by line items of expenditures. Although this particular example deals with changes in shares across time, you could also compare schools or districts of varying sizes. In a direct, side-by-side comparison of total spending, a larger school's instructional or operational expenditures might dwarf those of a smaller school; however, share analysis could reveal that a smaller percentage of these expenditures are allocated to instruction. Also, from individual, site-based data for schools within the district whose data are shown in Table 4–2, you could determine whether individual schools' shares are consistent with district-wide trends. The Excel syntax for these calculations is shown in Table 4–4, and tips for setting up this spreadsheet are as follows.

Graphically, shares can be represented in a variety of ways: pie charts, area charts, or the type of columns seen in Table 4–4. Unfortunately, pie charts do not work well when time

TABLE 4–1
Shares, Ratios, and Indicators

Type of Analysis	General Use	Examples
Share analysis	When a resource or pool of objects is finite (total budget, total enrollment) and contains subcategories of resources or objects (e.g., teacher salaries, administrative salaries, instructional support).	a. Instructional spending as a share (%) of total budget b. Low-income pupils as a share (%) of enrollment
Ratio analysis	When the value of a single number does not stand alone or lacks context. Used to create a *scale,* or basis of comparison.	a. Expenditures per pupil (= Total Budget/Pupils) b. Pupil-to-teacher ratio (= Total Pupils/Total Teachers)

Note: Shares are ratios of a part to the whole. However, ratios need not be shares.

TABLE 4–2

Expenditures by Function: City Schools Budget Summary for All Funds for 2000–2002

		Expenditures ($)		
Line	Instructional Service	FY2000	FY2001	FY2002
743	General Instruction	216,884,848	261,324,051	281,864,021
744	Other Instruction	9,789,667	11,544,290	12,318,240
746	Student Services	466,359	546,004	532,544
751	Special Education	3,462,541	3,945,690	4,419,091
754	Vocational Instruction	14,168,125	15,668,711	16,877,845
755	Adult/Alternative Instruction	3,287,378	4,709,036	7,078,461
756	Special Instruction	79,251,388	94,170,408	101,049,444
757	Special Vocational Instruction	3,204,536	3,913,946	5,789,540
758	G&T Instruction	2,070,918	2,405,432	2,607,489
	Total	332,585,760	398,227,568	432,536,675
		Expenditures ($)		
Line	Support Service	FY2000	FY2001	FY2002
725	General Fund Support	4,715,841	50,000	50,000
746	Student Services	2,832,455	3,855,085	4,394,908
762	Food Services	24,043,492	25,107,367	25,537,347
764	Pupil Transportation	22,537,505	24,991,943	24,847,703
767	Facilities	53,045,065	59,535,308	60,447,884
768	School Police	7,075,432	5,060,571	5,131,496
	Total	114,249,790	118,600,274	120,409,338

Note: FY = fiscal year; G&T = gifted and talented.

is a factor. One important feature of the graphic style used in Figure 4–1 is that the y-axis scale is in percentage units. As a result, column totals are 100%. Only the internal shares vary. When shares are the objects of interest, this approach is particularly effective. Allowing the height of the columns to vary by total budget volume makes visually assessing the relative changes in shares more difficult. By attaching data labels to these shares, we can see that pupil transportation and facilities costs are creeping up relative to the costs of the other categories.

Studying shares across time informs us of shifts or changes in resource use, perhaps alerting us to expense categories that are increasingly consuming a finite pool of resources. Similarly, we can perform share analyses when, rather than comparing one year with the next, we are comparing one school or district with the next. Cross-sectional comparisons of this type might reveal spending pattern differences between high- and low-performing schools or districts, or such comparisons might reveal different resource allocation strategies.

TABLE 4–3

Shares of Expenditures by Function: City Schools Budget Summary for All Funds for 2000–2002

		Share of Expenditures (%)		
Line	Instructional Service	FY2000	FY2001	FY2002
743	General Instruction	65.21	65.62	65.17
744	Other Instruction	2.94	2.90	2.85
746	Student Services	0.14	0.14	0.12
751	Special Education	1.05	0.99	1.02
754	Vocational Instruction	4.26	3.93	3.90
755	Adult/Alternative Instruction	0.99	1.19	1.64
756	Special Instruction	23.83	23.65	23.36
757	Special Vocational Instruction	0.96	0.98	1.34
758	G&T Instruction	0.62	0.60	0.60
	Total	100.00	100.00	100.00

		Share of Expenditures (%)		
Line	Support Service	FY2000	FY2001	FY2002
725	General Fund Support	4.13	0.04	0.04
746	Student Services	2.48	3.25	3.65
762	Food Services	21.04	21.17	21.21
764	Pupil Transportation	19.73	21.07	20.64
767	Facilities	46.43	50.20	50.20
768	School Police	6.19	4.27	4.26
	Total	100.00	100.00	100.00

Note: FY = fiscal year; G&T = gifted and talented.

Although share analyses are commonly applied with financial data, they can be particularly useful with a variety of educational data. The following student information is best reported in terms of shares:

Demographic

1. Proportions of students by ethnicity
2. Proportions of students who are economically disadvantaged

Performance

1. Proportions of students receiving 4.0 grade point averages
2. Proportions of students graduating, dropping out, or being retained

Staffing

1. Proportions of teachers with master's degrees
2. Proportions of teachers by gender or ethnicity

TABLE 4–4

Syntax for Share Analysis

	A	B	C	E	F
1					
2	**Line**	**Instructional Service**	**FY2000**	**FY2001**	**FY2002**
3	743	General Instruction	216884848	261324051	281864021
4	744	Other Instruction	9789667	11544290	12318240
5	746	Student Services	466359	546004	532544
6	751	Special Education	3462541	3945690	4419091
7	754	Vocational Instruction	14168125	15668711	16877845
8	755	Adult/Alternative Instruction	3287378	4709036	7078461
9	756	Special Instruction	79251388	94170408	101049444
10	757	Special Vocational Instruction	3204536	3913946	5789540
11	758	G&T Instruction	2070918	2405432	2607489
12		**TOTAL**	=SUM(C3:C11)	=SUM(E3:E11)	=SUM(F3:F11)
13					
14		**Support Service**	**FY2000**	**FY2001**	**FY2002**
15	725	General Fund Support	4715841	50000	50000
16	746	Student Services	2832455	3855085	4394908
17	762	Food Services	24043492	25107367	25537347
18	764	Pupil Transportation	22537505	24991943	24847703
19	767	Facilities	53045065	59535308	60447884
20	768	School Police	7075432	5060571	5131496
21		**TOTAL**	=SUM(C15:C20)	SUM(E15:E20)	=SUM(F15:F20)
22					
23					
24	**Line**	**Instructional Service**	**FY2000**	**FY2001**	**FY2002**
25	743	General Instruction	=C3/C$12	=E3/E$12	=F3/F$12
26	744	Other Instruction	=C4/C$12	=E4/E$12	=F4/F$12
27	746	Student Services	=C5/C$12	=E5/E$12	=F5/F$12
28	751	Special Education	=C6/C$12	=E6/E$12	=F6/F$12
29	754	Vocational Instruction	=C7/C$12	=E7/E$12	=F7/F$12
30	755	Adult/Alternative Instruction	=C8/C$12	=E8/E$12	=F8/F$12
31	756	Special Instruction	=C9/C$12	=E9/E$12	=F9/F$12
32	757	Special Vocational Instruction	=C10/C$12	=E10/E$12	=F10/F$12
33	758	G&T Instruction	=C11/C$12	=E11/E$12	=F11/F$12
34					
35					
36		**Support Service**	**FY2000**	**FY2001**	**FY2002**
37	725	General Fund Support	=C15/C$21	=E15/E$21	=F15/F$21
38	746	Student Services	=C16/C$21	=E16/E$21	=F16/F$21
39	762	Food Services	=C17/C$21	=E17/E$21	=F17/F$21
40	764	Pupil Transportation	=C18/C$21	=E18/E$21	=F18/F$21
41	767	Facilities	=C19/C$21	=E19/E$21	=F19/F$21
42	768	School Police	=C20/C$21	=E20/E$21	=F20/F$21
43		**TOTAL**			

Note: FY = fiscal year; G&T = gifted and talented.

Column D is hidden in this example.

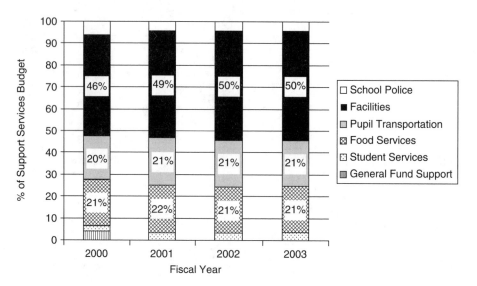

FIGURE 4–1
Analysis of Support Service Spending Shares Across Time

RATIO ANALYSES APPLIED

Ratios in Funding-Equity Analysis

Since the 1970s, fiscal equity has become an increasingly significant issue in public education. The need for equity measures has been fueled by court decisions requiring state legislatures to establish equitable funding formulas and then to prove statistically that they have applied them (*Abbott v. Burke* [NJ]; *Edgewood v. Kirby* [TX]; *Brigham v. State of Vermont*). In general, the sophistication of equity analysis has increased with each new wave of litigation. Yet, gaining a better understanding of fiscal equity is as simple as using ratio analysis.

In 1991–1992, consultants for the litigants in the case of *Mock v. Kansas* noted that the range in per-pupil spending between wealthy and poor districts in the state had dramatically increased from 1983–1984 to the end of the decade. The consultants used two indicators to make this argument. First, they looked at the simple difference between the highest and lowest spending districts in the state (range). Then, they reanalyzed the data, discounting outliers (extremely high or low spending schools) to get a better picture of the more typical discrepancies that exist (restricted range). Conclusion: Spending disparity increased by 47%.

However, overall spending for both poor and wealthy districts increased throughout the period. What if we compare the ratio of the difference (range or restricted range) with the base level of spending? This common approach, known as a *range ratio* or a *restricted range ratio*, works as follows: (MAX − MIN)/MIN. Table 4–5 displays how ratio versus range analysis changes the conclusions of this study. Because minimum values were not readily

TABLE 4–5
Data and Reanalysis from *Mock v. Kansas*

Year	Range ($)	%Δ	Restricted Range ($)	%Δ	Mean ($)	%Δ	UR/Mean	%Δ	RR/Mean	%Δ
1978–1979	2,546		1,282							
1983–1984	5,199	104	2,363	84	3,197		1.63		0.74	
1988–1989	6,020	16	3,469	47	4,388	37	1.37	−16	0.79	7

Note: Δ = change; UR/Mean = unrestricted range/mean; RR/Mean = restricted range/mean. Data from "The Kansas School District Equalization Act: A Study of Fiscal Equity of Funding Categories," by D. Thompson, D. Honeyman, and R. C. Wood, 1994, *Journal of Education Finance,* 19(1), pp. 36–68. Range ratios calculated from these data.

available, mean per-pupil expenditures were used as the base. The range ratio shows a dramatic decline in inequity during the period in question, and the restricted range ratio shows only a modest increase in inequity.

If you are looking at student test score data, as opposed to school finance data, consider the possible number of points attainable when you describe the point range on the test. A range of 20 points from high to low is twice as significant on a test with a maximum of 50 points as on a test with a maximum of 100 points.

Ratios in Cost-Effectiveness Analysis

Ratios can also be used to monitor cost-effectiveness in education. Table 4–6 exemplifies the concept of cost-effectiveness and its measurement by C/E (cost-effectiveness) ratio with four types of programs: small group instruction, individualized program instruction, computer-assisted instruction, and peer tutoring. Each program has an associated cost per pupil and an average test score of students. Although we might instinctively want to simply continue with the program that is least expensive (peer tutoring), or most effective (small groups), we would be wise to consider first the cost-effectiveness of the programs. By creating a ratio of cost per pupil to test score, we achieve a measure of cost per point. This measure becomes more valuable than either cost or points alone for comparing the programs.

TABLE 4–6
Cost-Effectiveness Analysis Example

Method	Cost per Student ($)	Effectiveness (Score)	C/E ($)
Small groups	600	20	30
IPI	200	4	50
CAI	300	15	20
Peer tutoring	100	10	10

Note: C/E = cost per student/effectiveness; IPI = individualized program instruction; CAI = computer-associated instruction. Adapted from *Cost-Effectiveness: A Primer* (1st ed.), by H. M. Levin, 1983, Thousand Oaks, CA: Sage.

THE CONCEPT OF VALUE ADDED

One of the difficult aspects of the cost-effectiveness example is the measure of effectiveness. In recent years, school leaders have begun to use the concept of *value added*. Value-added assessment recognizes that two points are better than one. Consider Figures 4–2 and 4–3, which describe the performance of Schools A and B. In Figure 4–2, School B appears to be the stronger school. In contrast, Figure 4–3 displays the two schools' 3-year trends in performance. Now School A appears to be improving dramatically, whereas School B's performance is declining. The value-added measures for these schools would be the differences between their performance from one point in time to a previous point in time. Although School B has the higher performance level, its value added is negative.

Value-added analysis is even more useful when you are analyzing data at the student level. Value-added analyses account for previous levels of student performance when you are assessing current levels. One goal of education is that students learn and accumulate knowledge, but more important is that they continue to learn. Increasingly, value-added assessment is combined with educational policy for the measurement of both individual and institutional performance.[1]

Value-Added Assessment in Policy and Practice

Perhaps the most significant example of value-added assessment in education policy is Tennessee's statewide Value-Added Assessment System, or TVAAS. The Tennessee State Department of Education currently tracks the annual performance of all students in the state. Using a collection of standardized assessments, the Department of Education calculates an annual scaled score for each child. This information can be used to assess a child's average performance across time, or it can be used to assess the average effectiveness of teachers or schools. Table 4–7 provides an example of how TVAAS data can be used to assess average classroom gains. In this case—an example adapted from the TVAAS teacher

FIGURE 4–2
Scholastic Aptitude Test (SAT)
Performance of High School Juniors

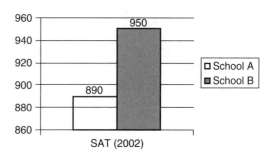

---

[1] One example of this is South Carolina's attempt in the early 1990s to provide incentive funding based on value-added assessment of school performance (Richards & Sheu, 1992).

FIGURE 4–3
Scholastic Aptitude Test (SAT)
Performance of High School Juniors:
Value Added

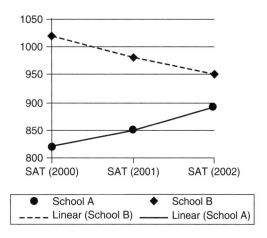

and principals' guide—students' scaled scores on entry and departure from a particular class are tabulated. Each student is assigned a gain (or loss) score by subtracting the entry score from the exit score. The average gain (or loss) score for the class may then be calculated.

This crude example has shortcomings; however, you will be able to overcome them as you develop your skills with more complex statistical tools. For instance, this type of analysis does not account for children's identities, skill levels, or background beyond their measured achievement. In response, William Sanders and colleagues at the Value-Added Research Center in Tennessee developed complex statistical models that more precisely identify which portion of the gains (or losses) is likely to be attributable to teacher effects by accounting for student and other differences in contextual variables.

TABLE 4–7
Computation of Gains at the Classroom Level

Student	Entry Score	Exit Score	Average Score	Net Gain/Loss
Aaron	783	782	783	−1
Aileen	734	774	754	+40
Adam	715	770	743	+55
Amanda	716	761	739	+45
Alan	721	743	732	+22
Amy	717	743	730	+26
Arnold	714	741	728	+27
			Average gain =	+31

Adapted from *Using and Interpreting Tennessee's Value-Added Assessment System: A Primer for Teachers and Principals,* by S. E. Bratton, Jr., S. P. Horn, and S. P. Wright, 1996, Knoxville, TN: Value-Added Research Center, University of Tennessee.

COHORT TRACKING

Just as variations in school structures present unique issues regarding data analysis, student flow through the system presents challenges as we analyze student performance data. Students typically pass through a school in clusters, or *cohorts*, from grade level to grade level. The flow of student cohorts and their respective performance data could be structured as in Table 4–8.

Value-added analysis may help you determine the annual body of knowledge or skills gained by either a cohort or individual students passing through the system. Such information is often missed when, for example, because state math assessments occur only in the fourth and eighth grades, we compare only this year's fourth grade with next year's and so on. Comparing each cohort with its predecessor might be valuable, but assessing the following is also prudent:

♦ Each cohort's value added from fourth to eighth grade
♦ The difference in fourth- to eighth-grade value added among cohort groups

IMPORTANCE OF STUDENT-LEVEL DATA

In this section, we provide a brief example of the significance of performance differences that can occur when you are using school-level data versus student-level data to calculate value added. Significant performance differences can be seen particularly in schools where high levels of student mobility occur. Ideally, the goal of a performance measurement system is to isolate the effects that teachers and other elements of the schooling environment have on individual student learning during a defined period. However, we have no way to control entirely for what students may be learning outside school during that period.

The example at hand involves an ongoing privately funded voucher program, in which nearly 2,000 inner-city children have been given the opportunity to attend primarily inner-city Catholic schools. In the state in question, both public and private schools participate in the state's testing system, which we will call the *State Test of Academic (k)Nowledge, Development, And other Really Difficult Stuff* (STANDARDS). Typically, school performance is evaluated by percentages of students passing criteria (criterion referenced) or by each school's median normal curve equivalent score, which is based on state or

TABLE 4–8
Tracking Cohorts of Students in Tabular Format

Grade	2000	2001	2002
1	67[a]		
2		72	
3			83

[a]This number may represent a class mean score on a standardized test or percentages of students who meet standards in a curricular area.

national norms (norm referenced). We discuss the meaning of norm-referenced assessment in greater detail in chapter 5. Value added, or what we call *pseudo value added*, is often inferred by observing the average performance of cohorts of students across time—for example, the percentage of 2001 eighth graders passing standards compared with the percentage of 1999 sixth graders passing standards.[2] Similar comparisons are also made with normal curve equivalent (NCE) scores.

What if large numbers of students who are low performing exit schools of choice between sixth and eighth grade? What if large numbers of students who are higher performing enter? What are the implications for the performance ratings of schools losing students who are lower performing and for the performance ratings of schools gaining those students? Are these effects trivial? Do all things balance out in the end? Individuals who support the continued use of school-level performance measures often adhere to such beliefs.

Table 4–9 presents the value-added performance of the 1999 sixth-grade cohort attending Catholic schools that was participating in the privately funded voucher program. Value added is calculated by using both school mean scores and student-level scores for the students who stayed in the schools from sixth to eighth grade (or "stayers"). The difference is primarily the order of the calculations. In school mean value added, 1999 scores are averaged, 2001 scores are averaged, then the difference of the averages is taken, which reveals improvements of more than 10 NCE points. That is, students' scores improved 10 points more than the score of the average student, when a score of 50 is the average. In the student-level value-added calculation, each student's value added is calculated first (eighth-grade score minus sixth-grade score), which results in the exclusion of students missing either

TABLE 4–9

Comparison of School Mean and Student-Level Value-Added Calculations

	Group	Reading	Math	Language	Total Battery
All students	1999 (N = 312)	53.85	56.87	55.54	55.44
	2001 (N = 1,446)	66.08	66.32	65.43	65.89
	School Mean Value Added	12.23	9.45	9.89	10.45
	Value Added − Stayers (N = 182)	0.46	−4.03	−2.60	−2.59
Scholarship students	1999 (N = 148)	46.48	48.91	49.73	48.41
	2001 (N = 74)	52.26	48.04	51.01	50.91
	School Mean Value Added	5.78	−.87	1.28	2.50
	Value Added − Stayers (N = 74)	1.55	−3.95	−2.74	−1.26
Nonscholarship students	1999 (164)	60.51	64.05	60.79	61.79
	2001 (1,372)	66.83	67.30	66.20	66.70
	School Mean Value Added	6.32	3.25	5.41	4.91
	Value Added − Stayers (108)	−0.30	−4.08	−2.50	−3.51

[2]At this point, we choose to ignore the even less reliable method of assessing different cohorts passing through the same grade level.

TABLE 4–10
Sources of Differences in Value-Added Calculations

Group	Reading	Math	Language	Total Battery
All leavers (N = 130)	47.82	51.62	50.25	49.95
Scholarship leavers (N = 74)	42.26	45.82	45.70	44.65
Nonscholarship leavers (N = 56)	55.18	59.28	56.27	56.95
Enterers (N = 1,265)	67.16	67.72	66.68	67.20

eighth- or sixth-grade scores. Then the value-added scores are averaged. The finding is that stayers performed slightly below, rather than significantly above, national averages.

Table 4–10 reveals the source of the changes in Table 4–9: The dramatic differences in school mean versus student-level value added are partially a function of attrition of students who were lower performing (both on and not on scholarship) but even more significantly a function of entry of students who were higher performing.

In fact, differences of similar magnitude are unlikely to exist in public systems, where fewer choices are available, which results in less student mobility. With the expansion of charter schools and publicly and privately funded voucher programs, we can expect mobility to increase with time. Further, in rural areas and small towns, where this type of mobility is less likely to occur, the movement of even a single family into or out of a school district may significantly influence performance evaluation because of very small school size.

CONSTRUCTION OF INDEXES

Constructing useful, efficient indexes that describe your school is a creative process. No preexisting standards will tell you which data to use and how to use data to paint the best picture of your institution. Thus, explore the possibilities with available data, construct various ratios and indexes, and assess their usefulness. Following are some examples of index design.

Efficiency

An *effort index* describes the flow of resources to their intended objective. Imagine we are considering the extent to which resources allocated to a new reading program are being directly applied to the program.

$$\text{Effort} = \frac{\text{Resources to Target}}{\text{Available Resources for Target}}$$

First, let us define Resources to Target and Available Resources, which may be ratios. Resources to Target are time and/or money spent with the students on the new reading skills, and Available Resources are the Resources to Target plus all resources consumed by implementation and administration of the new program. Perhaps only a small percentage of the newly allocated resources are being dedicated to the target. Tracking this indicator across time might be useful if we assume that the effort of the new program will improve.

Cost-Effectiveness

We already gave you one example of cost-effectiveness analysis. Now we expand Levin's concept. In the previous example, cost-effectiveness was defined as follows:

$$\text{Cost-Effectiveness} = \text{Cost/Effectiveness}$$

where Cost was defined by the dollars dedicated to the cause, and Effectiveness was typically an achievement measure.

$$\text{Cost-Effectiveness} = \text{Dollars Spent/Eighth-Grade Reading Score}$$

The preceding equation yields an intuitive measure of Dollars per Reading Point. We can integrate this concept with that of value added to enhance our index:

$$\text{CE} = \text{Dollars Spent/Value-Added Reading Score}$$

where CE is Cost-Effectiveness and

$$\text{Value-Added Reading Score} = \text{Eighth-Grade Reading Score} \\ - \text{Fourth-Grade Reading Score}$$

This yields the intuitive measure of Dollars per Point Gained.

Let us take the index one step further:

$$\text{CE} = \text{Dollars/Percent Gain}$$

where

$$\text{Percent Gain} = \frac{(\text{Eighth-Grade Reading Score} - \text{Fourth-Grade Reading Score})}{\text{Fourth-Grade Reading Score}}$$

Relative Share

What if you wanted to know whether a particular population of students was receiving its fair share of resources? You might create an index of Relative Share as follows:

$$\text{Relative Share} = \frac{\% \text{ of Total Dollars to Special Population}}{\% \text{ of Students in Special Population}}$$

In this case, let us begin with both proportions of students and proportions of dollars. The mathematical question is whether a given proportion of students receives an appropriate proportion of resources. Assuming all students to be alike, we would expect each 1% of students to receive 1% of resources. This is not the case, however, because students have different needs, which are accompanied by different costs. Always recognize that when more resources flow to some students, by necessity fewer resources are flowing to others, unless these extra resources are subsidized by an external source such as the state or federal government.

Following is another example. Assume an activity budget (x) and a total number of students participating in activities (y). Imagine 10 possible activities, each given the same budget (10% of x). Imagine further that one student activity has 20% of y students, whereas another has 5% of y students. In this case, the relative shares for the activities are as follows:

$$\text{Activity 1 Share} = 10\% \text{ Budget}/20\% \text{ Pupils} = 0.5$$
$$\text{Activity 2 Share} = 10\% \text{ Budget}/5\% \text{ Pupils} = 2.5$$

which indicates clearly that Activity 2 is receiving a disproportionately large share, whereas Activity 1 is receiving a disproportionately small share of the available resources. Similar indexes can reveal the shares of resources dedicated to instructional programs or student special needs.

TABLE 4–11

Useful Indexes for Measuring Institutional Performance

Name	Derivation
Cost indexes	
Budget per Pupil	BPP = Total Budget/Enrollment
Budget Share	SHARE = Expense/Total Budget
Cost per Classroom	CPC = Instructional Expenses/Classrooms
Costs per Instruction Staff	CPIS = Instructional Expenses/FTE Instructional Staff
Demographic indexes	
Poverty Index	PI = Pupils Receiving Free or Reduced Lunch/Total Enrollment
Enrollment Rate	ER = Number of School-Age Children Enrolling in Your School/Total Eligible School-Age Children
Performance indexes	
Gain Score	GAIN = Posttest − Pretest
Participation Rate	PARTICIPATE = Participants/Number Eligible
Percent Successful	%PASS = Number Passing/Number Participating
Performance relative to benchmark	P-INDEX = School Mean (Median)/State Mean (Median)
Performance Adequacy	ADEQ = Mean (pupils below median)/Median [ideal = 1.0]
Present Mastery	PM = Percent students above 80th percentile
Efficiency and C/E indexes	
Effort to Succeed	ES = Hours (or Personnel or Dollars) dedicated to a specific purpose/Success Rate (percentage of students passing, not dropping out, etc.)
Cost/Effectiveness	C/E = Unit Cost/Average "Effectiveness" Rate (student scores, value added)

Note: FTE = full-time-employed.

Cautions

Ultimately, the key to any index is that it must make sense. The objective of using an index is to more efficiently present the condition of your organization and to aggregate data in useful and meaningful ways. Thus, when you create a new index, you should bear in mind the following:

Define the index with its simplest intuitive meaning, a name that "says it all."

Field-test the index with your colleagues, providing them with minimal context on the index, to determine whether it is intuitively understandable.

Table 4–11 presents a framework for constructing indexes. You might calculate any or all of them, given the appropriate data on a school district or an individual school. Some of the indexes may be more useful than others. Consider your own possibilities within the four categories, as well as possibilities for entirely new categories.

SUMMARY

Unfortunately for school leaders, no one set of basic indicators is typically used to describe the health of a public K–12 educational institution. Thus, you must develop your own understanding of the meaningful uses of educational data and create your own descriptive or comparative indexes. You must remember to say as much as possible with as few numbers as possible.

One way to think about a basket of indicators is to decide which variables you want to monitor in your organization and the kind of indicators that would assist you. For example, in a high school setting, you may be interested in the following areas:

Safety

♦ Violent incidents
♦ Property damage reports
♦ Threats recorded
♦ Climate summary of teachers' and students' perceptions of safety

Academic Rigor

♦ Percentage of seniors who took at least one advanced placement (AP) class
♦ Percentage of AP class offerings to total class offerings
♦ AP scores
♦ Percentage of students graduating with honors
♦ Grade point averages across years

Academic Achievement

♦ Percentage of students taking the Scholastic Aptitude Test (SAT) or the ACT (American College Test)
♦ Student scores on the SAT or the ACT
♦ Scores on the state's high-stakes exit examination
♦ Percentage of students accepted at top-tier 4-year colleges

PROBLEM B

Shares and Indexes

Background: For the past 5 years, your school district has implemented 10 specialized reading programs in an effort to determine both the relative costs and the effectiveness of the programs. The school board and superintendent recently declared that the decision time is now and expressed the belief that the decision should be based on a combination of information on costs and effectiveness.

Your Mission: Use the data in the file listed at the beginning of this problem. Given the data on the 10 programs, prepare a brief summary with recommendations and a rationale regarding which program(s) should be considered for continuation. The superintendent has provided you with some guiding tasks:

Task 1: Determine the Shares of the Total Budget being spent on the select group of students and the Share of students being served in the program. Assess the extent to which these data line up. Does an appropriate proportion of students appear to be receiving an appropriate proportion of funding? Create an index that measures the appropriateness of the spending level. Provide a brief narrative of your major findings.

Task 2: Perform appropriate cost-effectiveness analysis of the data. Be sure to consider units and the concept of value added. Following are some indexes you should consider calculating:
a. Per-Pupil Cost per Point (Grade 4)
b. Per-Pupil Cost per Point (Grade 8)
c. Per-Pupil Cost per Point Gained (Grade 8 − Grade 4): Value Added
Provide a brief narrative of your major findings.

Task 3: Interpret the results and make a recommendation.

Sample Figure and Table for Problem B

FIGURE 4–B–1
Fourth- to Eighth-Grade Mean Value Added for 10 Reading Programs

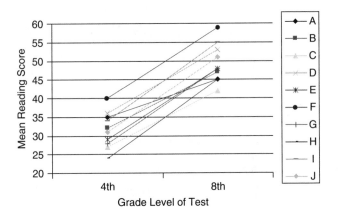

TABLE 4–B–1
Shares of Budget Spent and Shares of Population Served in 10 Reading Programs

Program	Budget Share (%)	Population Share (%)
A	0.9	9.2
B	2.1	11.7
C	1.2	5.7
D	1.1	7.2
E	1.3	5.6
F	1.4	4.9
G	1.5	5.2
H	2.0	6.2
I	3.7	8.9
J	2.1	5.0

5

Applying Descriptive Statistics to the Schooling Context

Researchers and statisticians have developed a formal set of tools for the description of data, or *context setting*. These tools are commonly referred to as *descriptive statistics*. With regard to traditional descriptive statistics, two key features need to be understood: (a) measures of central tendency and (b) measures of variance. In our careers as educators, most of us have used the terms *mean* and *standard deviation*, perhaps with regard to student Scholastic Aptitude Test (SAT) performance in our district, or even when comparing average salaries with those of instructors at neighboring schools. The mean is a measure of central tendency, whereas standard deviation is a measure of variance.

We often forget that underlying these apparently simple statistics is a set of basic rules of probability. The most basic rule is the assumption of a *normal distribution*, or *bell curve*, that serves as the foundation from which the meaning of *mean* and *standard deviation* is derived (Figure 5–1).

Because the goal of this book is not to provide you with a full course in probability and statistics, but to give you the necessary practical tools for school-level data analysis, we often provide you with rules of thumb and guidelines for interpreting statistics. For instance, when our sample size (number of scores, etc.) exceeds 30, we can confidently say that about 95% of the cases (or students in this case) fall between the two outside lines (shown in Figure 5–1), which are about 2 standard deviations away from the mean. Being caught in the 2.5% at either end would be considered an unlikely occurrence. Therefore, let us assume that the mean of a distribution is 75; the upper limit, 90; and the lower limit, 60. If we are given a child's test score of 27, we can assume either that the score is a highly unlikely occurrence from this distribution ($p < .05$, which is statistical jargon for a probability of less than 5%) or perhaps that the score came from a different distribution (e.g., another class).

Real data, such as test scores or salary data, do not always conform to a bell curve. For example, a common pattern of employment in public schools is a large mass of faculty at the top end of the step scale and a large number of relatively new teachers. If a simple mean were calculated for the faculty, we would achieve a value that represents the salary of few actual teachers. The best approach is usually to look at a scatterplot to get a pictorial view of the distributions prior to using statistical abstractions.

Table 5–1 provides an example of mean, median, and standard deviation calculations for grades assigned by a group of science teachers, and Table 5–2 shows the Excel syntax for analysis of the student grades. The question being asked is whether or not "grade inflation" exists in the science department. Notice that the mean and median in Table 5–1 are not the same for any of the years in question, which suggests that our distribution is not

FIGURE 5–1
Standard Normal Distribution

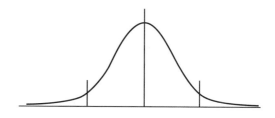

TABLE 5–1

Analysis of Student Grades: Average Mathematics Grades

Instructor	Year				
	1998	1999	2000	2001	2002
Baker	2.90	2.90	2.30	2.00	2.10
Seife	3.00	2.20	2.30	2.10	2.00
Chuckrow	2.70	2.60	2.60	2.50	2.50
Scully	3.50	3.50	3.40	3.30	3.10
Ketchum	3.10	2.80	2.90	3.00	2.70
Kuo	2.70	2.50	2.30	2.20	2.20
Stires	2.40	2.30	2.10	2.00	2.00
Sneider	3.10	3.20	3.10	2.90	2.90
Mahase	2.90	2.80	2.80	2.70	2.40
D'Allessandro	3.40	3.50	3.30	3.40	3.20
Mean	2.97	2.83	2.71	2.61	2.51
Median	2.95	2.80	2.70	2.60	2.45
Standard deviation	0.33	0.46	0.46	0.53	0.45

perfect. One instinctive response is to determine whether the mean or median appears to be changing with time. If we graph both trends, both appear to be headed downward. Yet, we are simply tracking one descriptor, a measure of central tendency, which may or may not characterize the population well. At this point, we are simply providing descriptive measures of the data.

In this particular situation, looking at the variance in scores across time might also be interesting. Often, when schools experience grade inflation, not all grades are rising. After all, some have already reached their upper limits. What we are more likely to see is a convergence of grades toward the high end, or disappearance of low grades. This trend would be more likely reflected in the standard deviation than in the mean because as the grades converge more and more, the mean continues to change only slightly. Mathematically, the standard deviation is a measure of the average distance of individual scores from the mean. As the standard deviation grows smaller, the shape of the bell curve changes: It grows taller and narrower, looking less like a "bell" and more like a tapered candle.

TABLE 5–2

Syntax for Analysis of Student Grades

	A	B	C	D
13	Mean	=AVERAGE(B3:B12)	=AVERAGE(C3:C12)	=AVERAGE(D3:D12)
14	Standard Deviation	=STDEV(B3:B12)	=STDEV(C3:C12)	=STDEV(D3:D12)
15	Median	=MEDIAN(B3:B12)	=MEDIAN(C3:C12)	=MEDIAN(D3:D12)

DIFFERENT-SIZE GROUPS: WEIGHTED ANALYSIS

What if Mr. Kuo's class has only 10 students, and Ms. Sneider's class has 20? The way that the calculations are performed in Table 5–2, the class is the basic unit, but it may not be the most appropriate unit. If we have widely different class sizes and want to see how the grades of the student population are changing, we have to either have student-level data or create weightings for each class average, according to the numbers of students in each class.

Consider another example in which the size of the groups being compared matters. In Table 5–3, we have 10 school districts of varying size and wealth (measured by property value per pupil). Two ways of calculating our measures are central tendency and variances. The first way is to consider each district as 1 and take a simple mean and standard deviation. Doing so does not seem fair when we consider that District A, the poorest, has more than 10 thousand students and District J has fewer than 1 thousand. Clearly, this fact will skew the mean upward. Notice that in the fourth column we multiplied the Property Value per Pupil (PVPP) by the number of pupils for each district. We then summed this column to determine the total property wealth (TPW) for all pupils. By dividing the TPW by the number of pupils, we determined a pupil-weighted mean property wealth per pupil, or the mean property wealth where the basic unit is the pupil, not the district.

TABLE 5–3

Weighted Means and Standard Deviations

District	Enter # of Pupils	Property Value per Pupil	Pupils × PVPP	Pupils × (PVPP − PVPPmean)^2	**Notes**
A	10,040	$56,670	$568,966,800	$3,438,189,660,288	
B	7,028	$46,845	$329,226,660	$5,640,746,973,804	
C	7,985	$55,203	$440,795,955	$3,185,184,956,420	
D	4,152	$64,875	$269,361,000	$440,518,368,281	
E	5,148	$71,762	$369,430,776	$59,980,263,601	
F	6,216	$81,913	$509,171,208	$282,178,390,636	
G	3,666	$92,949	$340,751,034	$1,158,094,864,822	
H	2,961	$106,195	$314,443,395	$2,849,123,619,571	
I	3,472	$135,496	$470,442,112	$12,633,139,118,625	
J	848	$306,776	$260,146,048	$45,485,741,559,000	
SUM	51,516		$3,872,734,988	$75,172,897,775,048	Sum of Squared Errors
Mean (Unit = District)		$101,868		$1,459,214,570	SSE/Pupils
Standard deviation (Unit = District)		$76,839			
Mean (Unit = Pupil)		$75,175			
Standard deviation (Unit = Pupil)		$38,200	Square Root (SSE/Pupils)		

Note: PVPP = property value per pupil; SSE = sum of squared errors.

Table 5–4 shows the Excel syntax for these calculations.

Determining the pupil-weighted standard deviation is somewhat more complicated. The basic equation is as follows:

$$SD = \sqrt{\sum_{i=1}^{N} P_i(x_i - \bar{x}_p)^2 \bigg/ \sum_{i=1}^{N} P_i}$$

where SD is the standard deviation, P is the number of pupils in district i, x_i is the district PVPP, x_p is the pupil-weighted mean PVPP, P_i is the total number of pupils, and N is the number of districts. Notice, in Table 5–3, that the pupil-weighted mean is significantly lower than the original mean. The change in the standard deviation is also substantial, but less meaningful. Most of this change can be attributed to the assumption inherent in the calculation that there is no variance in PVPP within any of the schools and that in raw calculation terms our total sample size is now more than 50 thousand, whereas it was previously only 10 thousand. The lack of variance within institutions may be a fact in this case, but we would be wise to rethink our methods if we wanted to determine the pupil-weighted standard deviation for the previous example by using grade point averages (GPAs).

TABLE 5–4

Syntax for Weighted Averages and Standard Deviations

	A	B	C	D	E	F
1	**District Summary Analysis**					
2	*District*	*Enter # of Pupils*	*Property Value per Pupil*	*Pupils × PVPP*	*Pupils × (PVPP − PVPPmean)²*	**Notes**
3	A	10040	56670	=(B3*C3)	=(B3*($C$16-C3)^2)	
4	B	7028	46845	=(B4*C4)	=(B4*($C$16-C4)^2)	
5	C	7985	55203	=(B5*C5)	=(B5*($C$16-C5)^2)	
6	D	4152	64875	=(B6*C6)	=(B6*($C$16-C6)^2)	
7	E	5148	71762	=(B7*C7)	=(B7*($C$16-C7)^2)	
8	F	6216	81913	=(B8*C8)	=(B8*($C$16-C8)^2)	
9	G	3666	92949	=(B9*C9)	=(B9*($C$16-C9)^2)	
10	H	2961	106195	=(B10*C10)	=(B10*($C$16-C10)^2)	
11	I	3472	135496	=(B11*C11)	=(B11*($C$16-C11)^2)	
12	J	848	306776	=(B12*C12)	=(B12*($C$16-C12)^2)	
13	SUM	=SUM(B3:B12)		=SUM(D3:D12)	=SUM(E3:E12)	Sum of Squared Errors
14	Average (Unit = District)		=AVERAGE(C3:C12)		=(E13/B13)	SSE/Pupils
15	Standard deviation (Unit = District)		=STDEV(C3:C12)			
16	Average (Unit = Pupil)		=(D13/B13)			
17	Standard deviation (Unit = Pupil)		=SQRT(E14)	Square Root (*SSE*/Pupils)		

Note: PVPP = property value per pupil; *SSE* = sum of squared errors; ^2 = excel code for squared.

MEAN AND MEDIAN DEVIATION AND z SCORES

In this section, we discuss methods of *centering* and standardizing data. Centering data enables you to compare groups that may be using vastly different scales or that may have very different mean or median scores on a given scale. Centering is a useful tool for comparing the relative performance of students across different classes with different teachers. For example, two teachers may have the same group of students during a school year, but the two teachers' grading practices may be substantially different. For instance, the median (middle) score in one class may be an 85, whereas the median in the other class may be a 78, or, conversely, their grading standards may be virtually identical but the two classes of students have different study habits. We could better compare the performance of the students in these classes by looking at each student's score relative to the median, or

$$mScore = Score - Median$$

Table 5–5 provides three examples of centering, and Table 5–6 shows the Excel syntax for these calculations. In the first example of centering in Table 5–5, (Score − Mean), mean-deviated scores are calculated by subtracting the mean from each score. Scores less than the mean appear negative, and scores greater than the mean appear positive. This is similarly the case for the median-deviated scores in the next column. The final column includes a z score, which is based on the probability framework of the bell curve. z Scores represent the number of standard deviations an individual score is away from the mean. Thus, the z score is calculated by taking the (Score − Mean), or distance from the mean, and dividing it by the standard deviation to determine the distance relative to standard deviations.

TABLE 5–5
Centered and Standardized Scores

Student	Score	Score − Mean	Score − Median	z Score
Bruce	2.90	−0.07	−0.05	−0.21
Tama	3.10	0.13	0.15	0.39
Robert	2.60	−0.37	−0.35	−1.12
Kevin	3.40	0.43	0.45	1.30
Carl	3.00	0.03	0.05	0.09
Kane	2.90	−0.07	−0.05	−0.21
Kenny	2.40	−0.57	−0.55	−1.73
Cheryl	3.10	0.13	0.15	0.39
Compton	2.90	−0.07	−0.05	−0.21
John	3.40	0.43	0.45	1.30
Mean	2.97			
Median	2.95			
Standard deviation	0.33			

TABLE 5–6
Syntax for Centered and Standardized Scores

	A	B	C	D	E
1	**Student**	**Score**	**Score − Mean**	**Score − Median**	**z Score**
2	Bruce	2.9	=B2-$B$12	=B2-$B$13	=C2/$B$14
3	Tama	3.1	=B3-$B$12	=B3-$B$13	=C3/$B$14
4	Robert	2.6	=B4-$B$12	=B4-$B$13	=C4/$B$14
5	Kevin	3.4	=B5-$B$12	=B5-$B$13	=C5/$B$14
6	Carl	3	=B6-$B$12	=B6-$B$13	=C6/$B$14
7	Kane	2.9	=B7-$B$12	=B7-$B$13	=C7/$B$14
8	Kenny	2.4	=B8-$B$12	=B8-$B$13	=C8/$B$14
9	Cheryl	3.1	=B9-$B$12	=B9-$B$13	=C9/$B$14
10	Compton	2.9	=B10-$B$12	=B10-$B$13	=C10/$B$14
11	John	3.4	=B11-$B$12	=B11-$B$13	=C11/$B$14
12	Mean	=AVERAGE(B2:B11)			
13	Median	=MEDIAN(B2:B11)			
14	STDev	0.33			

Note: Notice the dollar signs in the references to cell $B$12 in column C. The dollar signs indicate a *stationary* reference (as opposed to a relative reference). What this means is that as we copy the formula from one cell to the next (perhaps with the Autofill function), the new formulas continue to refer to B12 rather than changing to B13, B14, and so on. The $ can be placed in front of the letter, the number, or both, depending on which reference must remain stationary. In this case, in column C, we need only place a dollar sign in front of the 12, but we have included one in front of the B as well. STDev = standard deviation.

z Scores allow us to make judgments about the likelihood of an event. For example, if we have a large enough sample of students, a z score farther than 1.96 from the mean, either positive or negative, would be an unlikely event (<5% chance).

Another variation for centering is to take two groups of students with similar academic profiles (e.g., two honors classes) and estimate a combined mean and calculate z scores for both. Then we can re-sort the students into their original classes and compare the z scores of the two groups.

THE DESCRIPTIVE ANALYSIS TOOL

To conclude this chapter, we introduce the first two of a series of automated analysis tools available in Excel. These tools allow us to perform many of the functions that are available in specialized statistical software packages such as SPSS (Statistical Package for the Social Sciences) and SAS (Statistical Analysis System). For most institutional data analysis, this specialized software is unnecessary. First, we examine the Descriptive Statistics tool, which provides descriptive statistics summaries of data. We continue to make use of the student grades data discussed previously.

FIGURE 5–2
Installation of the Analysis Tools

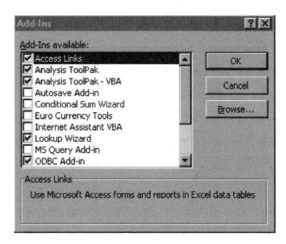

To perform the descriptive analysis of the student grades data, follow these seven steps:

1. Select Data Analysis from the Tools menu. If this item does not appear (bottom of the menu), select Add-Ins (Figure 5–2). From the list that appears, check off two items—Analysis ToolPak and Analysis ToolPak—VBA. Then click OK. The Data Analysis item should now appear on your Tools menu. If the Analysis ToolPak items do not appear on the Add-Ins list, you may need to reinstall your version of Excel, making sure to install "all components" or a "full" rather than a "typical" installation.
2. Select Descriptive Statistics from the Analysis Tools menu (Figure 5–3).
3. Place your cursor in the Input Range cell and highlight the block of data you want to analyze, including labels (Figure 5–4).
4. Click the Labels in First Row toggle box (if you highlighted labels in the first row).
5. Click the Output Range circle, and select a cell with ample room below and to the right. This will be the upper left-hand corner of your output table. Be careful not to overwrite any of your data. You can simply have your output appear on a new sheet, but having it available on the same sheet is sometimes handy.

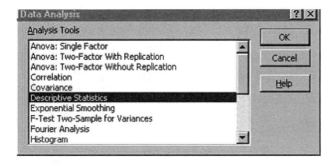

FIGURE 5–3
Analysis Tools Menu

FIGURE 5–4
Descriptive Analysis Tool Screen

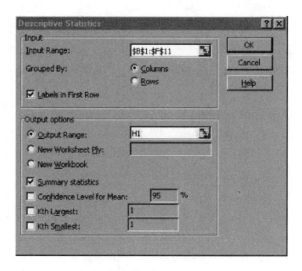

6. You can also select whether to group your data by Rows or Columns. The data in question can be analyzed either way (teacher or year; Tables 5–7 and 5–8).
7. Click OK.

You will likely pay attention to only certain numbers in the descriptive statistics output table. For example, you now have the mean (arithmetic average), median (midpoint), and mode (most frequent) for each variable. You also have the *standard error* of the mean, or

TABLE 5–7
Descriptive Statistics Output Tables (in Rows)

Baker		Seife		Chuckrow	
Mean	2.44	Mean	2.32	Mean	2.58
Standard Error	0.19	Standard Error	0.18	Standard Error	0.04
Median	2.30	Median	2.20	Median	2.60
Mode	2.90	Mode	#N/A	Mode	2.60
Standard Deviation	0.43	Standard Deviation	0.40	Standard Deviation	0.08
Sample Variance	0.19	Sample Variance	0.16	Sample Variance	0.01
Kurtosis	−3.02	Kurtosis	3.50	Kurtosis	−0.61
Skewness	0.34	Skewness	1.80	Skewness	0.51
Range	0.90	Range	1.00	Range	0.20
Minimum	2.00	Minimum	2.00	Minimum	2.50
Maximum	2.90	Maximum	3.00	Maximum	2.70
Sum	12.20	Sum	11.60	Sum	12.90
Count	5.00	Count	5.00	Count	5.00

TABLE 5–8
Descriptive Statistics Output Tables (in Columns)

1993		*1994*		*1995*	
Mean	2.97	Mean	2.83	Mean	2.71
Standard Error	0.10	Standard Error	0.14	Standard Error	0.15
Median	2.95	Median	2.80	Median	2.70
Mode	2.90	Mode	3.50	Mode	2.30
Standard Deviation	0.33	Standard Deviation	0.46	Standard Deviation	0.46
Sample Variance	0.11	Sample Variance	0.21	Sample Variance	0.21
Kurtosis	−0.12	Kurtosis	−0.98	Kurtosis	−1.45
Skewness	0.03	Skewness	0.30	Skewness	0.24
Range	1.10	Range	1.30	Range	1.30
Minimum	2.40	Minimum	2.20	Minimum	2.10
Maximum	3.50	Maximum	3.50	Maximum	3.40
Sum	29.70	Sum	28.30	Sum	27.10
Count	10.00	Count	10.00	Count	10.00

how much the mean is likely to vary (this is the $+/-$ figure commonly given in polling results), and you have the standard deviation. Measures of kurtosis and skewness relate to how well your data conform to the bell curve. However, for now, you can make some judgments by comparing your mean and median values. Notice, in Table 5–7, that Baker's median is less than the mean, which suggests that the midpoint of the data is to the left of the arithmetic average, or that the distribution is slightly skewed.

RANK AND PERCENTILE ANALYSIS

The second analysis tool is the Rank and Percentile tool. This tool will quickly and easily convert any list of data into a percentile classification of each element. For example, in Table 5–9, we can see that the United States fares well compared with other countries, such as Denmark, with regard to Age 9 reading scores. However, although ranking these countries will delineate their relative position, ranking alone will not convey the magnitude of the differences among the countries. Percentile analysis will place the countries on a range from 0 to 100, which allows you to interpret not only relative position, but, more precisely, how well or how poorly a particular country is doing.

To perform rank and percentile analysis on the preceding data, follow these seven steps:

1. Select Data Analysis from the Tools menu.
2. Select Rank and Percentile (Figure 5–5).
3. Place your cursor in the Input Range cell, and highlight the data you want to analyze, including the labels.
4. Check whether your data are organized in rows or in columns (as in our example).

TABLE 5–9
OECD Reading Score Comparison

Country	Reading Score (Age 9 yr)
Denmark	291.2
Netherlands	303.8
Germany	328.7
Spain	329.6
Greece	331.9
Belgium	334.4
Ireland	337.3
Switzerland	339.7
Iceland	350.2
Norway	357.9
New Zealand	363.9
Italy	365.4
France	367.0
Sweden	379.2
United States	388.6
Finland	418.8

Note: Data from *Education at a Glance*, by Organization for Economic Cooperation and Development, 1999, Paris: Author.

5. Select the Labels in First Row toggle box.
6. Click the Output Range circle, and select a cell.
7. Click OK.

Your rank and percentile output will appear as in Table 5–10. The Point column simply represents the original position of the data before sorting. The reading scores are now sorted from highest to lowest and ranked accordingly, and percentiles are assigned from the 0th percentile to the 100th percentile.

FIGURE 5–5
Rank and Percentile Tool

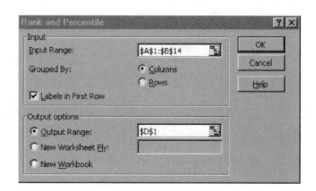

TABLE 5–10
Rank and Percentile Output

Country	Point	Reading Score (Age 9 yr)	Rank	Percentile
Finland	1	418.8	1	100.00
United States	2	388.6	2	93.30
Sweden	3	379.2	3	86.60
France	4	367.0	4	80.00
Italy	5	365.4	5	73.30
New Zealand	6	363.9	6	66.60
Norway	7	357.9	7	60.00
Iceland	8	350.2	8	53.30
Switzerland	9	339.7	9	46.60
Ireland	10	337.3	10	40.00
Belgium	11	334.4	11	33.30
Greece	12	331.9	12	26.60
Spain	13	329.6	13	20.00
Germany	14	328.7	14	13.30
Netherlands	15	303.8	15	6.60
Denmark	16	291.2	16	0.00

Note: "Point" is an Excel term for case number. Point and rank are only the same in this example because the countries were already sorted from highest to lowest score.

NOTES ON MEASURING VALUE ADDED WITH NORM-REFERENCED DATA

Figure 5–6 portrays the concept of norm-referenced value added. If a cohort of students, or an individual student, has achieved national average gains, the norm-referenced value added will be zero, which produces a horizontal line of performance in Figure 5–6. That is, the mean of the cohort, or individual score, will be in approximately the same position

FIGURE 5–6
Norm-Referenced Value Added

Note: In this example, the third-grade cohort showed no norm-referenced value-added growth on normal curve equivalent (NCE) scores.

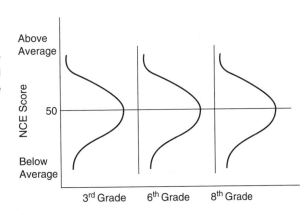

on the normal curve as it was previously. When norm-referenced value added is negative, the cohort or individual has progressed more slowly than the national average, which results in a downward-sloping line, and when norm-referenced value added is positive, the cohort or individual has exceeded the national average value added, which results in an upward-sloping line.

NOTES ON THE STRUCTURE OF DATA

Some basic dos and don'ts regarding the use of descriptive statistics apply. Students in different schools or classrooms are essentially receiving different *treatments*.[1] Thus, we can expect them to perform differently. For example, if we were interested in comparing male and female math performance across two schools, we should not compare the average female and male performance across both schools. One school might have higher overall performance in math. A solution is to first compare males and females within schools, or, in this case, within classrooms, and then compare the results at each level. Try the following:

1. Create z scores or median-deviated scores for all students at the classroom level for each classroom (using classroom-level means or medians) across both schools.
2. Compute the averages of the z scores or median-deviated scores for males and females.

This approach will balance any general differences in performance level from classroom to classroom or school to school, which will allow you to focus directly on the question of interest: male versus female performance in math. However, remember that all these efforts have elements that are beyond our control. We cannot easily control for differences in prior experiences with reading, parental support at home, hours of television watched, student motivation, peer group interactions, nutrition, learning disabilities, and many other possible causes of variation. With this caution in mind, we are only at the stage of using indicators to identify potentially meaningful differences. Further analysis may be necessary to determine which interventions are likely to be effective.

SUMMARY

In this chapter, you encountered a set of basic tools you might apply when you are constructing a descriptive overview of data on your school or district. We necessarily left out much of the formal discussion of probability theory that typically dominates statistics texts. At this point, we encourage you to test your skills by performing descriptive analyses on Problem C. Once you do so, we encourage you to then tackle the Part II Simulation and to prepare a data-driven policy brief on Where We Stand: U.S. Performance and Efficiency.

---

[1]*Treatment* is the research jargon that describes the agent assumed to cause change. In this case, the complex combination of student talent, teacher talent, curriculum, textbooks, and peer interactions in a classroom is the treatment.

PROBLEM C

Creation of a Descriptive Profile

Background: Two issues have recently been recurring in faculty meetings at your school. First, much concern has been expressed about differential grading practices. A small group of math and science teachers who perceive themselves as the "rigor regatta" have been suggesting that others in their departments are going easy on the students so that they will be liked. Test and quiz grade data have been compiled for four teacher teams across the math and science curriculum (see the Student Scores worksheet). Currently, math and science are taught in a block in your school, such that a team of two teachers has the same group of students for each content area. A board member, who is a retired engineer, raised a second issue, of somewhat less concern. The board member was concerned that reports of a schoolwide GPA of 3.07 were overstated because of the relatively high GPA of the large sophomore class and the unweighted method used to determine the schoolwide average (see the Weighted Analysis worksheet).

Your Mission: You need to prepare a full report to the board for the next meeting (next week). The report should include a comprehensive set of analyses to address the first question raised by the "rigor regatta" and a brief response, with appropriate recalculation, regarding the schoolwide GPA concern. Your superintendent wants you to complete the following tasks:

Task 1: Compute descriptive statistics for the student achievement data, for each teacher's students, for males and females separately. Prepare summary tables of your results. Provide a brief narrative of your major findings.

Task 2: Compute a series of mean- and median-deviated scores and z scores for all students. Provide a brief narrative of your major findings.

Task 3: Determine the ranks and percentiles for students within each class to see whether more students are achieving higher grades in specific classes. Provide a brief narrative of your major findings.

Sample Figure and Table for Problem C

FIGURE 5–C–1

Normal Distribution of Male and Female Math Scores Within a Class

Note: In Excel, choose the *Stock Chart* (High, Low, Close) option.

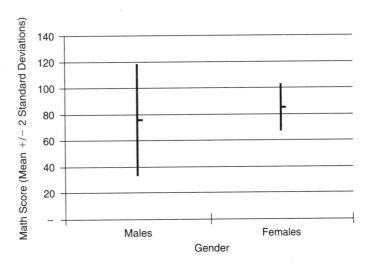

TABLE 5–C–1

Male and Female Math and Science Performance in Two Classrooms

		Math		Science	
Class	Student Gender	Mean	SD	Mean	SD
1	Male				
	Female				
2	Male				
	Female				

Note: SD = standard deviation.

PART II SIMULATION

Where We Stand: U.S. Performance and Efficiency

You have been called before the U.S. Department of Education to present a summary analysis of the relative performance and efficiency of U.S. schools in an international climate. You have been provided with data from the Organization for Economic Cooperation and Development (OECD; 1999). A standard set of indicators is requested for the report. The indicators are listed next. However, you are encouraged to construct additional indicators that may paint a different, or more comprehensive, picture of Where We Stand. Variable descriptions are given in the table that follows.

1. How does the United States compare with other OECD nations relative to the following indicators:
   a. Gross domestic product per capita (GDP/Capita)
   b. Expenditure per pupil (EXP/PUP)
   c. Pupils-to-teacher ratios (P/T Ratio)
   d. High school graduation rates (HS GRAD)
   e. Higher education graduation rate (HE GRAD)
   f. Reading performance (READING SCORE)
2. Calculate the following ratios:
   a. National Educational Effort (expenditure per pupil relative to GDP per capita).
   b. Rate of Return on Educational Investment (expenditure per pupil relative to high school graduation rate).
   c. Educational Efficiency (expenditure per pupil relative to reading score).
   d. Construct one additional and interesting indicator, define it, calculate it for each nation, and explain the results.

Variable Descriptions for International Education Exercise

Variable Name	Description
GDP/Capita	Gross domestic product per capita.
PPE	Per-pupil expenditure for various levels of education.
Graduation Rates (Upper Sec Grad, BA/BS Grad, MA Grad)	Graduation rates expressed as a ratio of students who completed the level of education by the expected age to the number of students in the given cohort (can exceed 100 if students younger than the expected age graduate along with those of the expected age).
P/T Ratio (Early Childhood, Primary, Secondary)	Pupils-to-teacher ratio for various levels of education.
Teaching Hr/Yr (Early Childhood, Primary, Secondary)	Average number of teaching hours per year for various levels of education.
Reading Score	Measure of reading literacy based on data collected between October 1990 and April 1991 for an IEA study (OECD, 1999, p. 207).

(continued)

Variable Descriptions for International Education Exercise (*continued*)

Variable Name	Description
Earnings (Male and Female earnings are repor- ted separately for Primary–Lower, Non- university, University, Secondary = 100)	Earnings are all expressed relative to the average earnings of high school graduates for the given country, where high school graduate earnings = 100.

Note. IEA = International Association for Evaluation of Educational Achievement. From *Education at a Glance,* by Organization for Economic Cooperation and Development, 1999, Paris: Author p. 207.

Sample Summary Table for Simulation

Wealth, Spending, and Effort Measures

Measure/Index	U.S. Rank	Mean (All)	U.S. z Score	Median	U.S.% of Median
Per-Pupil Spending					
Gross Domestic Product (GDP) per Capita					
Effort = PPE/GDP					

Note. You can add columns for measures like U.S. Percentile. You can also create similar tables for Outcome, Efficiency, and Effectiveness measures. It is important to establish a consistent reporting format to be carried through a brief. PPE = per-pupil expenditure.

PART II SUMMARY

Take a moment to examine the contents of your tool kit. In addition to the knowledge you gained from part I, you should now have a working knowledge of how to organize and summarize data. Consider your organization for a moment. How many types of data are available to your organization at this time? Are these data systematically collected or analyzed? If so, who uses them and why?

Data collection and analysis practices vary widely among states, districts, and even schools. We (the authors) recall one school district in which annual budget data were entered into a word-processing document, not a spreadsheet. Furthermore, only a hard copy of the current year's budget was kept in the computer. As a result, data comparisons from previous years were made all but impossible. You may not encounter such drastic setbacks to data access, but your system may require some attention.

Once you have the opportunity to examine your organization's data, use the tools from this part of the book to uncover information. Make sure you are comfortable using the following techniques. (Suggested data sets are in parentheses.)

- Calculation of percent change (student enrollment)
- Matrix operations (salary schedule)
- Ranking, sorting, and filtering data (gender differences on test scores)

- ◆ Share analysis (teachers with master's degrees as a share of total staff)
- ◆ Ratio analysis (educational efficiency, per-pupil expenditures)
- ◆ Value added (dollars spent per reading test score point gained)

In this part, we also explained how to construct useful indexes. Calculate three indexes from Table 4–9, using data from your organization. Then construct and calculate an additional index, not found in this part. This exercise is a preliminary information-gathering process designed to reveal story lines in your organization. In part III, you learn how to uncover relationships among the story lines.

Finally, review the seven statistical techniques listed next. Briefly explain how to use them in Excel; more important, practice putting them into use. These are the "nuts and bolts" of your newly expanded tool kit.

1. Normal distribution
2. Standard deviation
3. Weighted analysis
4. Mean, median, and z score
5. Descriptive analysis
6. Rank and percentile analysis
7. Value added and normed value added

With these skills added to your tool kit, you are ready for part III.

Part III
Searching for Relationships in Education Data

Both system linkages and statistical relationships are connections that exist between two variables. However, a statistical relationship between two variables within a system has embedded contextual meaning. A model of causality is implied even if it is not explicitly stated. One good habit of ecological thinking is to spend some time exploring your hidden assumptions about the meaning of relationships between variables. For example, does a statistical relationship exist between a student's math class average and his or her individual average rate of progress? Let us assume that the data suggest such a relationship and that the relationship is positive. In other words, as the average of the class increases (among many classes), an individual student's score is also likely to be better. What might explain the relationship? You might explore several notions about the relationship: (a) the *peer effect*, which involves the contention that a student will do better if he or she is surrounded by more academically able students; (b) the *grade inflation effect*, which involves the belief that teachers who give higher grades are more likely to give them to everyone independent of ability; or (c) the *statistical artifact effect*, in which the argument is that the statistical result is simply an artifact of the way the data are analyzed. How might you test the robustness of each of these causal models? We address methods for studying such differences in chapter 6.

You will also look at more complex issues in this part, such as the question of whether or not allocating more resources to classrooms is related to improved student performance. In this type of problem, multiple possible levels of resources can be allocated, perhaps from $1,000 per pupil up to $5,000 per pupil, and multiple levels of student outcomes are possible. The goal is to determine what the most cost-effective level of input might be given the varied outcomes to different inputs. When the analysis is simple and we are comparing the relationship between two variables, we can use *bivariate regressions*. These are also known as *multiple differences* and are addressed in chapters 7 and 8.

Understanding system linkages is a necessary first step in understanding relationships among various components of an entire system. The analytic tools in this part are traditional statistical tools, designed to help find relationships that exist in data. This is not a full course on formal inferential statistics, nor does this part include complicated code writing for statistical software packages. Rather, our goal is to prepare you to perform basic analyses, all of which can be done in Excel, so that you can reveal important relationships among the functions (or dysfunctions) of your school or district.

6

Similarities and Differences Among Groups

FIGURE 6–1
Comparing Two Distributions

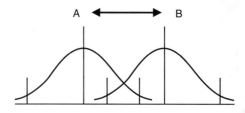

We begin our discussion with the concept of significant differences. For simplicity's sake, we begin with a discussion of methods for studying differences between two groups. Recall our discussion of the normal distribution and z scores in chapter 5. Remember that when the z score was more than 2 standard deviations from the mean, we could label it an unlikely occurrence. Let us continue to define *unlikely occurrence* as a less than 5% chance. In Figure 6–1, rather than looking at a single point in relation to a distribution, we are comparing two distributions. The goal is to determine whether the means of the two groups are different enough that their being the same would be a highly unlikely occurrence. In other words, we want to be 95% confident that the difference between the groups is not zero. Given Figure 6–1, we can easily see that the farther apart the means, and the "tighter"[1] the distributions, the lower and lower the probability that the two groups are the same.

Such a comparison might be applicable under a number of circumstances. Imagine that Bell Curve A, on the left, represents the scores of students on a pretest in math, and Bell Curve B, on the right, represents the scores of the same students on a posttest. We want to know whether A is different from B and if it is, how much different. In another situation, the two curves could represent students' reading scores after they tried two computer-assisted reading programs. To compare the relative effectiveness of each program, we would compare the means of the two groups to determine whether they are meaningfully different.

RESEARCH LITERATURE ON GROUP COMPARISON

In massive volumes of research literature in education, researchers have applied statistical tests of differences between groups. The popularity of these statistical methods originates from the use of statistical group comparisons in controlled experimentation, in which one group is a control group, receiving no treatment, and another group is an experimental group and does receive intervention. So that we can learn whether the treatment works, statistical analyses indicate whether the results from the experimental group and the control group are different. Few large-scale examples of experimental design research exist in the education policy literature. Too many logistical and ethical concerns arise about the treatment of children as experimental subjects. For instance, suppose we want to answer the question: Does preschool education have any positive effects? We would have to randomly assign half a large sample of children to a preschool program and deny the program to the other half, not permitting the parents to purchase it privately. Clearly, this is not a policy-acceptable research strategy.

---

[1]The distributions are tighter when their tails are closer to the middle of the chart.

One example that comes closest to a group comparison, experimental design study is the Tennessee Class Size Study (Finn & Achilles, 1999). This study has significantly affected public policy, from a presidential decree providing 100,000 teachers to help reduce class size to numerous state efforts to make class size reduction a central education policy objective. In 1985, the Tennessee legislature funded a multiyear study in which entering kindergarten students (about 6,000 in the first year and 12,000 during the 4 years) were placed in the following groups:

Group 1	Small classes (13–17 students)
Group 2	Regular-size classes (22–26 students)
Group 3	Regular-size classes with one teacher and a full-time aide

Students were randomly distributed within schools and a variety of factors were controlled for to ensure that each entering sample of students was comparable. In addition, teachers were assigned at random to the 329 classrooms in 79 schools and 46 districts. Student achievement was tracked across 4 years (K–Grade 3) with a variety of standardized measures and then statistically analyzed with the types of tests we discuss in this chapter. (We discuss some of the findings later in this chapter.)

SAME GROUP, TWO POINTS IN TIME

The example of comparing the same group at two points in time is a classic pretest-to-posttest comparison. The question is this: Is the gain from pretest to posttest different from zero?

Table 6–1 shows data for two classes of students, both of which have pretest and posttest scores. These data are used in each of the three following examples. Our first comparison

TABLE 6–1
Two Pretest-to-Posttest Comparisons

	Class A				Class B		
Students	Pretest	Posttest	Gain	Students	Pretest	Posttest	Gain
1	75	91	16	1	72	92	20
2	68	86	18	2	64	85	21
3	84	95	11	3	78	97	19
4	56	62	6	4	62	64	2
5	67	78	11	5	63	80	17
6	78	80	2	6	71	82	11
7	73	72	−1	7	69	75	6
8	70	76	6	8	70	75	5
9	64	82	18	9	63	86	23
10	60	86	26	10	58	91	33
Mean	69.5	80.8	11.3	Mean	67	82.7	15.7

FIGURE 6–2

t-Test Analysis Tool

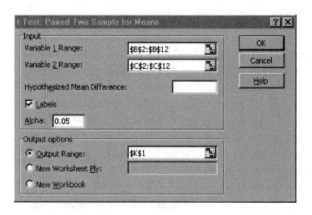

involves the boxed variables from Class A. In a pretest-to-posttest comparison, we generally have all the same participants (students). This allows us to line up their pretest and posttest scores and, by subtracting the pretest score from the posttest score, to ascertain how many students made improvements, or gains, and by how much. To rephrase, we are asking whether the average gain score is other than zero.

The tool we use for this type of analysis is the *t* Test for Paired Groups. The groups are paired because each posttest has a corresponding pretest. To run this test, follow these steps in Excel:

1. Select Data Analysis from the Tools menu.
2. Select *t*-Test: Paired Two Sample for Means (Figure 6–2).
3. Enter the cell range (click and drag) for Pretest scores as Variable 1 Range (include the label).
4. Enter the cell range for Posttest scores as Variable 2 Range (include the label).
5. Check the box that indicates that you included the labels.
6. If you want your output to appear on the same worksheet, specify an output range.
7. Click OK.

The result will look like Table 6–2. Only a few numbers from the table are of interest at this point. Notice that the means in the table match the means calculated in your spreadsheet. You could have similarly calculated the variance. Note that the hypothesized mean difference was zero. Always begin with the formal assumption that until evidence is found to the contrary, no meaningful difference exists between the groups.

To judge whether we have such evidence, we can take either of two approaches. The *t* Critical two-tail value is a measure of how different the groups must be for a less than 5% chance that they are the same. We use the two-tail value because we are not sure which group we expect to have higher or lower scores. So, we consider the possibility that the bell curves could overlap their tails on either end. The *t* Stat is the measure of how different the groups are. If the absolute value of the *t* Stat (−4.30 in Table 6–2) is larger than the *t* Critical two-tail (2.26 in Table 6–2), we can say with confidence that the difference between the groups is not zero. In this case, the *t* Stat is negative because the pretest group is the reference group, and the scores for the pretest group are lower than

TABLE 6–2
t-Test: Paired Two Sample for Means

	Pretest	Posttest
Mean	69.50	80.80
Variance	70.72	91.51
Observations	10.00	10.00
Pearson Correlation	.58	
Hypothesized Mean Difference	0.00	
df	9.00	
t Stat	**−4.30**	
p(T<=t) one-tail	.00	
t Critical one-tail	1.83	
p(T<=t) two-tail	**.00**	
t Critical two-tail	**2.26**	

Note: df = degrees of freedom.

those of the posttest group. If the scores of the pretest group had been higher, the *t* Stat would have been positive.

Another approach is to look at the $p(T<=t)$ two-tail (0.00). This value is the probability that the difference between the groups is zero. In this case, the probability has been rounded to zero. Therefore, the probability that the difference is not zero is high.

TWO GROUPS, SAME TEST

In the example of two groups, same test, we compare two groups of students. The question is this:

Is there a difference in student performance in Class A compared with Class B?

The test for this example is similar to the paired *t* test. However, in this case, we cannot look at the average difference among the students because we do not have scores matched to the identical students. Therefore, we must conceptually look at the difference of the averages of the two groups. Our new tool is the *t* test for unpaired groups (Table 6–3). Let us compare the pretest performance of Class A with the pretest performance of Class B. We could just as easily compare posttest performance.

Steps for performing the analysis in Excel are as follows:

1. Select Data Analysis from the Tools menu.
2. Select *t*-Test: Unpaired Two Sample for Means.
3. Enter the cell range (click and drag) for Pretest A scores as Variable 1 Range. (Include the label. You may want to add the A to your label so that both variables do not have exactly the same label. Doing so will make your results easier to read.)
4. Enter the cell range for Pretest B scores as Variable 2 Range (include the label).

TABLE 6–3
t-Test for Unpaired Groups

	Class A				Class B		
Students	Pretest	Posttest	Gain	Students	Pretest	Posttest	Gain
1	75	91	16	1	72	92	20
2	68	86	18	2	64	85	21
3	84	95	11	3	78	97	19
4	56	62	6	4	62	64	2
5	67	78	11	5	63	80	17
6	78	80	2	6	71	82	11
7	73	72	−1	7	69	75	6
8	70	76	6	8	70	75	5
9	64	82	18	9	63	86	23
10	60	86	26	10	58	91	33
Mean	69.5	80.8	11.3	Mean	67	82.7	15.7

5. Check the box that indicates that you included the labels.
6. If you want your output to appear on the same worksheet, specify an output range.
7. Click OK.

Your output from the analysis should look like Table 6–4. In this case, notice that the absolute value of the t Stat is not larger than the t Critical two-tail. In addition, the p value (p[T<=t] two-tail) is .45, which indicates a 45% chance that you would be wrong if you suggested that the groups were different. We do not think you want to take that kind of risk.

TABLE 6–4
t-Test: Two Sample Assuming
Equal Variances

	Class A	Class B
Mean	69.50	67.00
Variance	70.72	35.78
Observations	10.00	10.00
Pooled Variance	53.25	
Hypothesized Mean Difference	0.00	
df	18.00	
t Stat	0.77	
p(T<=t) one-tail	.23	
t Critical one-tail	1.73	
p(T<=t) two-tail	.45	
t Critical two-tail	2.10	

Note: df = degrees of freedom.

TABLE 6–5

Two Groups, Two Times

	Class A				Class B		
Students	Pretest	Posttest	Gain	Students	Pretest	Posttest	Gain
1	75	91	16	1	72	92	20
2	68	86	18	2	64	85	21
3	84	95	11	3	78	97	19
4	56	62	6	4	62	64	2
5	67	78	11	5	63	80	17
6	78	80	2	6	71	82	11
7	73	72	−1	7	69	75	6
8	70	76	6	8	70	75	5
9	64	82	18	9	63	86	23
10	60	86	26	10	58	91	33
Mean	69.5	80.8	11.3	Mean	67	82.7	15.7

TWO GROUPS, TWO POINTS IN TIME

In our final two-group comparison, we combine the ingredients of the two prior comparisons. The most valuable knowledge we can gain from the information is whether or not the gains of the students in Group A are different from the gains of the students in Group B. We could begin by performing the pretest-to-posttest analysis on each class to ensure that the gains for at least one group are significant. If neither group has significant gains, a significant difference between their gains is impossible.

Assuming that we validated the gains in at least one class and tested the gains in both, we proceed with an unpaired group t test of the gain scores of Class A to the gain scores of Class B (Table 6–5). Our results are shown in Table 6–6. What do you think?

DIFFERENCES WITHIN AND AMONG MULTIPLE GROUPS

What if we wanted to compare multiple groups of students simultaneously? We can no longer ask whether the means are different enough. We need to focus on group variances.[2] Again, we are trying to determine whether differences exist among groups. For these differences to be apparent, they must be relatively large compared with the differences within the groups. The t test is a ratio of between-group variance compared with within-group

---

[2]If you look at the t test and think carefully about what it takes for means to be "different enough," it all comes down to whether the variances (spread of the curves) within the two groups are so great that the groups overlap significantly. If the variance between the groups is large, telling whether they are different becomes more difficult.

TABLE 6–6
t-Test: Two Sample Assuming
Equal Variances

	Gain A	Gain B
Mean	11.30	15.70
Variance	69.12	92.23
Observations	10.00	10.00
Pooled Variance	80.68	
Hypothesized Mean Difference	0.00	
df	18.00	
t Stat	−1.10	
p(T<=t) one-tail	.14	
t Critical one-tail	1.73	
p(T<=t) two-tail	.29	
t Critical two-tail	2.10	

Note: df = degrees of freedom.

variance that generates a *test statistic*. In this case, because we have multiple groups, we use what is called the *F statistic*. *F* is compared with the *F*-crit value as *t* was compared with the *t*-crit value, and the probability of error is similarly reported. One shortcoming of this test is that although we determine whether significant variance exists among groups, we do not necessarily know which groups are doing better or worse than the others, or if any two groups in particular are about the same.

You might want to perform this type of analysis to determine whether the grading practices among teachers in your school vary. In this case, you probably do not want to see dramatic differences among groups. Alternatively, you might investigate whether a peer evaluation form actually allows students to discriminate among the performances of their peers. In this case, you might want to see differences in ratings of the students being assessed, but you would not want to see differences among the raters of an individual student. If the differences among the raters (variance within) were greater than the differences in the ratings of different students (variance between), the variance-within raters would cancel out the effectiveness of the peer evaluation.

Table 6–7 indicates the grading practices of various science teachers. In this case, our tool is the single-factor analysis of variance (ANOVA). The analysis is single factor because only one type of group (i.e., a class) is involved. If we wanted to further study gender differences within and among classes, we could use the two-factor ANOVA. To run the ANOVA test in Excel, do the following:

1. Select Data Analysis from the Tools menu.
2. Select ANOVA: Single Factor (Figure 6–3).[3]
3. Highlight the range of your data (and the labels).
4. Proceed as you did for the *t* test.

---

[3]*Single factor* simply means that your data is organized into only one type of grouping, in this case by year. It would be possible, given alternative data, to determine whether males or females within each of five groups show differences. This would be a two-factor ANOVA.

TABLE 6–7
Single-Factor Analysis of Variance (ANOVA) Data

Kuo	Seife	Levin	Scully	Chuckrow
2.90	2.90	2.30	2.00	2.10
3.00	2.20	2.30	2.10	2.00
2.70	2.60	2.60	2.50	2.50
3.50	3.50	3.40	3.30	3.10
3.10	2.80	2.90	3.00	2.70
2.70	2.50	2.30	2.20	2.20
2.40	2.30	2.10	2.00	2.00
3.10	3.20	3.10	2.90	2.90
2.90	2.80	2.80	2.70	2.40
3.40	3.50	3.30	3.40	3.20

Note: This is a poor layout for these data unless we presume that each teacher has the same students, where each student's grades can be read across the row. However, this layout is needed for us to use Excel's ANOVA feature, which does not presume pairing.

After clicking OK, our table of results appears as in Table 6–8. Again, far more information is provided than is needed. The SUMMARY portion of the table provides the means and variances for each teacher's grades. As with the *t* test, we can make our final judgment by either of two methods. First, we can compare the absolute value of the *F* stat with the *F* crit. In this case, notice that the *F* stat is not as large as the *F* crit, which indicates that we cannot be confident that differences exist. Just how *not* confident are we? The *p* value indicates that if we were to suggest that the groups are different, we would have a 19% chance of being wrong. We probably do not want to take such a risk.

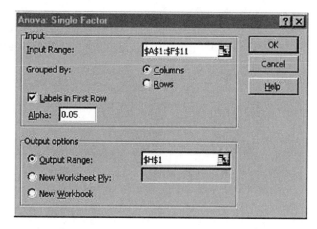

FIGURE 6–3
Analysis of Variance (ANOVA) Analysis Tool

TABLE 6–8
ANOVA: Single Factor

SUMMARY

Group	Count	Sum	Average	Variance
Kuo	10	29.7	2.97	.11
Seife	10	28.3	2.83	.21
Levin	10	27.1	2.71	.21
Scully	10	26.1	2.61	.28
Chuckrow	10	25.1	2.51	.20

ANOVA

Source of Variation	SS	df	MS	F	p Value	F Crit
Between groups	1.31	4	0.33	1.61	.19	2.58
Within groups	9.11	45	0.20			
Total	10.42	49				

Note: ANOVA = analysis of variance; *SS* = sum of squares; *df* = degrees of freedom; *MS* = mean square.

STATISTICAL SIGNIFICANCE VERSUS POLICY RELEVANCE

In formal inferential analysis, researchers use guidelines that determine whether or not to accept a group difference. For example, you are studying whether a new reading program (Group B) has any advantage over an existing reading program (Group A). In formal research, you would be required to hypothesize the expected outcome—that Group B will outperform Group A—or you would accept the default hypothesis of no difference. You would also be expected to indicate what level of probability you are willing to accept. That is, if you hypothesize that B will outperform A, are you willing to accept a 1, 5, or 10% chance of being wrong? Most often, the choice is 5%, and a two-tailed test (2.5% in either direction) is used.

Although this approach is fine for research literature, it is restrictive for making policy decisions. In the previous example, if Group B students appeared to outperform Group A students but even a 6% chance that the scores were statistically the same existed, you would be required to say they are the same. Yet, from a policy perspective, such a strong indication of difference in performance would suggest that you should explore continuing the new reading strategy and continue to gather data. Thus, leaders are interested in policy significance rather than statistical significance. Another way to understand the difference between policy significance and statistical significance is that with very large data sets you can obtain statistical significance at the .0001 level. On the face of it, this seems like a significant result. However, the actual difference might be one more test question answered correctly between two groups—definitely policy insignificant.

RESULTS FROM THE RESEARCH LITERATURE: TENNESSEE FINDINGS

At the beginning of this chapter, we discussed the underlying design of the Tennessee Class Size Study. Table 6–9 (Finn & Achilles, 1999, Table 1) displays some of the findings.

The numbers in the table represent *effect sizes* rather than simple mean differences. Given the methods we discussed in this chapter, we could look at Small-Class Mean − Other-Classes Mean = Difference. However, there are ways to include the importance of variance, or standard deviation, in measuring the difference between two means. For this analysis, we (the authors) take Finn and Achilles's (1999) approach:

> Each effect size is the difference between the mean of small classes and the mean of the two other class types, divided by the standard deviation of students in regular classes; separate standard deviations were used for White and minority effect sizes. The particular contrast was chosen to maximize precision after it was discovered that there were no significant differences between regular and teacher aide classes. (pp. 99–100)

As you can see in Table 6–9, Finn and Achilles's data show positive effects in all cases for students in small classes versus those in larger classes. For all students, across curricular areas, these effect sizes seem to increase as students move from kindergarten to first grade, then level off.

This is only one set of results from a large, growing body of literature in which researchers are debating the importance and effectiveness of class size reduction. According to Hanushek (1999),

> No support for smaller reductions in class size (i.e. reductions that do not attain the critical threshold of less than 17) or for reductions in later grades is found in the STAR [Standardized Testing and Reporting] results. (p. 143)

TABLE 6–9

Small Versus Larger Effect Size

		Grade Level			
Scale (Test)	*Group*	*K* *(N = 5,738)*	*1* *(N = 6,572)*	*2* *(N = 5,148)[a]*	*3* *(N = 4,744)[a]*
Word study skills	White	.15	.16	.11	na
	Minority	.17	.32	.34	na
	All	.15	.22	.20	na
Reading	White	.15	.16	.11	.16
	Minority	.15	.35	.26	.35
	All	.18	.22	.19	.25
Math	White	.17	.22	.12	.16
	Minority	.08	.31	.35	.30
	All	.15	.27	.20	.23

Note: Adapted from "Tennessee's Class Size Study: Findings, Implications, Misconceptions," by J. D. Finn and C. M. Achilles, 1999, *Educational Evaluation and Policy Analysis, 21*(2), p. 99.

[a]Excluding pupils whose teachers received STAR (Standardized Testing and Reporting) training.

na = not available.

Yet, Nye, Hedges, and Konstantopoulos (1999) stated the following:

> The STAR experiment demonstrated that small classes lead to significantly higher achievement for students in reading and mathematics. Analyses of the data collected by the Lasting Benefits Study demonstrate that the positive effects of small classes in early grades result in mathematics, reading and science achievement gains that persist at least through the eighth grade. (p. 137)

As with much of the research literature, the debate on class size continues. Sometimes the debate centers on the subtle difference between statistical significance and policy significance. In policy research, economics and politics are always factors. For example, a study might show statistically significant but very small effects. At the same time, implementing the new policy might be extremely costly (in terms of either dollars or other effort). When applying research to policy, we must ask whether the statistically significant effect is worth the price, a consideration we are not necessarily held to in educational research.

SUMMARY

In this chapter, you learned basic methods for making two- and multiple-group comparisons. As you acquire new tools, each with subtle differences in purpose, and, as a result, subtle differences in design and interpretation, your challenge becomes knowing which tool to use and why. Subsequent to meeting the first challenge, you must then be able to determine what it all means. Although statistical tools can help us to understand data, they are ultimately only as good as the data you are trying to understand and your capacity to interpret them correctly. Your interpretations of data and the results of your analyses should always be accompanied by a good dose of common sense. For example, is a 1% difference in performance, though statistically significant, of enough practical or policy significance to warrant the cost of implementation? With this in mind, try your hand at Problem D.

PROBLEM D

Group Comparisons

Background: You are the principal of a high school within a large city district, and it is again time for your annual report to the district office. A few issues have been of particular interest this year. First, accusations have been flying (from other high school principals in your district) that the only reason your school looks as good as it does on paper is that you and your faculty are participating in organized grade inflation among the teaching teams you have established. You have gathered data on average grade point averages given out by each team during the past 5 years. Second, concerns have been raised that male students are significantly outperforming female students in science and math and that the problems are much greater among some of your teams. Finally, the middle school principals in your district have been raising serious concerns that their schools are underfunded compared with the high schools in the district, and, for that matter, when compared with elementary schools.

Your Mission: You need to prepare a policy brief for your meeting next week. You should be sure to address the major questions raised, but feel free to include additional points you find interesting about the data you have gathered. Remember that although responsiveness to concerns is good, it does not always lend itself to comprehensive analysis. Your superintendent has provided you with some guiding tasks:

Task 1: Use the data on the Grade Inflation worksheet to address the inflation question. For example, you could use paired two-group comparisons between years to see if significant differences exist from year to year. Try this from one year to the next, and from the first year to the last year. You could also use the ANOVA function to compare the variance among all years. Provide a brief narrative of your major findings.

Task 2: To address the question of male versus female performance in math and science, you need to begin by extracting the necessary data from the Student Groups worksheet and creating new worksheets specifically for the analyses you want to perform. Use the Autofilter function to select male students, and copy and paste them on a separate sheet; do the same for female students. You will be able to make comparisons using the unpaired t-test function. Provide a brief narrative of your major findings.

Task 3: For your last task, extract different school types. Compare mean expenditures per pupil of elementary and middle schools, and of middle schools and high schools, using a t test. Then use ANOVA to compare all means. Provide a brief narrative of your major findings.

Note: As you use more advanced tools, do not forget your basic descriptive tools. For example, plot a chart of the grades across time. This will be much easier to explain to the central office and board. Also, calculate means, medians, and standard deviations for all groups before comparing them.

Sample Tables for Problem D

TABLE 6–D–1

Comparison of Male and Female Mean Performance Within Classes

		Males			Females			
Class		N	Mean	SD	N	Mean	SD	t[a]
Class 1	Science	7	85.9	7.0	9	84.7	6.6	−0.3
	Math							
Class 2	Science							
	Math							

Note: SD = standard deviation.

[a]This column indicates a significant group mean difference ($p < .05$).

TABLE 6–D–2

Comparison of Mean Per-Pupil Spending Levels by School Type[a]

School Type	N	Mean	SD
Special facilities	11	14,488	8,241
Middle/high schools	2	13,795	6,667
High schools	18	5,553	3,397
Elementary schools	105	4,338	761
Middle schools	24	4,026	461
Elementary/middle schools	4	3,856	417
Other	2	3,682	459
F statistic	32.9[b]		

Note: SD = standard deviation.

[a]Sorted from high to low mean expenditures per pupil. [b]This figure indicates a significant between-group difference ($p < .01$).

7

Education Data and Statistical Relationships: I

This chapter is about a type of system linkage that we refer to as *relationships*. Just as it was easiest to begin a discussion of differences by studying differences between two groups, it is easiest to begin a discussion of relationships by studying relationships between two features of the system. We can consider the two variables, or features, as if they were two dimensions of a system. However, ultimately, an entire system has multiple dimensions, with varying and complex linkages among them.

As some of you may remember from algebra class, we call our dimensions x and y. In this chapter, we first discuss the xy scatterplot, which represents variable relationships in a two-dimensional plane. Then, we discuss the correlation analysis method for sifting through numerous variables so that we can seek out potentially relevant two-dimensional relationships.

RESEARCH LITERATURE ON ORGANIZATIONAL INPUT–OUTCOME RELATIONSHIPS

Analyses of the xy relationship are particularly useful for studying the relationship between organizational inputs (x) and organizational outcomes (y), such as educational spending and student performance.

The debate about the existence of input–outcome relationships in education can be traced to a study, titled *Equality of Educational Opportunity*, conducted by Coleman et al. (1966) for the federal government. Though not the first such study, the Coleman Report was the largest and most influential of its time, in which 600,000 students in 3,000 schools across the United States were studied. The Coleman Report explored the distribution of student performance across various types of student populations and various types of schools. In Coleman's study, the researchers concluded that family characteristics are the primary determinant (x) of student performance (y) and that schooling (as an x) has a negligible relationship with performance. This finding spurred many debates about the value of increased spending on public education and stimulated a massive proliferation of input–outcome research literature that still continues.

Research on the input–outcome relationship since the Coleman Report falls into a few basic categories. One is the choice of the outcome measure (y). If we ascribe to the idea that spending on education is an economic investment, we should expect our investment to yield an economic return. In several studies, researchers attempted to find a relationship between school quality (x) and earnings (y). Critics contend that many other factors beyond schooling are likely to influence an individual's financial success. (For a summary and critique of many of these studies, see Betts, 1996.)

In another, larger body of research, investigators measured academic achievement— presumably a desired outcome of schooling and a measure expected by some individuals to be related to financial success. Yet, as time passes, less agreement exists on just how academic achievement should be measured. Should we study performance on college entrance exams like the Scholastic Aptitude Test (SAT)? One problem with this approach is that not all students take the same tests, especially in some regions of the country.[1] All too often, we lack adequate standardized test data on uniform populations of students.

The increasing prevalence of major national efforts—such as the National Assessment of Education Progress (NAEP), the National Educational Longitudinal Study of 1988 (NELS '88), and the Third International Math and Science Study (TIMSS)—is providing researchers and policy makers with more detailed information on educational inputs and outcomes. Although state departments of education are becoming more involved in developing outcome assessment systems, many have been slow to develop sophisticated data sets. One current trend is to reduce student performance on standardized assessments to a simple pass-or-fail measure and to report school-level performance in terms of percentage passing or percentage failing. A modest improvement on this approach is the three-level outcome that typically includes a high-pass, or honors, category in addition to the other two. Some states, like Tennessee, have displayed strong leadership by moving in the opposite direction, providing increasingly detailed analyses of annual student achievement on a portfolio of standardized assessments.[2]

We can also delineate input–outcome studies by the choice of input measures (x). In response to the results of studies suggesting that money alone does not directly predict student outcomes, researchers have started exploring whether different schooling inputs that have cost implications affect student performance. As discussed in part II, class size is one such input. If class size does affect achievement, and class size reduction costs money, we can establish an indirect link between spending and performance. Other alternative cost-related inputs studied include teacher characteristics, such as level and type of education (Goldhaber & Brewer, 1996) or years of experience, and administrative and facilities costs.

With this background on input–outcome analysis, we now demonstrate how to construct an xy scatterplot.

DATA IN TWO DIMENSIONS: x AND y

To construct an xy scatterplot, we first need data on two dimensions, or features, of a system. Let us assume we know the number of hours students have prepared for a particular test. Let us call this dimension, or variable, x. We also have data on the students' performance on that test, variable y, as shown in Table 7–1.

---

[1]This fact explains why, for example, students from Iowa typically have among the highest average SAT scores. Their high average (relative to that of students in eastern states) is a result of the fact that few midwestern high school students take the SAT (<10%), and those who do intend to apply to highly competitive (Ivy League, etc.) colleges out of their region. In contrast, as many as 80 to 90% of students in some eastern states take the SAT.

[2]Tennessee uses a program called the *Tennessee Value-Added Assessment System*, or *TVAAS*. More information on the TVAAS can be found in Bratton, Horn, and Wright (1996).

TABLE 7–1
xy Scatterplot Data

Hours Studied (x)	Test Score (y)
1	52
2	67
3	60
4	80
5	68
6	90
7	82
8	100

We can now plot these data on our *xy* plane, setting a scale for *x* data on the horizontal axis and a scale for *y* data on the vertical axis. To construct the *xy* scatterplot in Excel, follow these five steps:

1. Enter your data in two columns on the spreadsheet, with the data you intend to match to the horizontal axis in the left-hand column. Enter labels in the top row.
2. Highlight (click and drag the cursor) your data and labels.
3. Click on the Chart Wizard toolbar (the small blue, yellow, and red bar graph).
4. Select the *xy* scatterplot graph format and continue the Chart Wizard steps.
5. Be sure to label your horizontal and vertical axes, including both the variable names and the units.

Remember from part II that you can easily change most features of your graph simply by double clicking on the feature you want to change, or by clicking once on the chart, then selecting Chart Options from the Chart menu.

Your chart should look like Figure 7–1. (We changed some formats, adding grid lines and data labels.) Two types of questions can be answered with this type of chart:

1. Does a relationship exist between the two variables, and if so, how strong is it?
2. If a relationship does exist, what is the nature of the relationship?

The second question becomes moot if no relationship or a weak relationship exists between the two variables. In this particular case, you might presume that a linkage will exist. However, if the content covered on the test is somehow inconsistent with the material studied, or the material presented in preparation for the test was inaccurate or poorly communicated, you might find a weak linkage. Visual assessment of Figure 7–1 reveals a direction to the points: a diagonal line. Although not a perfect line, a pattern emerges. We find an association between the students who studied for longer periods and improved performance on the test; or, as *x* increased, so did *y*.

Appendix A displays the types of potential relationships between variables.

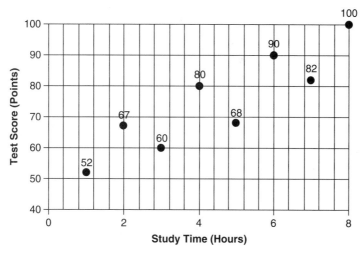

FIGURE 7–1
Study Time Versus Performance

INTERPRETATION OF RELATIONSHIPS BETWEEN *x* AND *y*

To begin to more confidently answer questions about the strength and nature of the relationship between variables, we need to add a few new tools to our kit. The scatterplot shown in Figure 7–2 is a replica of the scatterplot previously discussed, but it contains two new analytic options: a *trend line* and a statistic called the R^2. First, the trend line represents the average straight-line pattern created by the dots. Mathematically, the trend line

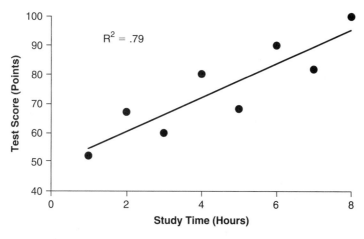

FIGURE 7–2
Study Time Versus Performance: Strong Relationship

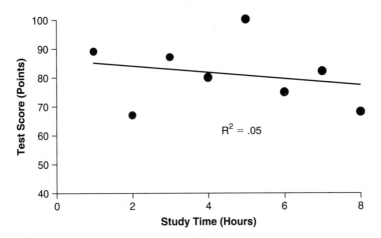

FIGURE 7–3
Study Time Versus Performance: Weak Relationship

is drawn such that the average distance from the line to the points above is equal to the average distance from the line to the points below. When the points make a relatively tight line, as in Figure 7–2, the average distances are relatively small, so finding the best-fit line is easy, and the best-fit line represents the data well. When the points are more randomly scattered, the best-fit line is both difficult to determine and meaningless. Figure 7–3 illustrates this scenario.

The R^2 is a measure of how well the line fits the data and an assessment of the strength of the relationship between the two variables. The R^2 can range from 0 to 1, where 0 = no calculable relationship and 1 = a perfect linear, or straight-line, relationship. You can see in Figure 7–2 that the $R^2 = .79$, a relatively strong relationship, whereas the R^2 in Figure 7–3 is only .05, which indicates a weak relationship.

To insert the trend line and R^2 on your graph from the previous exercise, follow these six steps:

1. Click once with the right mouse button on one of the points on your graph. A drop-down menu will appear.
2. From this menu, select Add Trendline (Figure 7–4).
3. Select the "linear trend line" option (this should already be selected as the default).
4. Click on the Options folder tab on the Add Trendline menu.
5. Click on the box next to Display R-squared value on chart (Figure 7–5).
6. Click on OK.

Another method that is useful for interpreting relationships between variables is called the *correlation function*. Using the correlation function, at least when we are dealing with two variables, is equivalent to taking the square root of R^2—or R. This value, the *correlation coefficient*, can range from −1 to +1. A negative (−) R indicates a downhill-sloping line, and a positive (+) R indicates an uphill-sloping line. We can deduce that R^2 values range only from 0 to 1 because when you square the negative R values, they become positive. We

FIGURE 7–4
Add Trendline Menu

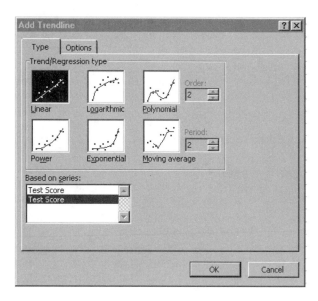

can also deduce that R^2 values will be smaller than R values because when you multiply a fraction by a fraction, the result is a smaller fraction.

Table 7–2 shows the correlation analyses for Figures 7–2 and 7–3. The table is set up such that each variable is correlated first with itself, which in all cases should yield $R = 1$, then with each other variable. We can easily see, as was shown in the graphs, that the relationship in the first data set (Figure 7–2) is much stronger ($R = .89$) than that in

FIGURE 7–5
Display R^2 Option

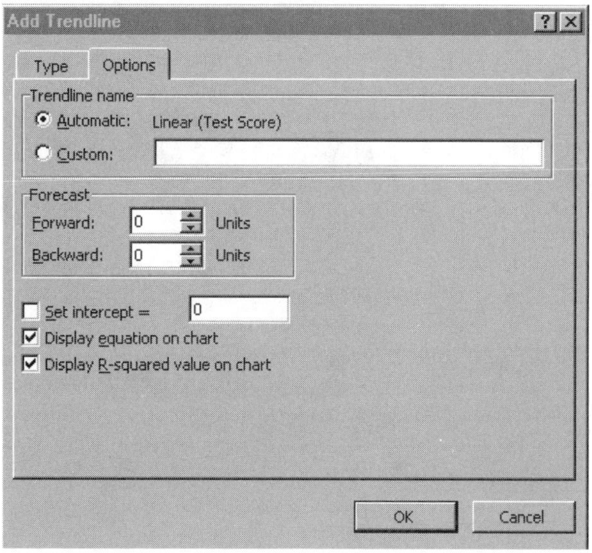

TABLE 7–2
Correlations for Figures 7–2 and 7–3

FIGURE 7–2		
	Hours Studied	*Test Score*
Hours studied	1	
Test score	.89	1
FIGURE 7–3		
	Hours Studied	*Test Score*
Hours studied	1	
Test score	−.23	1

Figure 7–3 ($R = -.23$). Also note that the correlation coefficient is positive for Figure 7–2, which confirms our uphill-sloping line. The second correlation analysis displays a negative coefficient, which suggests a downhill-sloping line, but the relationship is weak, which calls into question whether a line even exists.

These correlation functions are performed by following seven steps:

1. Select Data Analysis from the Tools menu.
2. Select Correlation from the Analysis Tools menu (Figure 7–6).
3. For the Input Range, highlight both columns of data with their labels.
4. Select Grouped By Columns.
5. Click on the box that acknowledges that you included labels.
6. Select an output range.
7. Click on OK.

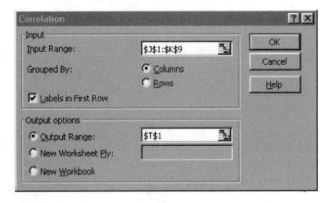

FIGURE 7–6
Correlation Analysis Tool

One shortcoming of a correlation statistic is the inability to visualize a relationship between variables when the relationship is reduced to a single number. However, a correlation statistic is useful for sifting through large sets of variables to find potential relationships to explore in more detail.

THE SEARCH FOR RELATIONSHIPS IN LARGER DATA SETS

When you are searching for relationships in large data sets, the tool to use is, again, the correlation function, except in this case you will sift through multiple correlations simultaneously. In the end, you will have a *correlation matrix*: a list of several variables and their relationships to themselves and one another. Table 7–3 contains data on a variety of dimensions, or variables, for several schools. These variables include the following:

- ◆ Average enrollment per grade level (Enroll)
- ◆ Length of school year (LSY)
- ◆ Length of school day (LSD)
- ◆ Pupil-to-teacher ratio (PTR)
- ◆ Proportion of students in special education (Speced)
- ◆ Percentage of students who drop out annually (Dropout)
- ◆ Ratio of pupils per computer (Computers)
- ◆ Average teacher salaries (Salaries)
- ◆ Percentage of parents with postsecondary education (ParentEd)
- ◆ Per-pupil expenditures (Spending)
- ◆ Average combined SAT score for the school (SATT)

As you can see, constructing *xy* scatterplots of all possible combinations of two variables would be extremely time consuming. However, creating a table that displays the correlation between each possible set of two variables is not difficult (Table 7–4). Such a table is simply an extension of the single-comparison tables we created previously with the correlation function. Notice in Table 7–4 that the correlation between each variable and itself is always 1.00 and is seen as a diagonal line through the table. Also, the upper wedge of the table is left blank because these numbers would simply replicate the numbers below the diagonal of 1.00s. This table is created by first entering your data as shown, anywhere on the spreadsheet. Then, you must follow these seven steps:

1. Select Data Analysis from the Tools menu.
2. Select Correlation from the Analysis Tools menu.
3. For Input Range, highlight the entire section of data and the labels (the labels are especially important when you are studying many variables).
4. Select Grouped By Columns.
5. Remember to click on the box that acknowledges that you included labels.
6. Select an output range (or, because the matrix will be large, you may want to have your output appear on a new sheet).
7. Click on OK.

TABLE 7-3
Data for Multiple Correlation Analysis

PSID	Enroll	LSY	LSD	PTR	Speced	Dropout	Computers	Salaries	ParentEd	Spending	SATT
PS211	77	175	7.00	13.5	14.0	1.7	20.8	34588	22.2	3740.6	918
PS287	57	175	6.50	10.7	8.6	1.0	2.3	42043	41.6	5534.1	1104
PS344	46	178	6.50	13.5	9.1	6.0	7.3	32632	9.5	3284.0	1000
PS346	44	176	6.80	13.3	10.8	1.8	5.3	40637	26.3	4138.1	996
PS351	60	175	6.50	13.8	11.9	10.3	10.0	38579	17.8	4117.6	856
PS011	90	177	6.50	13.3	8.9	4.7	4.8	34718	23.4	3682.5	936
PS035	67	175	6.50	12.9	6.3	8.2	4.1	35357	16.0	4542.8	896
PS098	54	175	6.50	12.4	17.4	7.2	7.9	33766	9.4	3663.2	944
PS124	52	182	6.75	12.4	13.4	2.6	3.9	38016	17.4	4620.6	995
PS138	70	180	6.50	12.6	11.6	2.3	13.6	37735	29.3	4870.6	1075
PS139	50	175	6.33	11.6	13.7	4.5	6.1	32377	17.8	4668.9	956
PS158	46	175	7.00	11.7	12.5	6.0	10.2	31234	21.7	4226.8	982
PS161	82	178	7.00	10.8	5.2	4.5	5.7	35828	26.9	4891.6	1016
PS183	78	175	6.00	14.4	11.6	3.1	7.2	34922	20.5	3532.2	1066
PS187	120	180	6.50	13.8	10.4	5.1	12.6	52844	10.2	3689.7	935
PS195	69	176	7.00	12.9	11.9	5.0	6.6	37766	23.4	3535.1	1012
PS219	143	180	6.50	12.9	14.1	4.4	8.0	38665	16.8	3721.3	1037
PS220	69	175	6.50	11.4	11.8	4.6	7.1	34392	20.9	4026.3	964
PS224	133	180	6.50	14.8	9.6	3.5	9.5	36640	15.8	3878.0	944

Note: PSID = public school identification number; Enroll = enrollment per grade level; LSY = length of school day (hours); PTR = pupil-to-teacher ratio; Speced = percent special education; Dropout = percent dropouts; Computers = pupils-per-computer ratio; Salaries = average teacher salaries; ParentEd = percentage of parents with college education; Spending = instructional spending per pupil; SATT = average combined SAT score.

TABLE 7-4
Correlation Matrix

	Enroll	LSY	LSD	PTR	Speced	Dropout	Computers	Salaries	ParentEd	Spending	SATT
Enroll	1.00										
LSY	.51	1.00									
LSD	−.17	.03	1.00								
PTR	.41	.21	−.30	1.00							
Speced	−.10	−.07	−.06	.09	1.00						
Dropout	−.09	−.26	−.10	.13	−.01	1.00					
Computers	.24	.05	.22	.36	.35	−.07	1.00				
Salaries	.40	.40	−.05	.18	−.15	−.16	.07	1.00			
ParentEd	−.20	−.20	.22	−.49	−.31	−.57	−.18	.06	1.00		
Spending	−.29	.00	.10	−.69	−.32	−.28	−.31	.08	.67	1.00	
SATT	−.03	.21	−.09	−.34	−.07	−.66	−.26	.06	.57	.32	1.00

Note: Enroll = enrollment per grade level; LSY = length of school year (days); LSD = length of school day (hours); PTR = pupil-to-teacher ratio; Speced = percent special education; Dropout = percent dropouts; Computers = pupils-per-computer ratio; Salaries = average teacher salaries; ParentEd = percentage of parents with college education; Spending = instructional spending per pupil; SATT = average combined SAT score.

131

Interpretation of Table 7–4 can be approached in either of two ways: deductively or inductively. Given this data set and the particular variables involved, you may have some questions: Do schools that spend more money have students with higher SAT scores? You might go directly to this connection in the table and see that the relationship has an R of .32. You should consider both the size and the sign of the R when you are scanning through the table. This approach is *deductive*. You have a theory in your mind, so you look to test the specific theory. Conversely, the *inductive* approach is to scan the table to find R values that are notable. Doing so might lead you in some interesting directions in studying linkages in your school or district. You would probably want to follow up any questions raised by your correlation matrix with *xy* scatterplots and trend lines, as well as some of the tools we address in chapter 8.

SUMMARY

In this chapter, we moved from assessing data in a single dimension to assessing data in two dimensions. We suggest the following basic framework for exploring relationships in your data:

1. Prepare a correlation matrix of your data.
2. Search for (a) strong relationships, those that have among the highest correlations in the matrix (positive or negative), and (b) relationships related to potentially interesting questions. Many of your strongest correlations in a data set may be obvious, such as discovering that students' math SAT scores are highly related to their total SAT scores. If this relationship is not strong, you may still have something interesting to explore. You may also find that some of the interesting questions in a database do not have correlations that are notable. For example, you might hope that computer access would help math performance; thus, you might want to check out this correlation in the matrix. Always remember that a weak relationship where you would expect a strong one can be as interesting as a strong correlation.
3. Once you determine the correlations you want to explore, you should construct *xy* scatterplots. An R or any single number is no substitute for the visual, two-dimensional representation of the data.
4. Summarize your findings on your questions of interest in a summary table, like the examples given throughout this chapter, and explain your findings in intuitive terms (e.g., "More students seem to pass standardized assessments in schools with lower pupil-to-teacher ratios"). Remember that you are reflecting on patterns in the data, not absolute situations. Also, always keep in mind the unit of analysis. Our example is based on data collected at the school level; thus, we cannot say anything specifically about individual students.

This exercise will be useful not only in developing your understanding of linkages, but also in explaining them to other people, especially less informed audiences (such as those who will read your policy briefs).

PROBLEM E

Finding System Linkages

Background: For the past 4 years, your state has implemented a new assessment program to determine the mathematical competencies of elementary school students. The program is standards based and linked with a statewide portfolio assessment program. Performance data are starting to enter the state department, and some individuals have expressed concern that particular elementary schools have low success rates. The state department has formed a committee of elementary school principals to explore the problem. You have been selected for the committee.

Your Mission: Determine which elementary school characteristics seem to be related to success rates on the math standards assessment. By next week, you and your team should be prepared to report on your findings to the state board of education. The commissioner has provided the following guiding tasks:

Task 1: Pursue your intuitions first. Construct visual representations (*xy* scatterplots) of relationships you suspect might be interesting. Provide a brief narrative of your major expected findings.

Task 2: To make sure you have not missed anything, run a correlation matrix on all the data to determine which relationships emerge with math performance. Also, check to see which other variables display strong relationships. For example, does community wealth affect the number of computers available, and does the number of computers in turn affect math performance? If so, an equity problem might exist. Provide a brief narrative of your major findings.

Sample Figure and Table for Problem E

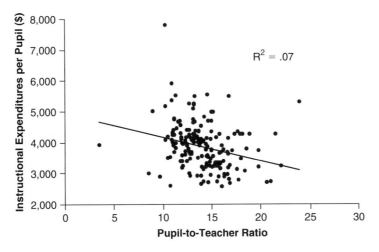

FIGURE 7–E–1
Relationship Between Instructional Spending and Pupil-to-Teacher Ratio

TABLE 7–E–1
Relevant Correlation Coefficients
Exceeding .80[a]

Variable 1	Variable 2	R

[a]Ranked from highest to lowest.

APPENDIX A

Possible Scatterplot Variations

Strong, Direct

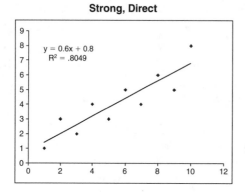

Strong, Indirect

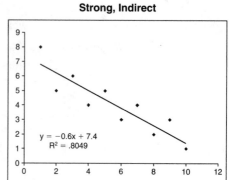

Weak, Direct

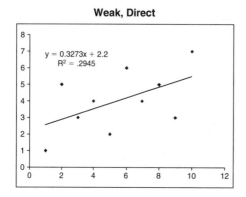

Weak, Indirect

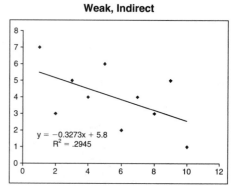

8

Education Data
and Statistical
Relationships: II

The analysis of causal linkages is an extended interpretation of the relationship analyses performed in chapter 7. In chapter 7, x and y were on equal footing, and we questioned their relationship. In this chapter, x is the independent variable, which may be manipulated in some cases. Variable x affects y, the dependent variable. We can now ask questions such as this: What are the differences in y that result from differences in x? For example, do smaller class sizes (x) yield higher average student performance (y)? The assumptions of causality you make when you analyze your data are entirely up to you. However, the tools in this chapter do not establish which is cause and which is effect.

MORE CONCEPTS FROM THE INPUT–OUTCOME LITERATURE

Let us return to the relationship between schooling inputs and schooling outcomes and focus on the relationship between per-pupil spending and student achievement. In this chapter, we discuss two questions that are relevant to the input–outcome relationship. First, what is the magnitude of the relationship between spending and learning? Second, how do we involve multiple xs with respect to y—that is, study the effects of spending on learning while controlling for student background characteristics?

We begin our discussion with the issue of magnitude. A statistically significant relationship can exist between two variables that has little policy relevance. For instance, although increased spending may relate to increased performance, $1,000 might be required to achieve a 1 to 5% performance increase. Figlio (1999), using National Educational Longitudinal Study of 1988 (NELS '88) data, found the following: Although the results are statistically significant, they seem small in magnitude. Ten percent increases in student-to-teacher ratios apparently result in only 1% lower changes in student performances, or less than 2% decreases in cumulative student achievement. Ten percent increases in starting salaries are also associated with small changes in student performance—about 1.4% higher performance growth from the eighth-grade level, or less than a 3% increase in cumulative student achievement. Only instructional hours seem to have substantial effects on student achievement, with 5% increases in cumulative student achievement associated with 10% increases in instructional hours (Figlio, 1999).

In contrast, in many previous studies—such as those repeatedly discussed by Hanushek (1999) in which researchers found no statistically significant relationship among spending, related factors, and achievement—overly restrictive analytic tools may have been applied. Figlio (1999), using less restrictive analyses, found the significant relationship but found it to be small and perhaps questionable with respect to policy relevance.

Another issue of major importance is how to structure an analysis that involves more than one x. Most input–outcome analyses involve many xs. Yet, we must be careful to not use too many xs or xs that measure the same or highly related factors. In most input–outcome studies, researchers apply a formal model known as the *education production function*. Rooted in economic principles, the education production function strictly tests for the relationship among school-related inputs (x_1), student-related inputs: peers and family (x_2), and performance gains (y). From a manufacturing perspective, it is as if we are measuring the performance of the business by relating the cost of the manufacturing process to the quality of the raw materials and the quality of the product. This approach is more telling than is a scatterplot or a correlation, but interpreting the results of these analyses is more difficult.

DEPENDENCE AND INDEPENDENCE: THE RELATIVE ROLES OF x AND y

You may have noticed, when adding the R^2 value to your scatterplots in chapter 7, that you could also display an equation. This equation is your next tool. First, let us establish which variable should be x and which should be y. Figure 8–1 demonstrates the relationship between community wealth and school spending. We assume that the wealthier (x) a community is, the more it will spend (y) on its schools.

Property Wealth (x) $\longrightarrow$ Per-Pupil Spending (y)

Now consider the relationship in reverse. It is possible that better funded schools (y) yield more productive citizens, develop the local economy, and increase property wealth (x). In later chapters, and more complex models, you will learn to consider both possibilities simultaneously. For now, in keeping with the first assumption—x yields y—enter property wealth data in the left-hand column of your Excel spreadsheet and construct the scatterplot shown in Figure 8–1. To obtain the equation, follow these four steps:

1. Click once with the right mouse button on one of the points in the series.
2. From the drop-down menu, select Add Trendline, or if you already have a trend line, click once with the right mouse button on the trend line and select Format Trendline.

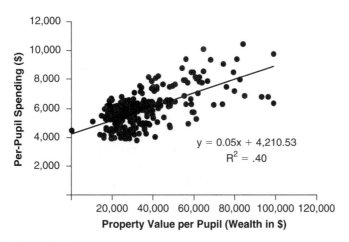

FIGURE 8–1
Relationship Between Wealth and Spending: A Positive, or Direct, Relationship

3. Click the Options folder tab and select Display Equation.
4. Click OK.

So now you see an equation, but what can it possibly mean? Remember that the equation is only as good as the R^2 that accompanies it. The equation expresses the mathematical relationship between x and y and requires two numbers to do so. The first number is called the *intercept*, or b, which in this case is \$4,210.53. This is the number that y equals if x is zero. If x is zero, the following equation is true:

$$y = (0.05 \times 0) + 4{,}210.53 \qquad \therefore \; y = 4{,}210.53$$

Note that in this example x (property wealth per pupil) is unlikely to equal zero unless you live on either a military base or an American Indian reservation (not that either has no property of value, but because both do not assess property taxes in most instances).

The intercept sets a base value for the calculation of the other number in the equation, m, which in this case is 0.05. Now the equation takes the following form:

$$y = mx + b$$

The m value is referred to as the *slope* of the trend line. Slope is the measure of how many units the line goes up (rise) divided by how many units the line goes across (run), or the unit change in y for every 1-unit change in x. In Figure 8–1, $m = 0.05$ tells us that for every \$1 change in property wealth per pupil, on average, a \$.05 (or 5-cent) change in spending per pupil occurs. Because m is positive, the line slopes upward. Given this information, we can now predict how much money a school district with a certain amount of wealth (x) would be likely to spend.

ANALYSIS OF TYPES OF LINEAR RELATIONSHIPS

Let us now explore system linkages by using the xy scatterplot, the R^2, and the linear equation. Figure 8–2 shows the relationship between the proportion of students receiving free or reduced-price lunches and average Scholastic Aptitude Test (SAT) performance in a group of schools. The measure of students receiving free or reduced-price lunches provides us with an index of the poverty level of the school that is likely to affect student achievement. Thus, we frame our analysis as follows:

$$\text{Poverty } (x) \longrightarrow \text{Performance } (y)$$

Both visual assessment and the R^2 value suggest that a linear relationship exists between the two variables. This scatterplot has some oddities, however. For example, in a "perfect" scatterplot, the points would be evenly and randomly distributed around the trend line. In this case, the data points within the middle range of the data show much greater variance. In the equation, b suggests that for the school with 0% poverty, the expected average SAT score would be 1,061.49. More important, $m = -2.78$ indicates that, on average, for each 1.0% increase in poverty, a 2.78-point decrease (negative slope) in SAT performance occurs. However, the relationship is not strong, which reduces the magnitude of policy implications.

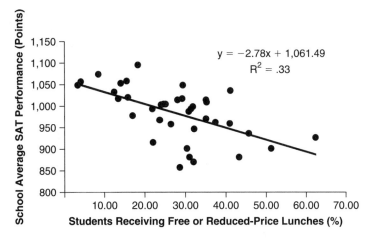

FIGURE 8–2
Relationship Between Poverty and Student Performance: A Negative, or Inverse, Relationship

Figure 8–3 relates school size, measured by the average number of students per grade level, and student performance, measured by average SAT scores. In this case, the R^2 value indicates that the linear relationship is incredibly weak, if it even exists. Thus, an equation is probably not useful for characterizing the relationship. Also, the points are not evenly distributed. However, although the R^2 is weak, the equation meaningless, and the variance uneven, the graph still tells a story. In fact, the uneven variance is the most interesting part of the story. The fanning out of the variance in performance among small

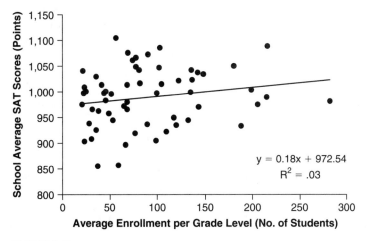

FIGURE 8–3
Relationship Between School Size and Student Performance: Uneven Variance, a Questionable Relationship

schools suggests that far greater variations in performance exist among small schools relative to those of large schools. Although no linear trend exists to suggest that either small or large is better in terms of performance, we might want to further explore the differences between high- and low-performing small schools.

FORMAL LINEAR REGRESSION ANALYSIS

Just as ways exist to test, in probability terms, when a difference is different enough, ways exist to test whether the equation that represents the linear trend line is a significant representation of the data. First, we must reexpress the equation $y = mx + b$ in its more formal representation:

$$y = \beta_0 + \beta_1 x_1 + e \qquad \text{or}$$

(Formally, this version of the equation represents the theoretical model of the entire population.)

$$y = b_0 + b_1 x_1 + e$$

(This model represents the actual equation, for which we will determine the values of b_0 and b_1 by using our data sampled from the population.)

In this reexpression, β_0 is now the intercept (b); β_1 is now the slope, or regression coefficient (m); and e is the leftover error in the model, or the distances from the points to the line. The more scattered and less linear the points, the greater the leftover error and the less meaningful the model.

Imagine that, depending on the "scatteredness" of the points, the line that fits the points becomes either more tightly or more loosely fixed in place. In a highly scattered example, such as the school size and performance relationship, the line is extremely loose, and could swivel around, which would yield a range of possible reasonable slope values. In some cases, when the relationship is loose enough, the line could swivel all the way to being horizontal, or slope = 0, or even swivel back and forth between positive and negative. In formal regression analysis, the question is this: What is the probability that the slope of the line is *not* zero? Or, how likely is it that the swivel room for the line includes the zero-slope option?

To answer this question, you must run a formal regression analysis on the relationship between property wealth and spending from the first xy scatterplot in the chapter (Figure 8–1). To do so, follow these seven steps in Excel:

1. Select Data Analysis from the Tools menu.
2. Select Regression analysis (Figure 8–4).
3. For the Input Y Range box, highlight your dependent variable data and labels.
4. For the Input X Range box, highlight your independent variable data and labels.
5. Check the Labels box.
6. Select an output range if you want to include the regression output on the same sheet as your data.
7. Click on OK.

The regression output appears in Table 8–1. The Summary Output section of Table 8–1 provides more information than is needed. Focus on the important features of this

FIGURE 8–4
Regression Analysis Tool

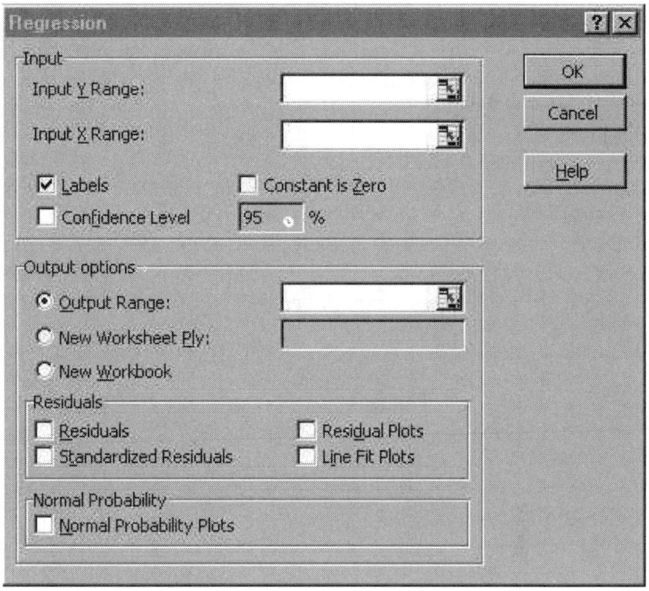

TABLE 8–1
Regression Analysis of Property Wealth Versus Spending

SUMMARY OUTPUT

Regression Statistics	
Multiple *R*	.635
R^2	.403
Adjusted R^2	.401
Standard error	943.575
Observations	288

ANOVA

	df	SS	MS	F	Significance F
Regression	1	171,632,591.40	171,632,591.4	192.77	.000
Residual	286	254,635,293.37	890,333.19		
Total (df)	287	426,267,884.77			

SLOPE AND INTERCEPT

	Coefficients	Standard Error	t Stat	p Value
Intercept	4,210.53	130.81	32.19	.00
APVPP96	0.047	0.003	13.884	.000

Note: ANOVA = analysis of variance; *df* = degrees of freedom; *SS* = sum of squares; *MS* = mean square; APVPP96 = adjusted property value per pupil (1996).

section of the table. First, the R^2 value indicates the overall fit of the line. More formally, the R^2 value is the percentage of variance explained in y by knowing x. Consider the total variance in y to be 100%. If you knew nothing of y or anything related to it and tried to explain y and guess its value, you would have approximately a 0% chance of being correct. However, if x is related to y, and you know something about x, you improve your chances of explaining y. In this case, the relationship is strong enough between the two so that by knowing x, you can explain about 40% of y. As might be expected, the adjusted R^2 is a modified version of this explanation of variance. It is based on two pieces of information: (a) the amount of data on both x and y, and (b) how many x variables are used to help explain y. For now, only one x helps explain y. Because there are 288 data points ($N = 288$), you can accurately explain y from x, and the R^2 and adjusted R^2 values are almost identical.

The next section of Table 8–1 is an analysis of variance (ANOVA) portion and takes the same form as the ANOVA presented in chapter 6. This section of the table indicates whether the equation is a worthwhile representation of the data. As with the earlier ANOVA, note the F statistic (F stat) and the significance of the F stat—in this case, $p < .001$. We can be fairly confident that the equation does explain something about the dependent variable.

The final section of the table includes β values, or slope and intercept. They are listed in the column titled Coefficients. Note that they are the same values that appeared in Figure 8–1. The advantage of this method over the trend-line equation is that the table also tells whether the swivel room for the line is likely to include a slope of zero. The probability that the β_1 can be zero in this case is nearly zero itself ($p < .001$), as seen in the p-Value column of the table.

Sometimes the scales of the x and y variables are extremely different. Property values (x) in the example are as much as 10 times the size of per-pupil spending levels (y). As a result, the slope can appear to be deceptively small. One alternative is to convert the data into standardized scores, or z scores, as discussed in part II. Table 8–2 is a reanalysis of the wealth-to-spending relationship with the data rescaled to z scores.

Table 8–2 displays the z scores of the first six school districts in the sample. Recall that z scores always range around a mean of zero.

TABLE 8–2
z Scores of Six Schools

PVPP ($)	PPE ($)	PVPP (z)	PPE (z)
21,174	5,374	−0.84	−0.39
37,306	5,628	0.14	−0.19
82,996	7,979	2.92	1.74
59,906	8,472	1.52	2.15
70,030	6,208	2.13	0.29
23,556	4,891	−0.69	−0.79

Note: PVPP = property value per pupil; PPE = per-pupil expenditure.

FIGURE 8–5

Normalized Comparison of Wealth and Spending

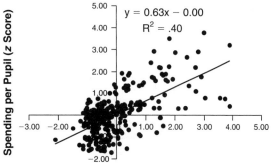

Figure 8–5 shows the plot of the z scores of property wealth against the z scores of per-pupil spending. Notice that the pattern is visually the same as in our original analysis (Figure 8–1), as is the R^2 value. The linkage between the variables has not changed; the relationship is just represented on a different scale. As a result, some features of the scatterplot have changed. In particular, both the intercept (b) and the slope (m) of the trend line are different. When you are plotting z scores against z scores, the intercept of the trend line should always be zero. Notice that the slope (0.63) is much larger than it had been (0.05). The rescaling suggests that the magnitude of the effect of wealth on spending is perhaps larger than was originally assumed because of the differences in scale. With standardized data, a slope of 1 would indicate a 1-unit change in y for every 1-unit change in x. The new slope indicates a 0.63-unit change in y for every 1-unit change in x.

THE EFFECTS OF MANY xs ON A GIVEN y

One goal in regression analysis is to see how much of the variance in y can be explained by the variance in xs. With only one x and one y, the equation is simple:

$$y = \beta_0 + \beta_1 x_1 + e$$

With more x values, the equations begin to look like the following:

$$y = \beta_0 + \beta_1 x_1 + \beta_2 x_2 + \cdots + \beta_i x_i + e$$

or

$$y = b_0 + b_1 x_1 + b_2 x_2 + \cdots + b_i x_i + e$$

This equation expresses that each x variable has its own relationship to the y variable. If each additional x variable significantly covaries with the y, we should be able to explain more variance in y as the equation becomes more complex. Before, the question was Is x related to y? Now, the question is Are the xs collectively or individually related to y?

The data in this case are similar to the multiple correlation analysis in chapter 7. However, in this example, the average total SAT score (SATT) is y, or the dependent variable. Your goal

TABLE 8–3
Characteristics of High Schools

ENROL/GRD	LSD96	ATTEND95	PUPTEA96	SPECED94	FRLUN96	EDUC67	INSPP95	SATT
41.0	6.8	95	14.6	10	41	28	3,466	1,037
72.1	6.0	96	15.2	12	16	28	3,033	1,021
23.0	6.8	96	13.0	4	30	10	3,026	902
23.3	6.5	94	11.6	11	43	16	3,243	882
18.5	6.5	93	11.3	10	63	8	3,827	927
16.5	6.5	94	10.3	9	22	30	4,490	994
36.4	6.5	95	13.8	9	24	24	3,256	968
20.4	7.0	95	13.2	13	46	20	3,943	936
41.3	6.5	95	13.8	9	32	22	2,622	946

Note: ENROL/GRD = enrollment per grade level; LSD96 = length of school day (hours); ATTEND95 = average daily attendance rate; PUPTEA96 = pupil-to-teacher ratio; SPECED94 = proportion of special education students; FRLUN96 = proportion of students receiving free lunch; EDUC67 = proportion of parents with postbaccalaureate degrees; INSPP95 = instructional spending per pupil ($); SATT = average total SAT score.

is to determine which of the x variables has the greatest effect on, or shares the strongest relationship with, SAT performance in Vermont schools (Table 8–3). Please note the following two cautions:

1. In multiple linear regression (MLR) analysis, be careful not to choose xs that are highly related to one another because they may mask one another's effects. Make xy scatterplots for each relationship before you move on to the MLR analysis.
2. This method will identify only the strongest straight-line relationships in the data. A variety of interesting nonlinear relationships among variables may exist.

To run a multiple regression analysis in Excel, use the same analysis tool as in the previous example. The only difference is that the x range encompasses all columns of x variables—in this case, from column A to column H. The output is displayed in Table 8–4. Note that we indicated the adjusted R^2, rather than the R^2, in bold, and that the adjusted R^2 is smaller than the R^2. This difference occurs because we have multiple inputs, and the quality of the R^2 is penalized by the addition of each input because the test is stricter. Likewise, the F test becomes stricter, but in this case the model is still significant.

Let us now pause to discuss more characteristics of the ANOVA portion of Table 8–4. The df column refers to the degrees of freedom, SS to the sum of squares (variance), and MS to the mean square. There are 37 schools in the entire list (only an abbreviated list is displayed), and eight x variables; hence, the degrees of freedom are defined as follows: df–Regression = #xs; df–Residual = N − #xs. In the SS column, the SS–Regression (SSR) is the amount of variance that is explained, the SS–Residual (SSE) is the amount of variance left unexplained, and the SS–Total (SST) is their sum. Thus, the R^2 value is the ratio of SSR/SST. Table 8–5 and Figure 8–6 display the calculation of variance explained for the data set.

The MS column of Table 8–4 is calculated by dividing the SS value by the df. The F stat is then the ratio of MSR/MSE. Why? The overall significance of a regression model depends on explaining significant portions of variance with a given number of inputs.

TABLE 8–4
Multivariate Regression of School Characteristics

SUMMARY OUTPUT				

Regression Statistics				
Multiple R	.731			
R^2	.534			
Adjusted R^2	**.405**			
Standard error	46.421			
Observations	38			

ANOVA

	df	SS	MS	F	Significance F
Regression	8	71,508.034	8,938.504	**4.148**	**.002**
Residual	29	62,491.440	2,154.877		
Total (df)	37	133,999.474			

SLOPE AND INTERCEPT

	Coefficients	Standard Error	t Stat	p Value
Intercept	**426.394**	483.703	**0.882**	.385
ENROL/GRD	**0.282**	0.153	**1.849**	.075
LSD96	**11.455**	29.225	**0.392**	.698
ATTEND95	**4.413**	4.964	**0.889**	.381
PUPTEA96	**−1.680**	5.573	**−0.301**	.765
SPECED94	**0.279**	2.482	**0.112**	.911
FRLUN96	**−0.615**	0.979	**−0.628**	.535
EDUC67	**3.113**	1.315	**2.367**	.025
INSPP95	**0.002**	0.014	**0.150**	.882

Note: ANOVA = analysis of variance; df = degrees of freedom; SS = sum of squares; MS = mean square; ENROL/GRD = enrollment per grade level; LSD96 = length of school day (hours); ATTEND95 = average daily attendance rate; PUPTEA96 = pupil-to-teacher ratio; SPECED94 = proportion of special education students; FRLUN96 = proportion of students receiving free lunch; EDUC67 = proportion of parents with postbaccalaureate degrees; INSPP95 = instructional spending per pupil ($).

TABLE 8–5
Determining the Variance Explained

Variance	SS	Calculation
Portion explained	71,508.034	71,508/133,999 = .53
Portion not explained	62,491.440	62,491/133,999 = .47
Total	133,999.474	

Note: SS = sum of squares.

FIGURE 8–6
Graphic View of Variance Explained

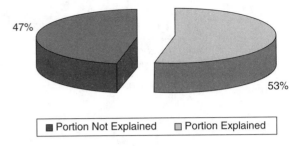

Now, back to the question we originally set out to answer: Which variables are the strongest predictors of SAT performance in Vermont schools? To answer this question, look at the last section of Table 8–4, which lists the coefficients and their respective t statistics and p values. We find that parent level of education (EDUC67) is the only predictor that displays significance with 95% confidence. Enrollment per grade (ENROL/GRD) appears to be close, but a 7.5% chance that the coefficient is zero still exists. However, we may find, if we eliminate other variables, that enrollment per grade level becomes significant.

ALTERNATIVE RELATIONSHIPS

One complicating factor in finding and analyzing linkages among variables is that straight lines cannot represent all linkages. Trend lines are meant to provide the best generalized explanation of the linkage. In our previous analysis of wealth and spending, the straight line seemed to provide a good explanation. With the data that follow, we may find that the straight-line option does not serve our purposes. Table 8–6 lists per-pupil expenditures on 10 reading programs and the respective gains in achievement of students from each program. By browsing the data, we can see that programs are sorted by increasing spending levels, but not all programs show an increase in performance for the additional spending. This finding suggests that several slopes may occur within the linkage. That is, among the

TABLE 8–6
Reading Programs Gains
Comparison

Reading Program	PPE ($)	Gains (points)
A	500	10
B	750	15
C	800	15
D	900	17
E	1,000	19
F	1,100	19
G	1,200	20
H	1,500	21
I	1,750	21
J	2,000	20

Note: PPE = per-pupil expenditure.

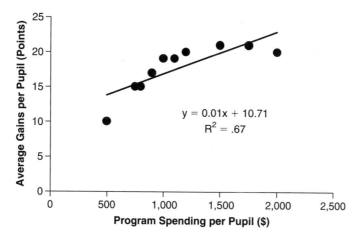

FIGURE 8–7

Relationship Between Spending and Gains

less expensive programs, increased spending yields positive gains (*slope* > 0), but the more expensive programs do not feature performance gains for additional dollars spent (*slope* = 0). This scenario is a classic diminishing marginal returns pattern in economics. However, how do we account for multiple slopes in one linkage, and what complicates a linear representation under these circumstances?

Let us begin by analyzing the linear representation of these data. In Figure 8–7, the pattern of dots is curved. (These data are synthesized, so the curve is much more "clean" than would be expected with real data.) If we had simply run a regression analysis, we might have been led to believe, by the R^2 value of .67, that we have a fairly strong linear relationship between the two variables. However, visually, a straight-line representation misses important features of the linkage.

You can take either of two approaches to better understanding the linkage between these two variables. First, you can try to break down the curve into straight-line segments. Your goal is to dramatically improve the fit and representation while using as few straight segments as possible. Notice in Figure 8–8 that the data can be modeled precisely with three linear segments. The first line has the largest positive slope. In the second segment, the slope reflects diminishing, but still positive, returns, and in the third segment of only two points, the slope has turned negative.

An alternative to decomposing the curve into straight-line segments is the use of *polynomial equations*. Polynomial equations relate x to y by including additional representations of x, such as x^2 or x^3. The use of these different factors can create a curved representation of the relationship. The basic structure of a polynomial equation is as follows:

$$y = b_1x + b_2x^2 + b_3x^3 + \cdots + \beta_ix^I$$

The *second-order* polynomial, as it is called, includes the squared term and generally results in a rapid growth curve pattern or a rapid decline curve pattern, depending on the sign of the *slope*. The third-order polynomial, $y = b_1x + b_2x^2 + b_3x^3$, can result in either even

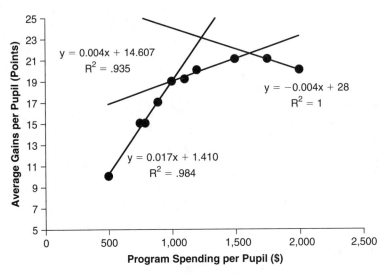

FIGURE 8–8
Spending Versus Gains: Three Slopes

more rapid growth or decline curves, or **U**- or **S**-shaped curves, depending on the signs of the *slope*. Rarely will data require more than a third-order polynomial for adequate representation of a linkage.

As with the linear decomposition, the goal of polynomial fitting is to find the simplest, best fit. You can continue adding higher order polynomial terms to improve the fit of the curve, but you may reach a point at which your representation is not generalizable or your equation may become so complex that it cannot be interpreted. With the program spending and achievement gains data, insert a third-order polynomial equation, which provides a much better representation of the linkage between the variables. To fit the polynomial equation to the data, follow these six steps:

1. Click once with the right mouse button on one of the points in your chart.
2. Select Add Trendline from the drop-down menu.
3. Select the "polynomial trend line" option.
4. Set the order of the polynomial you want to fit.
5. Click on the Options tab and then click on the Display Equation and R-squared boxes.
6. Click on OK.

The result should be as shown in Figure 8–9.

FINDINGS FROM THE RESEARCH LITERATURE

Many multiple regression versions of the production function equation exist. Choosing any one set of results to present would be difficult, if not impossible. Most seek statistically significant, rather than policy-significant, straight-line (or slightly bent logarithmic)

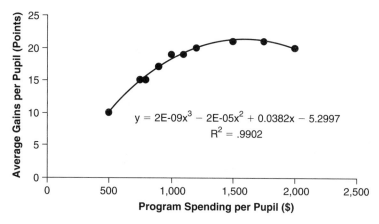

FIGURE 8–9
Spending Versus Gains: Curved Trend Line

relationships.[1] Tables 8–7 and 8–8 present two scorecards of the current research, decisively answering the question Does money matter? Unfortunately, as you can see in the scorecards, the definitive answer is "It depends." Specifically, it depends on how you keep score, which games you choose to count, and how big a win (slope) is really a win.

TABLE 8–7
Hanushek's Scorecard

Resources	Total No. of Estimates	Significant		Nonsignificant
		Positive	Negative	
TP ratios	277	15	13	72
Teacher education	171	9	5	86
Teacher experience	207	29	5	66
Teacher salary	119	20	7	73
PPE	163	27	7	66
Administrative inputs	75	12	5	83
Facilities	91	9	5	86
Total	1,103	121	47	532
% of total		11	4	48

Note: TP = teacher-to-pupil; PPE = per-pupil expenditure. Adapted from "School Resources and Student Performance," by E. Hanushek, in *Does Money Matter?* (p. 54), edited by G. Burtless, 1996, Washington, DC: Brookings Institution.

---

[1]The 1999 Figlio study is among the few in which researchers attempted to search for flexible polynomial relationships.

TABLE 8–8
Hedges and Greenwald's Scorecard: Summary of Results of Combined Significance Tests of Longitudinal Studies

Input Variable	Effects[a,b] Positive	Negative
TP ratio[c]		
Hanushek	No	No
Hedges et al.	**Yes**	**No**
Teacher education		
Hanushek	No	Yes
Hedges et al.	No	Yes
Hedges et al.[d]	**Yes**	**No**
Teacher experience		
Hanushek	Yes	No
Hedges et al.	**Yes**	**No**

Note: Bold emphasis added. TP = teacher-to-pupil. Adapted from "Have Times Changed? The Relation Between School Resources and Student Performance," by L. Hedges and R. Greenwald, in *Does Money Matter?* (p. 82), edited by G. Burtless, 1996, Washington, DC: Brookings Institution.
[a]Evidence of positive effects indicates that the null hypothesis was rejected at the $\alpha = .05$ level; evidence of negative effects indicates that the null hypothesis was rejected at the $\alpha = .05$ level.[b]These effects were seen in robustness samples, which are the middle 90%, with 5% trimmed from each side of the distribution.[c]The signs have been reversed in the studies that use the variable pupil-to-teacher (PT) ratio, or class size, for consistency with the TP ratio, so that $\beta > 0$ means that smaller classes have greater outcomes. [d]Represents a dichotomous sample created by using only the equation that indicated the teacher's possession of a master's degree. Equations with continuous variables (e.g., BA to PhD) were excluded from this subsample (Hedges and Greenwald, 1996).

Hanushek's (1996) general conclusion, based on his count of positive and negative significant and nonsignificant slope coefficients from several hundred studies, was that the evidence is inconclusive or that no systematic relationship exists. Certainly, the balance of significant and nonsignificant coefficients presented on his scorecard would suggest that we are far from a definitive answer.

Expressing skepticism about Hanushek's simple tally of coefficients, Hedges and Greenwald (1996), in several studies, presented a reanalysis of Hanushek's and additional findings. Hedges and Greenwald's scorecard is less skeptical. Most notably, they found consistent evidence, highlighted in bold, of positive effects for all three input measures (teacher-to-pupil ratio, teacher education, and teacher experience). They found no evidence of negative effects when expanding the sample to a dichotomous sample and trimming the ends (5% at each end) of the sample of studies to produce a "robust" sample.

SUMMARY

In this chapter, you learned the concept of causality as another type of linkage. Regression analysis is one tool for analyzing and interpreting causality. Again, note the importance of balancing analytic tools with common sense. Regression analysis is the "chainsaw" in our analytic tool kit. Although regression analysis can be incredibly useful for exploring and characterizing linkages, it can also be "dangerous" when it is allowed to blindly cut, typically in a straight line, through everything in its path. In other words, use your regression tool carefully, guiding around curves when necessary. Look closely at results to determine whether your product seems reasonable, comparing your results with those of other analyses of the same data. Unlike a chainsaw, your regression tool can be used on your data as many times as you need.

For your reference, Appendix A shows six analysis results and their possible interpretations.

PROBLEM F

Finding System Linkages

Background: For the past 4 years, your state has implemented a new assessment program to determine the mathematical competencies of elementary school students. The program is standards based and linked with a statewide portfolio assessment program. Performance data are starting to enter the state department, and some individuals have expressed concern that particular elementary schools have low success rates. The state department has formed a committee of elementary school principals to explore the problem. You have been selected for the committee.

Your Mission: Determine which elementary school characteristics seem to be related to success rates on the math standards assessment. By next week, you and your team should be prepared to report on your findings to the state board of education. The commissioner has provided the following guiding tasks:

Task 1: Pursue your intuitions first. Construct visual representations (*xy* scatterplots) of relationships you suspect might be interesting. Provide a brief narrative of your major expected findings.

Task 2: To make sure you have not missed anything, first run a correlation matrix on all the data to determine which relationships emerge with math performance. Also, check to see which other variables display strong relationships. For example, does community wealth affect the number of computers available, and does the number of computers in turn affect math performance? If so, an equity problem might exist. Provide a brief narrative of your major findings.

Task 3: Use your strongest correlations (and beware of independent (*x*) variables that are correlated with each other) to run your regression model.

Sample Figure and Table for Problem F

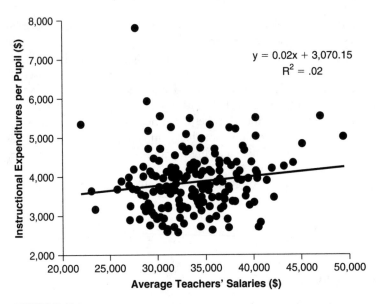

$$y = 0.02x + 3,070.15$$
$$R^2 = .02$$

FIGURE 8–F–1
Effect of Average Teachers' Salaries on Instructional Expenditures per Pupil

TABLE 8–F–1
Sample Regression Output

Variable	Coefficients	Standard Error	t
Percent special education	−2.91	13.27	−0.22
Students-per-computer ratio	−15.23[a]	8.24	−1.85
Length of school year	18.78[b]	4.74	3.96
Length of school day	−11.57	98.18	−0.12
Average teachers' salaries	0.02	0.01	1.67
Enrollment per grade	1.29	2.13	0.61
R^2	.04		
Adjusted R^2	.003		

[a]Indicates significance at $p < .10$. [b]Indicates significance at $p < .05$.

APPENDIX A

Interpretation of Your Results

A. *Diminishing Returns.* Increased inputs along the horizontal axis yield positive gains until a certain point, after which results decline. A classic example is that of a farmer who is fertilizing his field. The increasingly rich soil yields bountiful crops to a point; beyond this point, the overfertilized soil begins to kill the crops.

B. *Exponential Effect.* Increased inputs along the horizontal axis seem to yield few re-sults for a long time, until a certain point, after which the results skyrocket exponen-tially. Beware of indicators that seem stable for a long time and suddenly express positive change every year for several years. This system may shortly become out of con-trol. Cancer cells operate under the exponential effect, and, sometimes, so does school violence.

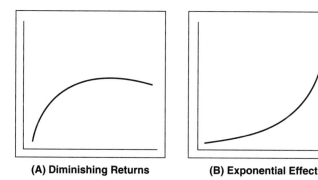

(A) Diminishing Returns   **(B) Exponential Effect**

C. *Perfect Positive Correlation.* A one-to-one positive relationship exists between input and outcome. Few perfect positive correlations exist in the real world; one simplified strong correlation is bacon double cheeseburgers eaten to ounces of fat gained.

D. *Perfect Negative Correlation.* A one-to-one negative relationship exists between input and outcome. For instance, for every carrot eaten, 1 pound is lost (if only!).

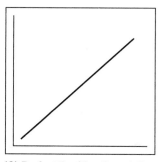 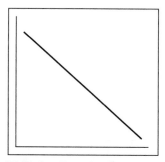

(C) Perfect Positive Correlation   **(D) Perfect Negative Correlation**

E.   *Bimodal Effect.* Inputs along the horizontal axis yield high results in two places and decline in the middle.

F.   **S**-*Shaped Curve.* Dollars spent on a new reading program (horizontal axis), for example, may have little effect on students' reading scores (vertical axis) until a certain level of spending occurs. At this time, the reading scores shoot up and level off at the highest levels of spending.

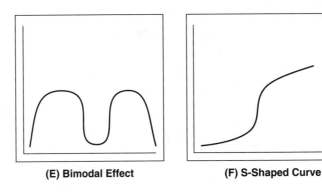

(E) Bimodal Effect   **(F) S-Shaped Curve**

PART III SIMULATION

Redesigning Schooling in Vermont

In the two problems in chapters 7 and 8, you dealt with comprehensive data on Vermont elementary schools. The current circumstances and recent history of the state are interesting. The state has been progressive in implementing curriculum reforms during the past several years, promoting new approaches to special education, integrating technology into the classroom, and implementing alternative assessment programs. In addition, the state is now redesigning its school funding formula so as to be fairer to the residents and students in wealthy and poor towns—to create "equal educational opportunity." As a result, two major issues need to be addressed:

1. If the state is going to channel more money toward different school districts, it would like evidence that the money can make a difference. (This may not mean that the money itself affects performance, but that expensive factors [pupil-to-teacher ratios or computers] may be related to performance.)
2. What is the fairest way to redistribute money for both the schools receiving the money and the taxpayers in wealthy and poor towns?

You have two data sets: (a) financial data on spending, wealth, and tax rates, and (b) school, structural, and community characteristics, and student outcome data for Vermont high schools. For your analyses, you will need to use nearly all the tools you developed thus far. Begin with the following steps:

1. Perform descriptive analyses (charts and statistics) on key variables. Doing so might help you to determine whether spending variance exists from school to school, or available computers vary from school to school. Do certain types or sizes of schools spend more, have students who achieve at a higher rate, or have more computers? How equal are student outcomes?
2. One of your key concerns is to determine which factors most affect the spending level of schools. Currently, the state legislature believes that because school funds are raised by property taxes, property wealth must be the best predictor of school spending. A local taxpayer group from a wealthy town has revolted against this idea because it means that the proposed new funding system will cause the group's tax rates to be unfairly high. *Focus on this issue in particular.* Determine which factors affect local spending first, then determine which factors affect total spending. Total spending includes state aid. Local spending is based on local voters' decisions. Do these voters vote with the value of their home in mind? Or with their annual income in mind?
3. On the performance data: In Problems E and F, your objective was to determine which factors were most related to performance. The question in this simulation is Where should the money go?

Your policy brief should summarize, but not be limited to, the following 3 issues:

1. How equitable is the current system in terms of available resources and student outcomes?
2. Which factors truly influence how much is spent on schools?

3. Which factors affect student performance? Which of these factors also affect costs? (That is, where should the money go?)

Variables for Simulation III

State Financial Data	High School Data
Per-pupil expenditures	Grade levels
Local school revenues	Total enrollment (1998)
Local revenues (residential property)	Students per grade level
Local revenues (nonresidential property)	Length of school year
State aid	Length of school day
Average adjusted gross income	Average daily attendance rate (%)
Resident taxes as a percentage of income	Percentage of students held back
Property wealth per pupil	Pupil-to-teacher ratio
Resident ownership ratio	Percentage in special education
Equalized tax rate	Percentage in technical education
Average daily membership (enrollment)	Percentage dropping out
	Students-per-computer ratio
	Average teachers' salaries
	Average teaching days
	Professional days
	Percentage of parents who dropped out of K–12
	Percentage of parents with a higher education
	Percentage of students in poverty
	Percentage receiving free lunch
	Property value per student
	Average adjusted gross income
	Income of joint head of household
	Current expenditures per pupil
	Percentage allocated to instruction
	Instructional expenditures per pupil
	Proportion passing advanced placement exams
	Advanced placement courses offered per 12th-grade student
	Average SAT verbal score
	Average SAT math score
	SAT verbal (males)
	SAT math (males)
	SAT verbal (females)
	SAT math (females)
	School average SAT combined

Note: SAT = Scholastic Aptitude Test.

Approaching a Complex Study of Linkages

Exploratory Phase

Your first phase analysis is to explore the data and see what they tell you. Your best tools for exploration are descriptive statistics tools, followed by a correlation matrix to use to search for relationships, then some scatterplots of interesting relationships. This process will acquaint you with your data. It will raise questions, not provide answers.

Constructing and Following a Rational Path

In Problem F, following your exploratory phase, try to construct a rational path to follow through the data: a potential story line of linkages. You might be interested in knowing the following:

1. How do community wealth variables relate to school spending variables? *Wealth variables* include parent education, income, and property wealth, and *school spending variables* include total expenditures per pupil, instructional expenditures per pupil, and teachers' salaries.
2. How do school spending variables relate to opportunities available to students? *Opportunities available* might refer to pupil-to-teacher ratio, pupils-per-computer ratio, and so on.
3. Do opportunities available to students relate to student performance? *Student performance* might be measured by student dropout rate, retention rate, or standardized test performance.

By following this path, you are telling how different communities support their schools, and how different opportunities may relate to better or worse performance. Keep in mind that community characteristics directly influence the performance of a community's children.

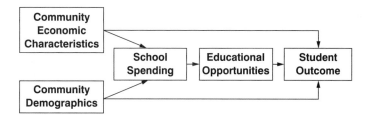

To help the reader of your policy brief follow your logic, you might present a diagram similar to that shown in this section. You should also clearly organize your analyses and summary tables so that they reflect this logic. For example, tables pertaining to the diagram presented in this section should be labeled like this:

TABLE 1. Relationships Between Community Economic Characteristics and School Spending

TABLE 2. Relationships Between School Spending and Educational Opportunities

⋮

TABLE X. Direct Relationships Between Community Economic Characteristics and Student Performance

The analyses could be organized so that you have a small table of descriptive statistics to represent each box in the diagram and a table of correlation and regression analyses data to represent each of the arrows that connect the boxes. Formally, such analyses are referred to as *path analyses*.

PART III SUMMARY

This part began with making connections in one dimension by analyzing simple differences. You might use this tool immediately to compare two or more fourth-grade classes' performance on tests administered to an entire grade level. States use the same analysis to compare school districts for annual educational report cards. Knowing how to analyze simple differences is akin to learning to distinguish pitches in baseball or music.

You also gained the tools necessary to examine data in two dimensions: correlation analysis. What association does input *x* have with outcome *y*? Correlation analysis is performed frequently in all fields of research. However, the warning that correlation does not imply causation has too often gone unheeded: Orange juice prevents cancer! Listening to Mozart makes you smarter! These claims have been exaggerated, and oversimplified, not by the researchers but by marketers who want to capitalize on the positive correlation between two variables. Correlation is an important, intermediate step toward determining the structure of your organization, but unless a meaningful mental model underlies these associations, you risk assuming a causal relationship that does not exist.

Do not stop there, however. Common sense indicates that nothing is so simple. Rarely, if ever, does one input yield one output—end of story. An underperforming school's test scores are likely the result of a combination of factors, including low teacher quality and commitment, lack of student support at home, a weak curriculum, poor school leadership, high rates of absenteeism, and inadequate funding, to name a few. What can be undertaken to account for multiple variables is to test the relationship of many inputs on a single output. One such tool, which you explored in chapter 8, is called *multivariate regression*.

Familiarity with these tools will enable you to more comfortably acquire the systems tools discussed in part IV.

Part IV
Measuring Time and Change in Schools

To this point, we used institutional data to define the positions of educational systems at given points in time. You also analyzed linkages between system components at given points in time. Now you will set the system into motion: You will study its dynamics. To accomplish this, you must introduce an often ignored dimension into your educational research, analysis, and planning—*time*.

Kofman and Senge (1993) implied that as a species, human beings are conditioned against perceiving change across time. These researchers noted, "Throughout our history as a species, the primary threats to our survival came as sudden dramatic events" and "Today, the primary threats to our survival are slow gradual processes." As a result, Kofman and Senge argued, "We are poorly prepared for a world of slowly developing threats. We have a nervous system focused on external dramatic events."[1]

Beer (1980) also observed, in his analyses of organizational entropy, that organizations much more commonly suffered unknowingly from a slow decay with time than were

---

[1]See also http://home.nycap.rr.com/klarsen/learnorg/kof_sen.html.

dramatically affected by any one event. We introduced this notion of *incremental entropy* at the beginning of part II, using the parable of the boiled frog.

Schein (1992) suggested that the way an organization perceives time, collectively and as individuals, is also significant. He stated:

> There is probably no more important category for cultural analysis than the study of how time is conceived and used in a group or organization. Time imposes a social order, and how things are handled in time conveys status and intention. The pacing of events, the rhythms of life, the sequence in which things are done, and the duration of events all become subject to symbolic interpretation. (pp. 113–114)

As a result, Schein also observed, "Misinterpretations of what things mean in a temporal context are therefore extremely likely unless group members are operating from the same sets of assumptions" (p. 114). Though Schein did not directly incorporate his views of time into a systems thinking context, he clearly indicated that time and the perception of time are significant factors affecting the cultural dynamics of an organization.

Richmond and Peterson (1996) also agreed that organizations are often not self-aware of their changes across time: "In the temporal domain, organizations continue to operate as if 'next quarter' were the finish line. Local time perspectives cause organizations to mortgage the future in order to achieve next quarter's targets" (pp. 1–3). Like Senge and Kofman, these researchers suggested that human beings have developed certain habits of thought that undermine the long-term ecological health of the organization they seek to improve because they have an excessively narrow focus on short-term results.

In simple, physical terms, for an object to move from Point A to Point B, the element of time is involved. If Points A and B are far apart, the object will require longer to make the trip. Yet, educational organizations suffer from the same problems as other organizations by underestimating the importance of long-term, steady work in the achievement of educational results. Moving student performance from Point A to Point B will take time. With the tools and models in this part, and a little ingenuity, we can begin to think about and analyze educational systems in motion.

In chapter 9, we explore characteristics of time-series data and explain how to inductively generate stories from patterns and trends revealed by such data. In chapter 10, we look closely at how things change with time and delve into the study of objects in motion, or *kinematics*. In chapter 11, we apply our understanding of time-series data by presenting various ways to construct time-series forecasts of the future.

9

Time: The Forgotten Dimension

Time is often ignored as an independent variable in the study of organizations and change. It is ignored because many people presume that time is something that just happens; it is inconsequential with regard to organizational processes. Yet, time is the only truly independent variable, unaffected by changes in other variables in the system. As time passes, things change; often, they change simply as a result of passing time. In dynamic systems, no true stasis exists. When institutional leaders suggest that they will "maintain the status quo," or "hold the line," all they can truly do is allow the system to continue its time-driven path. Consequently, understanding the time-driven paths of a system becomes important. In what direction is the system going? How fast is it moving? Is it accelerating or decelerating? Are cycles of acceleration or deceleration apparent?

In many ways, the tools for studying change across time are different from the analytic tools you developed in chapter 8. When studying time-series data, we are not concerned with whether y at a given point in time is different from y at another point in time. Rather, our concerns should be centered on describing patterns in data across a series of historical time periods (e.g., days, weeks, months, or years).

TOOLS FOR ANALYZING CHANGE ACROSS TIME

First, you will use a simple tool known as the *time-series plot*. The time-series plot is an *xy* scatterplot in which x = time and y = the variable of interest. Examples of y are student enrollment, standardized test scores, and per-pupil spending. Table 9–1 shows the average national spending per pupil from 1981 through 1998 (the dollar values are constant in

TABLE 9–1
Average National Spending per Pupil (1981–1998)

Year	CUREXP(9394)	Year	CUREXP(9394)
1981	4,226	1990	5,715
1982	4,236	1991	5,741
1983	4,405	1992	5,737
1984	4,561	1993	5,741
1985	4,800	1994	5,825
1986	5,047	1995	5,939
1987	5,219	1996	6,049
1988	5,352	1997	6,148
1989	5,606	1998	6,285

Note: CUREXP(9394) = current expenditures per pupil in 1993–1994 dollars. Data from *Projections of Education Statistics to 2006,* by D. Gerald and W. Hussar, 1996, Washington, DC: National Center for Education Statistics, U.S. Department of Education.

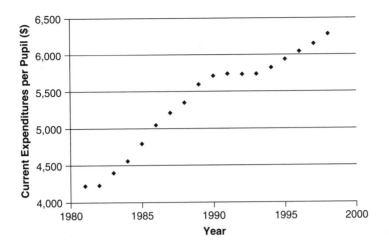

FIGURE 9–1
Changes in Educational Spending (in Constant Dollars Adjusted to 1993–1994; Data from Table 9–1)

1993–1994 U.S. dollars). The *xy* scatterplot of these data appears in Figure 9–1. Because these data occur across time, a line connecting the dots of the series might be appropriate. A less appropriate approach would be to apply a trend line. The unit of time is 1 year, or school year. This unit is the most typical unit of time for educational data. The unit may also be referred to as the *sampling frequency*. For instance, in a retail sales industry, a typical sampling frequency would be 1 month. In contrast, in the stock market, sampling frequencies have been reduced to a fraction of a second in an effort to keep nearly constant tabs on the pulse of the economy.

THE SEARCH FOR EVENTS

As mentioned previously, studying time-series data is different from the types of statistical tests discussed in part II. The study of time series is typically more descriptive and exploratory. We might look at a picture, such as the plot of spending across time, and ask ourselves "What's going on here?" One place to begin a series exploration is to look for events that stand out, or places where series behavior changes. In Figure 9–1, you might divide growth in spending across time into three segments. From the early 1980s through early 1991, growth appears to be significant. Then, from 1991 to 1993, growth in spending levels off. This section represents a change, or an event, in growth. Ultimately, growth in spending resumes from 1995 through 1998.

Remember that whatever you are measuring across time must exist in a broader context. Finding events in a single time series enables you to question how the context of the series has changed. In the case of Figure 9–1, a general economic slowdown between 1991 and 1993 is the likely cause.

FIGURE 9–2
The Level-Shift Change

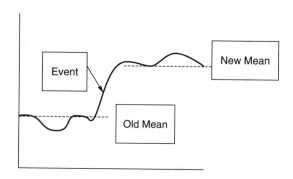

Events often elicit responses that include, but are not limited to, the following: (a) the level-shift change, (b) the temporary change, and (c) the one-time response.[1] In each case, an external or environmental change has occurred, and the series responds. For example, see Figure 9–2. Note that in a level shift, the time series is initially wandering around an identifiable mean, perhaps an average reading performance level for fourth-grade students in a school district. Following a certain event—for example, the implementation of a new reading curriculum—the scores jump upward, then level off at a new mean. Although continual growth in reading performance is ideal, this response is not unexpected.

Another typical response is known as the *temporary change* (see Figure 9–3). First, a strong, initial response to an event occurs, but then the response subsides and the series reverts to its original mean. Such a response might be less desirable than a level shift, yet such a response to environmental stimuli is common. Consider the effects of many staff development efforts on curriculum innovation or staff motivation. The response pattern might appear as in Figure 9–3. In this case, the initial response to the policy intervention, staff development, is strong and positive, yet with time, the response decays or subsides until the measure reverts to its original mean level.

FIGURE 9–3
The Temporary Change

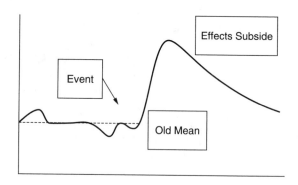

---

[1]These are our generic terms, which would formally be called *outliers* in time-series analysis.

FIGURE 9–4
The One-Time Response

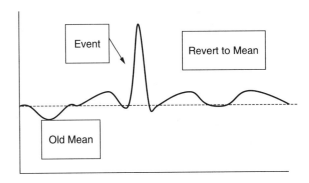

Similar to the temporary change is the *one-time response*, or "blip in the system." Rather than subsiding with time, the blip comes and goes almost immediately. This scenario might be the case when you are measuring daily attendance in an elementary school and the flu season hits. You would likely see a momentary spike in absences but would not expect the average number of absences to remain at the new level for long. Figure 9–4 might represent this situation.

We point out in these examples *positive* changes in response to an environmental stimulus, using the term *positive* to simply mean that the indicator under study (whether spending, absenteeism, or test scores) increases in number or percentage as a result of an environmental stimulus. We do not mean *positive* in the sense of *good*. For example, a positive increase in absences from school is not typically perceived as good, even though the response to the flu has been positive.

Finally, we note that environmental responses can have negative results as well. Some examples include these: A change in leadership causes violence to decline at a high school; an aging community causes enrollments to decline; or a new tax law (e.g., Proposition 13 in California) causes per-pupil spending to decline.

As an exercise, you might practice graphing your own examples of a positive and negative level-shift change, temporary change, and one-time response.

THE STUDY OF EVENTS IN EDUCATIONAL SYSTEMS

How might this approach to analyzing changes across time be different from usual methods? Often, schools take major policy leaps, such as into new curriculum-design or community-based programs, whatever the most popular current educational reform may be. The presumption is that these policy shifts, or events, will yield positive outcomes for students, most often in terms of student performance. Typically, educators and educational researchers attempt to study the effects of events, as shown in Figure 9–5, by using statistical tools from part II.

This approach has a number of shortcomings. Most important, when students take the pretest (A), then some intervention (Event) occurs, and they take a posttest (B) following the event, we cannot be sure whether the event has had sufficient time or conditions to yield a change. More often, the event is actually a lengthy process that involves several

FIGURE 9–5
Pretest, Event, Posttest

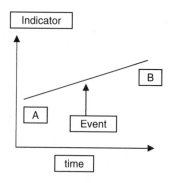

important steps, including these: (a) a commitment to making the recommended change on the part of the individuals who will implement it; (b) the training and skill acquisition necessary to implement the change; (c) the procurement of necessary materials, technology, and resources; and (d) a process of error correction and adaptation to local circumstances during implementation.

Too frequently, educators move on to the next reform before any possible effects of the previous reform can be realized. The initial response may be gradual, not yet yielding an apparent difference in the posttest, yet possibly creating a dramatic change in the direction of the system. Thus, a more sensible approach would be to continually monitor the system prior to, throughout, and following any major reforms (see Figure 9–6).

Note that the gestation period in Figure 9–6 can also be known as *lag time*. The subtle difference between *dead time* and lag time is that *lag time* refers to relationships in which a change in conditions (or *x* variables) results in later changes in a measured variable (*y*). Variables *x* and *y* may be continually moving but offset by one or more time periods. *Gestation* specifically refers to the period after an event, or intervention, during which no observable response occurs.

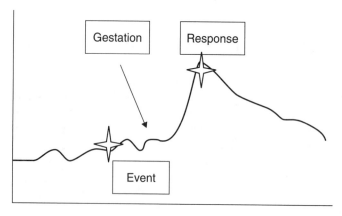

FIGURE 9–6
Monitoring, Event, Gestation, Response, Monitoring

TRENDS AND PATTERNS

The distinction between a *trend* or *pattern* and an *event* is extremely important. Events, as previously discussed, take many forms and yield many responses, but they do not necessarily represent permanent change in a system. Events tend to be one-time variants in the behavior of a system, whereas trends are represented by continuous change in the level of a system, as indicated by the two lines in Figure 9–7. Although not perfectly linear, both the black line and the gray line represent measures that are changing with time.

A level shift also changes its level with time. The difference is that the level shift reestablishes equilibrium at the new level, rather than continuing to change. In fact, the black line in Figure 9–7 displays characteristics of a level shift. Consider the black line to represent pupil enrollments in your school district. Continuance of the pattern as a trend, as might result from sustained regional economic growth, will have a much different meaning with respect to classroom space and building needs than would a level shift, perhaps resulting from a one-time transfer of employees and families to a local firm.

Cycles are another type of pattern that emerges from data-generating processes (Figure 9–8). Cycles are characterized by repeating patterns, generally oscillating around a stable level, or an *equilibrium*. We need to understand cycles and cyclic behavior because too narrow a snapshot of a system may deceive us into thinking that we are looking at a trend or an event. We might perceive a snapshot of the upswing of a cycle to be a segment of an upward trend.

Cycles are repeated events that occur at regular or defined intervals. In the example in Figure 9–8, we present three types of cycles. The first, Cycle A, continues to reach the same peaks and valleys (maxima and minima) through time, around a constant equilibrium. Cycle B oscillates with decreasing magnitude, converging toward its equilibrium state, and Cycle C represents an explosive oscillating pattern.

Because education data are typically measured annually, we often miss the cycles that appear in other kinds of data, such as sales or environmental data. Yet, one simple example might be the *third-quarter slump*: a dip in academic performance for certain students during the third quarter of grading (where such systems are still in place). Drawing a line from student performance from the first quarter to the third quarter of the school year might lead us to extrapolate that fourth-quarter performance is likely to be dismal.

FIGURE 9–7
Trends

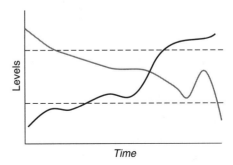

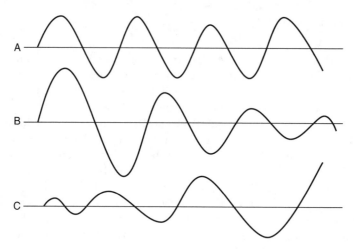

FIGURE 9–8
Three Cycles

Figure 9–9 displays a cycle with a trend. Annual atmospheric carbon dioxide levels, the driver of the greenhouse effect, is an environmental example. The Mauna Loa Observatory, Hawaii, data set displays seasonal peaks and valleys of atmospheric carbon dioxide, yet the level of atmospheric carbon dioxide has increased substantially since the 1950s.

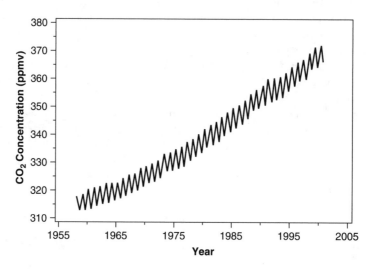

FIGURE 9–9
Cycle With a Trend: Mauna Loa, Hawaii

Note: Data from D. Keeling and T. Whorf, Scripps Institution of Oceanography, San Diego, CA.

An example relevant to education is housing development, which is usually seasonal, with increases in housing sales in the spring and summer. These patterns may oscillate around a stable equilibrium, but where economic growth and continued development occurs, a trend likely underlies the seasonal cycles.

MEASUREMENT OF DATA ACROSS TIME

If we plan to plot variable y across time, y should be measured in the same way throughout the time period. Doing so might seem simple when we are measuring a variable like enrollment; the basic unit is one person. However, some changes in enrollment counting processes might create false impressions of change. For instance, if a policy for school finance funding shifts from periodic (e.g., monthly) to a single, high-stakes count day such as October 31, districts are likely to make every effort to maximize enrollment for that day. Mapping student achievement across time is another example. Changes in the structure or scoring of tests, such as the recent rescaling of the Scholastic Aptitude Test (SAT), or to the numbers and types of students participating in the testing can complicate the interpretation of trends. Likewise, many other kinds of complications can set in. For instance, student scores on a statewide fourth-grade test have vacillated wildly from year to year. Of course, the same students are not taking the test, the test content may not be the same, the scoring procedure may not be the same, and the teachers preparing students for the test may not be the same. These cautionary notes underscore the importance of knowing the culture of your system extremely well before you seek to tell the story of the numbers.

SUMMARY

In this chapter, you learned that effective institutional leaders include time as a variable in their analyses of their systems and the importance of discerning patterns in data across time. You developed tools for creating time-series plots and learned to identify the three main types of responses resulting from events: the level-shift change, the temporary change, and the one-time response.

Also covered were the shortcomings of the traditional—pretest, event, posttest—approach to studying the effects of events. In this approach, educators often move on to the next reform before possible effects of the previous reform are realized. An alternative—monitoring the system prior to, throughout, and following any major reforms—was proposed.

Trends and patterns were distinguished from events, and cycles were discussed. Finally, you were cautioned that when you measure data across time, you must ensure that the variables are measured in the same way throughout the period for your analyses to be relevant and valid.

PROBLEM G

Storytelling with Time Series

Background: You are the assistant superintendent for business in a suburban school district. Recently, you and the superintendent decided to analyze long-run enrollment patterns in your district, growth rates in your community, and enrollment trends in the United States. These issues have become more prevalent of late because your district has decided to build a new elementary school. At a recent board meeting, at which these plans were announced, a local activist who works in construction pointed out that during the last 6 months, new housing sales and starts have declined. He used this fact to argue that no need exists for a new building.

Your Mission: By the next board meeting, you need to prepare a report on (a) local enrollment trends by grade level, (b) national patterns in enrollment during the past few decades, and (c) patterns of new construction and housing sales in your district. Following are two guiding tasks:

Task 1: Create time-series plots by using the data provided. For enrollment data, try creating time-series plots for individual grade levels, for clusters of grade levels (you will need to sum these), and for total enrollment. For the housing data, you may want to characterize the long-run trends with a linear trend line to determine whether a slowdown is occurring (as argued by the activist).

Task 2: Prepare descriptive discussions of the various time-series plots. Feel free to speculate on the meaning of different patterns you find, and where you think the future is headed, but be cautious.

10

Studying Change with Data

SYSTEM KINEMATICS

You may recall Newton's laws of motion from your introductory physics class: An object in motion will stay in motion unless acted on by an outside force. Conversely, an object at rest will stay inert unless acted on. Let us define the initial position of an object as D_0. If the object were to move to position D_1, our system would become dynamic. This motion could be described as follows:

$$D_1 - D_0 = \Delta D$$

where ΔD = change in location or distance.

Note that our object cannot instantaneously appear at D_1 (presuming we do not yet possess the capacity to "beam" the object from one location to another in Star Trek fashion). For the object to get from D_0 to D_1 takes time, or T. Time starts at T_0 when the object is at D_0 and ends at T_1 when the object is at D_1. Thus, both a change in distance and a change in time occur. The two together can be used to describe the motion of the object:

$$(D_1 - D_0)/(T_1 - T_0) = \Delta D/\Delta T = V$$

where V = velocity.

If an object is in motion through time, it has a velocity that is greater than zero. Given Newton's first law and assuming no force acts on the object, the velocity will remain constant.

What happens when a force acts on the object? The velocity of the object changes, by slowing or speeding up. The object that initially traveled at a velocity V_0 is now traveling at a velocity V_1, which is either greater or less than the original velocity. We can express the change in velocity as follows:

$$V_1 - V_0 = \Delta V$$

where ΔV = change in velocity.

However, again, the object cannot instantaneously change its velocity, just as it could not instantaneously change its position. Thus, we must include the change in time that occurred as well. As a result, we have this expression:

$$(V_1 - V_0)/(T_1 - T_0) = \Delta V/\Delta T = A$$

We call the change in velocity over the change in time *acceleration* (A). When no force is on the object (or mass), no acceleration exists; that is, $A = 0$. However, assuming that the object was initially in motion ($V > 0$), the object continues to be in motion ($V > 0$).

We draw our opening discussion of analyzing change from the physical world because we can easily see how physical objects cannot instantaneously change either their velocity or their position. As a result, time, or change in time, always finds its way into the denominator of ratios that involve the motion of physical objects. Yet, we do not always transfer our understanding of the physical world to our understanding of organizations in motion. Consider that an organization, like an object, will continue in motion unless forces act on it. Organizationally, we must determine how to apply the appropriate forces to yield acceleration in the proper direction. However, unlike in the pure Newtonian world, both internal forces and external forces may alter the speed or direction of an organization.

Recall that the time-series plot of the educational spending data in chapter 9 (Figure 9–1) could be divided into three sections. In the first section (1981–1991), significant positive growth appeared to occur. Second, from 1991 to 1993, growth appeared to slow, or perhaps recede. Finally, positive growth resumed around 1995. If we translate this example to physics terminology, per-pupil spending for any given year is the *position* of the system. Likewise, the rate of change, or growth, is the *velocity* of the system. We can determine the velocity of the system (educational spending) from 1981 to 1982 as follows:

(Spending in 1982 − Spending in 1981)/(1982 − 1981)

As long as we study velocity from only 1 year to the next, or 1 unit of time to the next, the number in the denominator will remain 1. Thus, we need only calculate the difference in spending between 1981 and 1982. The resulting velocity for 1981 to 1982 is $10 per year (see Table 9–1). This approach of subtracting current values from previous values is called *differencing*. We can use this approach, as in Table 10–1, to create an entirely new series of differenced values (CUREXP-D). The differenced values of the position data provide us with the velocity between each two points in time. We could also create another column—the differences of the differences—to study the acceleration of the series through time.

TABLE 10–1
Differencing

Year	CUREXP(9394) ($)	CUREXP-D ($)	CUREXP %D
1981	4,226		
1982	4,236	10	0.24
1983	4,405	169	3.99
1984	4,561	156	3.54
1985	4,800	239	5.24
1986	5,047	247	5.15
1987	5,219	172	3.41
1988	5,352	133	2.55
1989	5,606	254	4.75
1990	5,715	109	1.94
1991	5,741	26	0.45
1992	5,737	(4)	−0.07
1993	5,741	4	0.07
1994	5,825	84	1.46
1995	5,939	114	1.96

Note: CUREXP(9394) = current expenditures per pupil in 1993–1994 dollars; CUREXP-D = current expenditures differenced; CUREXP %D = percent change in current expenditures. Data from *Projections of Education Statistics to 2006,* by D. Gerald and W. Hussar, 1996, Washington, DC: National Center for Education Statistics, U.S. Department of Education.

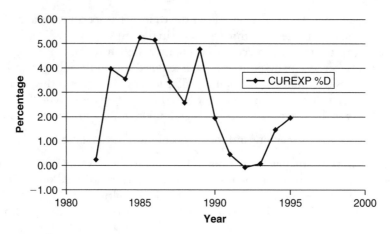

FIGURE 10–1
Plot of Percent Change

An alternative approach to calculating differences is to determine the percent change from year to year. As discussed previously, eliminating inconsistencies in scale is useful. For example, a system with a velocity of $10 per year might be significant if we started with only $50, but in our example a $10 gain per year represents only a 0.24% change. Percent change is determined as follows:

$$(\text{Spending in 1982} - \text{Spending in 1981})/(\text{Spending in 1981})$$

Plotting the differenced series or the percent-change series can reveal new information about changes in the system. The plot of the percent-change series for educational spending is displayed in Figure 10–1. Note that the plot of the differenced series would share the same shape as that of the percent-change plot, differing only in the values on the y axis. From Figure 10–1, we can assess the annual rates of change (velocity) relative to zero. For the differenced series, spending fluctuations are much greater than those in the time-series plot shown in Figure 9–1. Although the rates of change varied throughout the 1980s, the average rate of change seems to have been about 4% per year. In the early 1990s, the rate of change decreased dramatically, slipping momentarily into negative values in 1992. By 1995, the rate of change increased again. We cannot tell in Figure 9–1 whether the 1995 growth was equivalent to that of the 1980s. However, in Figure 10–1, we can easily see that the 1995 average rate of change was hovering around 2% per year, or approximately half the rate in the 1980s.

RELATIVE MOTION

Have you ever been sitting on a bus or a train parked at the station next to another bus or train? Suddenly, the adjacent bus or train starts to back out. As you look out the window, you appear to be moving forward, until you realize that the adjacent vehicle is going backward. Another example that typifies many of our efforts to promote educational reforms is

TABLE 10–2
Salary Projections Through 2006

Year	Salary ($)	CPI	Salary/CPI ($)
1997	29,500	1.591	18,547
1998	30,600	1.630	18,772
1999	31,800	1.683	18,895
2000	33,000	1.739	18,979
2001	34,400	1.795	19,163
2002	35,800	1.852	19,334
2003	37,200	1.906	19,517
2004	38,600	1.957	19,720
2005	40,000	2.010	19,898
2006	41,650	2.064	20,177

Note: CPI = consumer price index.

that of walking up the "down" escalator. We often feel as if we are getting nowhere, or trying harder and harder to move faster and faster, only to achieve slow incremental change. We may not recognize that our system is rapidly moving in the opposite direction from that in which we intend to go. If we were to stand still, we would unquestionably face a literal and rapid decline. Under such circumstances, maintaining position is not entirely undesirable.

Teacher salaries is an example of information that has an isolated rate of change with time. Table 10–2 lists a planned series of salary step increases for 10 years. At first glance, the step increases, or the data velocity, appear reasonable. However, do not forget that the larger system of the economy is in motion. One index used to track this motion is the *consumer price index*, an approximate measure of the cost of goods to consumers that reflects general changes in the cost of living. Figure 10–2 displays the upward trend for salary increments. According to the linear trend line, the salaries are moving upward at an average rate (velocity) of $1,352 per year.

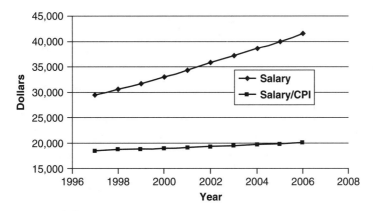

FIGURE 10–2
Salary and Salary/CPI (Consumer Price Index)

If the economy data were moving as quickly as the salaries, the velocity of the salaries would equal zero. In this case, the salaries appear to be moving slightly faster than the economy. However, the relative motion of the salaries is still vastly different from the absolute motion. Figure 10–2 also displays the motion of the salaries relative to changes in the consumer price index (Salary/CPI). From this figure, we can see that the average relative rate of change is only $173 per year.

Case Example

In the preceding example, we might assume that if the economy is moving at rate x and salaries at rate y, the relative motion of salaries is simply $y - x$, or change in y minus change in x. However, understanding relative change becomes more difficult when more than two rates of motion are occurring in a system at once. Consider the following scenario.

The Mission Valley Springs schools are in a rapidly growing district on the fringe of a metropolitan area. They have good, competitive teacher salaries and want to keep them that way (Table 10–3). The district is in a fiscally conservative state where per-pupil

TABLE 10–3

Mission Valley Springs Data

Year	No. of Pupils	Desired Pupil-to-Teacher Ratio	Average Teacher Salary ($)	Total Budget ($)
1980	1,200	20:1	23,500	2,400,000
1981	1,212	20:1	23,970	2,448,240
1982	1,236	20:1	24,449	2,522,177
1983	1,273	20:1	24,938	2,623,821
1984	1,324	20:1	25,437	2,756,061
1985	1,390	20:1	25,946	2,922,803
1986	1,474	20:1	26,465	3,129,153
1987	1,577	20:1	26,994	3,381,675
1988	1,703	20:1	27,534	3,688,731
1989	1,857	20:1	28,085	4,060,924
1990	2,042	20:1	28,646	4,511,687
1991	2,267	19:1	29,219	5,058,052
1992	2,539	19:1	29,804	5,721,669
1993	2,869	18:1	30,400	6,530,141
1994	3,271	18:1	31,008	7,518,804
1995	3,761	17:1	31,628	8,733,091
1996	4,363	17:1	32,260	10,231,689
1997	5,105	16:1	32,906	12,090,787
1998	6,023	16:1	33,564	14,409,800
1999	7,168	15:1	34,235	17,319,139

budget allocations have not kept up with desired levels. At the same time, a massive effort to dramatically reduce pupil-to-teacher ratios (class size) is ongoing in the district.

How do the various rates of change—(a) growth in pupil population, (b) declining pupil-to-teacher ratio, (c) increasing salaries, and (d) slow total budget growth—all come together? You must determine each individual and relative rate of change, construct indexes and ratios (see chapter 4), and determine their rates and relative rates of change.

Let us begin by looking at the rates of change. The population is growing rapidly, and salary rate of change has been constant at 2% per year. Note, in Table 10–4, that per-pupil expenditure (PPE) is growing at only 1% per year. Against salary data alone, this rate could cause a problem. However, remember that the district also has a plan to reduce pupil-to-teacher ratios. This plan means that not only will the district have more expensive teachers, it will have many more of them, which will compound the total staffing costs to the district.

Let us examine how staffing costs change with time. Determine the total number of teachers needed by dividing the total number of pupils by the desired pupil-to-teacher ratio. Then, multiply the number of full-time-equivalent (FTE) teachers by the average salary, a matrix activity (see chapter 3).

TABLE 10–4
Percent-Change Data

Year	PUP % Change	Salary % Change	PPE ($)	PPE % Change
1980			2,000	
1981	1	2	2,020	1
1982	2	2	2,040	1
1983	3	2	2,061	1
1984	4	2	2,081	1
1985	5	2	2,102	1
1986	6	2	2,123	1
1987	7	2	2,144	1
1988	8	2	2,166	1
1989	9	2	2,187	1
1990	10	2	2,209	1
1991	11	2	2,231	1
1992	12	2	2,254	1
1993	13	2	2,276	1
1994	14	2	2,299	1
1995	15	2	2,322	1
1996	16	2	2,345	1
1997	17	2	2,369	1
1998	18	2	2,392	1
1999	19	2	2,416	1

Note: PUP = pupils; PPE = per-pupil expenditure.

TABLE 10–5
Teacher Cost as a Percentage of Budget

Year	No. of Teachers Needed	Total Teacher Cost ($)	Teachers as % of Budget
1980	60	1,410,000	59
1981	61	1,452,582	59
1982	62	1,511,266	60
1983	64	1,587,736	61
1984	66	1,684,271	61
1985	70	1,803,854	62
1986	74	1,950,327	62
1987	79	2,128,587	63
1988	85	2,344,851	64
1989	93	2,607,006	64
1990	102	2,925,060	65
1991	119	3,486,056	69
1992	134	3,982,470	70
1993	159	4,845,206	74
1994	182	5,634,006	75
1995	221	6,997,435	80
1996	257	8,279,365	81
1997	319	10,498,132	87
1998	376	12,635,552	88
1999	478	16,359,501	94

You have two choices for determining whether total teacher costs are likely to be a problem. First, you could compare the rate of change of total teacher costs to the rate of change of the total budget. Second, you could look at a single rate of change—teacher cost as a percentage of the total budget (see chapter 5; Table 10–5).

From Table 10–5, we can see that the combination of the various rates of change in this model resulted in serious problems for the district. By 1999, teacher costs reached an unreal 94% of the total budget and continued to accelerate.

SPECIAL SECTION: A PRIMER ON FINANCIAL TOOLS IN EXCEL

In the fields of finance, financial accounting, and economics, practitioners have developed an extensive set of tools through time to determine the following:

- The value of an investment, made periodically at regular intervals, at a given year in the future: $T + x$
- The value of an asset, perhaps a new building or a school bus, purchased at time T, with a depreciation rate of r, at a future time $(T + x)$

◆ The amount of equity accrued or interest paid on a loan for the purchase of an asset by a given year in the future

Excel includes the preceding formulas as standard fare for calculation of rates of return or depreciation. However, note that formulas for multiple-year financial planning, savings, and investment are irrelevant in the context of public education. Many states deny public schools the opportunity to roll over savings from one year to the next and forbid deficits, although bonds are a legitimate means of distributing cost across time.

Present and Future Value

Let us say we have a plan to save $1,000 annually by putting lights on the flagpole outside each school in the district rather than having maintenance crews lower the flags every night. We might assume that in 5 years we will save $5,000. Alternatively, if we invest the money in a money market account that yields a 5% average annual return, we would expect to have more than $5,000 at the end of 5 years. We could calculate the interest manually, as in Table 10–6.

We can use Excel's Future Value (FV) function as well:

$$FV = (\text{interest rate, number of periods, \$ periodic investment})$$

TABLE 10–6
Manual Interest Calculation

Year	Annual Investment	Interest Rate	Cumulative Value (current dollars)
1	1,000	0.05	1000
2	1,000	0.05	= B4 + (D4*C4) + D4
3	1,000	0.05	= B5 + (D5*C5) + D5
4	1,000	0.05	= B6 + (D6*C6) + D6
5	1,000	0.05	= B7 + (D7*C7) + D7

FV Formula = −FV(C4, A8, B4)

= −FV(C4, A8, B4)

Value at period 5 = $5,526

Same as:

Year	Annual Investment	Interest Rate	Cumulative Value (current dollars)
1	$1,000	5.0%	$1,000
2	$1,000	5.0%	$2,050
3	$1,000	5.0%	$3,153
4	$1,000	5.0%	$4,310
5	$1,000	5.0%	$5,526
FV Formula	$5,526		

FV works both ways: If you pay out $1,000 per year, your loss is $5,526 in 5 years. In fact, the FV function calculates on the basis of this assumption and automatically returns a negative value—simply put, a negative sign in front of the FV (= −FV(rate, nper, pmt)).

Amortization

Other financial tools in Excel deal with payments toward debts or loans. In school management, these tools may help you decide whether to lease or purchase equipment, determine the costs and benefits of new construction, or decide whether to lease portable classrooms.

You may be familiar with amortization schedules from car or home loans. Basically, you are paying off a cost, x, at a given interest rate, r, during a period of years, T. Payback schedules are designed so that payments at the beginning of the loan period cover interest. As time passes, a larger proportion of each payment is applied toward the principal, which may be referred to as *equity*, or *ownership*. Similar payment issues exist when we are making capital purchases for schools (where laws do not prohibit accrual purchasing and accounting). Excel has functions that calculate (a) the periodic payment on a loan of amount x, at interest rate r, for T periods; (b) the amount of interest paid on a payment at period T, given a loan of x dollars, at interest rate r, for T periods; and (c) the amount paid to principal under similar circumstances.

For example, suppose your district would like to buy a new van for $40,000 to transport students between schools. You prefer to pay off the van in 5 years. However, you could lease the van. The lease estimate is $8,500 per year for 5 years. The interest rate estimate is 10%.

Consider relative motion in this example. Although you will have annual savings if you compare lease payments with purchase payments, the interest you will earn on these savings will likely be less than the interest you will pay on the loan, say 5%. Also, automobiles depreciate in value from year to year, so that by Year 5, a $40,000 van will not be worth $40,000 anymore. The purchasing-option yearly payments are $10,552 if we use the =PMT formula (see Table 10–7). Use the =PPMT formula (principal payment) to determine the equity for a given year (period). In the Equity column, sum the principal payments.

TABLE 10–7
Purchasing-Option Payments

Purchasing Option	Amount	
Price ($)	40,000	
Interest rate (%)	10.0	
Term (yr)	5	
Year	Yearly Payment ($)	Equity ($)
1	10,552	6,552
2	10,552	7,207
3	10,552	7,928
4	10,552	8,721
5	10,552	9,593
Total	52,759	40,000

Note: Totals are approximate because of rounding.

TABLE 10–8
Leasing Option

Year	Yearly Payment ($)	Savings ($)
1	8,500	2,052
2	8,500	2,052
3	8,500	2,052
4	8,500	2,052
5	8,500	2,052
Total	42,500	10,259
	Interest rate	5.0%
	Future value	$11,338

Note: Savings total is approximate because of rounding.

TABLE 10–9
Equity Value

Year	Asset Value ($)	Depreciation	Equity Value ($)
1	40,000	.2	40,000
2	32,000	.2	32,000
3	25,600	.2	25,600
4	20,480	.2	20,480
5	16,384	.2	**16,384**

If you choose the lease option ($8,500/year), you will save $2,052 per year (Table 10–8). Use the FV formula to determine the FV in 5 years. Assuming an interest rate of 5%, the savings in Year 5 are worth $11,338. If the van is worth more than that in 5 years, your best option may be to buy.

Next, assume that the van is worth 20% less each year (linear depreciation). Expect that the van you paid $40,000 for is worth $16,384 in 5 years. The equity in the van is worth more than what you would have saved with the lease option (Table 10–9).

Table 10–10 shows the Excel syntax for this lease-or-purchase example.

SUMMARY

The most important concepts you learned from this chapter are that (a) change must occur across *time* and (b) all change or motion is relative. Because organizational change lacks the concreteness of physical change, we often overlook these two basic, universal rules of kinematics. Problem H provides you with opportunities to explore motion and relative motion in an educational context.

PROBLEM H

Storytelling with Time Series

Background: You are the assistant superintendent for business in a suburban school district. Recently, you and the superintendent decided to analyze long-run enrollment patterns in your district, growth rates in your community, and enrollment trends in the United States. These issues have become more prevalent of late because your district has decided

TABLE 10–10
Syntax for Lease-or-Purchase Analysis

	A	B	C	D
1	**Leasing Option**			
2	**Year**	**Yearly Payment**	**Savings**	
3	1	8500	=B19-B3	
4	2	8500	=B20-B4	
5	3	8500	=B21-B5	
6	4	8500	=B22-B6	
7	5	8500	=B23-B7	
8				
9	**Totals**	**=SUM(B3:B7)**	**=SUM(C3:C7)**	
10		Interest Rate	0.05	
11		Future Value	**=-FV(C10,5,C3)**	
12				
13	**Purchasing Option**			
14	Price	40000		
15	Interest Rate	0.1		
16	Term	5		
17				
18	**Year**	**Yearly Payment**	**Equity**	
19	1	=-PMT (B$15,B$16,B$14)	=-PPMT (B$15,A19,B$16,B$14)	
20	2	=-PMT (B$15,B$16,B$14)	=-PPMT (B$15,A20,B$16,B$14)	
21	3	=-PMT (B$15,B$16,B$14)	=-PPMT (B$15,A21,B$16,B$14)	
22	4	=-PMT (B$15,B$16,B$14)	=-PPMT (B$15,A22,B$16,B$14)	
23	5	=-PMT (B$15,B$16,B$14)	=-PPMT (B$15,A23,B$16,B$14)	
24				
25	**Totals**	**=SUM(B19:B23)**	**=SUM(C19:C23)**	
26				
27				
28	**Year**	**Asset Value**	**Depreciation**	**Equity Value**
29	1	=B14	0.2	=C$25/B$14*B29
30	2	=B29-C29*B29	0.2	=C$25/B$14*B30
31	3	=B30-C30*B30	0.2	=C$25/B$14*B31
32	4	=B31-C31*B31	0.2	=C$25/B$14*B32
33	5	=B32-C32*B32	0.2	**=C$25/B$14*B33**

to build a new elementary school. At a recent board meeting, at which these plans were announced, a local activist who works in construction pointed out that during the last 6 months, new housing sales and starts have declined. He used this fact to argue that no need exists for a new building.

Your Mission: By the next board meeting, you need to prepare a report on (a) local enrollment trends by grade level, (b) national patterns in enrollment during the past few decades, and (c) patterns of new construction and housing sales in your district. Following are two guiding tasks:

Task 1: Create time-series plots (including differenced series) by using the data provided. For enrollment data, try creating time-series plots for individual grade levels, for clusters of grade levels (you will need to sum these), and for total enrollment. For the housing data, you may want to characterize the long-run trends with a linear trend line to determine whether a slowdown is occurring (as argued by the activist).

Task 2: Prepare descriptive discussions of the various time-series plots (including differenced series). Feel free to speculate on the meaning of different patterns you find, and where you think the future is headed, but be cautious.

11

A Look into the Future

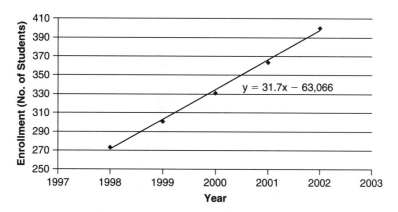

FIGURE 11–1
Enrollment Data for Mission Valley Springs School

One good reason to seek to understand your organization's past through time-series data is to develop a better understanding of the future. In this chapter, we generate several time-series data forecasts. The example involves enrollment data for a K–6 school. We begin by performing a test comparison of linear extrapolation and moving-average forecasts. The enrollment data for Mission Valley Springs School are displayed in Figure 11–1, along with a trend line. To this point, the trend line was not used with time-series data because of its limited appropriateness. In fact, in Table 11–1, the linear forecast explicitly reveals its inappropriateness. The trend line in Figure 11–1 indicates a slope of 31.7, or a gain of 31.7 pupils per year. However, each year the number of pupils is increasing: The early years underestimate. We could set a linear trend to only the last three points on the graph. However, we can expect that the moving-average forecast will do a better job of picking up this upward swing.[1]

LINEAR EXTRAPOLATION FORECAST

One way to perform the linear trend forecast is to use the equation that defines the trend line and enter new values for x to produce subsequent outputs. Another way is to ensure

TABLE 11–1
Linear Extrapolation Forecast of Enrollments

Linear Forecast	$y = 31.7x - 63,066$
1998	273
1999	301
2000	331
2001	364
2002	400

---

[1]The moving average is the equivalent of a localized, moving slope. Thus, the starting point for the moving-average forecast is the average slope of the last two periods of actual data.

TABLE 11–2

Calculation of Linear Extrapolation Forecast of Enrollments

	L	M
1	Linear Forecast	$y = 31.7x-63066$
2	1998	=31.7*L2-63066
3	1999	=31.7*L3-63066
4	2000	=31.7*L4-63066
5	2001	=31.7*L5-63066
6	2002	=31.7*L6-63066

that the slope value represents the average change in number of pupils per year. To do so, simply add m (in this case, 31.7) pupils per year (Tables 11–1 and 11–2).

MOVING-AVERAGE FORECAST

Tables 11–3 and 11–4 display the method for the moving-average forecast. The second column shows the enrollment figures for all years. The percent change (differenced series) is calculated in the third column. You can calculate the differences only through 1997. From this point forward, you must estimate expected change. Your only basis for such estimates in univariate time series is the history of the series. So, we must average the past two percent-change values, then multiply this value by the 1997 enrollment and add the product to the 1997 enrollment. This calculation creates a two-period, or 3-year, moving average.

The results are double those of linear trend analysis. This fact does not suggest that either method is superior. Although the pitfall of linear trend analysis is that it does not account for local variation in the pattern, a pitfall of moving-average forecasting is that it

TABLE 11–3

Moving-Average Forecast of Enrollments

Year	Enrollment	%Change
1990	255	
1991	251	−1.57
1992	249	−0.80
1993	248	−0.40
1994	227	−8.47
1995	209	−7.93
1996	225	7.66
1997	250	11.11
1998	273	9.38
1999	301	10.25
2000	331	9.82
2001	364	10.03
2002	400	9.92

TABLE 11–4

Syntax for Moving-Average Forecast

	L	M	N
9	**Moving Average Forecast**		
10	**Year**	**Enrollment**	**%Change**
11	1990	255	
12	1991	251	=(M12-M11)/M11
13	1992	249	=(M13-M12)/M12
14	1993	248	=(M14-M13)/M13
15	1994	227	=(M15-M14)/M14
16	1995	209	=(M16-M15)/M15
17	1996	225	=(M17-M16)/M16
18	1997	250	=(M18-M17)/M17
19	1998	=(N19*M18)+M18	=AVERAGE(N17:N18)
20	1999	=(N20*M19)+M19	=AVERAGE(N18:N19)
21	2000	=(N21*M20)+M20	=AVERAGE(N19:N20)
22	2001	=(N22*M21)+M21	=AVERAGE(N20:N21)
23	2002	=(N23*M22)+M22	=AVERAGE(N21:N22)

amplifies local pattern variation. In this case, the moving-average forecast does pick up the upward swing of enrollment, continues this swing, and amplifies it until enrollment has nearly doubled.

MOVING-AVERAGE/LINEAR EXTRAPOLATION SHORTCUT

Excel allows you to extrapolate a forecast by using the Autofill function. The extrapolation is a linear extrapolation of the average increments of the data. For example, using the preceding data, highlight the last three enrollments (209, 225, 250), then place the cursor on the lower right-hand corner (small square) of the highlighted section and drag down. You achieve a linear extrapolation based on an average rate of change of 21 ([16 + 25]/2) pupils per year. You can highlight a larger segment of the series to pick up a longer-run average rate of change.

EXPONENTIAL SMOOTHING

An alternative approach to studying and forecasting a single time series is *exponential smoothing*. Exponential smoothing involves generalizing the trends of a fluctuating time series without reducing it entirely to a straight-line representation. To create this

TABLE 11–5
Exponentially Smoothed Data

Year	Enrollment	α		
		.25	.5	.75
1990	255	255	255	255
1991	251	252	253	254
1992	249	250	251	253
1993	248	248	250	252
1994	227	232	238	245
1995	209	215	224	236
1996	225	222	224	233
1997	250			

generalized representation, use the following formula to generate predicted values of variable y:

$$\text{Predicted } y_T = (1 - \alpha)y_T + \alpha(\text{Predicted } y_{T-1})$$

In this equation, the predicted y at time T is based on the actual y at time T and y at the previous time period. A special multiplier, known as the *smoothing factor*, creates the smoothing effect on the data. Smoothing factors range from 0 to 1. When the smoothing factor is set to 0, no smoothing occurs, or the original pattern is replicated: $y_T = y_T$. As the smoothing factor moves toward 1, the trend becomes more generalized, or smoothed. See Table 11–5 for a comparison. The problem with using the smoothing factor is that it allows forecasters to manipulate the forecasts to accomplish other policy goals, such as justifying a new school building—or justifying not building a new school.

TABLE 11–6
Formulas Generated by Exponential Smoothing Function

	A	B	C	D	E
1	Year	Enrollment	Alpha=.25	Alpha=.5	Alpha=.75
2	1990	255	=B2	=B2	=B2
3	1991	251	=0.75*B3+0.25*C2	=0.5*B3+0.5*D2	=0.25*B3+0.75*E2
4	1992	249	=0.75*B4+0.25*C3	=0.5*B4+0.5*D3	=0.25*B4+0.75*E3
5	1993	248	=0.75*B5+0.25*C4	=0.5*B5+0.5*D4	=0.25*B5+0.75*E4
6	1994	227	=0.75*B6+0.25*C5	=0.5*B6+0.5*D5	=0.25*B6+0.75*E5
7	1995	209	=0.75*B7+0.25*C6	=0.5*B7+0.5*D6	=0.25*B7+0.75*E6
8	1996	225	=0.75*B8+0.25*C7	=0.5*B8+0.5*D7	=0.25*B8+0.75*E7
9	1997	250			

To generate exponentially smoothed data, follow these six steps:

1. Select Data Analysis from the Tools menu.
2. Select Exponential Smoothing.
3. Enter a Damping Factor (α).
4. Select an output range adjacent to your input range.
5. Select Chart Output and check the Labels toggle box if desired.
6. Click on OK.

Table 11–6 shows the formulas generated by the Exponential Smoothing function.

SMOOTHED FORECASTS

One purpose of smoothing is to produce a generalized forecast of data. When data sharply twist and turn, they can be particularly difficult to forecast because recent abrupt events can affect the direction of the forecast. These events and their effects are not negated by smoothing (unless we choose a smoothing factor of one), but their effects on forecasts can be lessened by either of two approaches, which are described next.

Option 1: Forecast Data, Then Smooth Forecasted Data

In the first approach, you generate a forecast of the nonsmoothed data with a moving-average method or a linear extrapolation method. Then, you use exponential smoothing to smooth the actual and forecasted data. In this case, the original forecast is still subject to abrupt, recent changes, depending on how many periods you track for average rates of change (Table 11–7).

TABLE 11–7
Forecasted, Then Smoothed Data

Year	Enrollment	α		
		.25	.5	.75
1990	255	255	255	255
1991	251	252	253	254
1992	249	250	251	253
1993	248	248	250	252
1994	227	232	238	245
1995	209	215	224	236
1996	225	222	224	233
1997	250	243	237	238
1998	269	263	253	245
1999	290	283	271	256
2000	310	303	291	270
2001	331	324	311	285

TABLE 11–8
Smoothed, Then Forecasted Data

Year	Enrollment	α		
		.25	.5	.75
1990	255	255	255	255
1991	251	252	253	254
1992	249	250	251	253
1993	248	248	250	252
1994	227	232	238	245
1995	209	215	224	236
1996	225	222	224	233
1997	250	243	237	238
1998	269	255	242	237
1999	290	269	249	238
2000	310	283	255	238
2001	331	297	262	239

Option 2: Smooth Data, Then Forecast Smoothed Data

In the second approach, you begin by smoothing the data, then you generate forecasts from the smoothed data. Again, you use either a linear extrapolation method or a moving-average method for extrapolating the smoothed data. This approach is generally more acceptable than the first. However, notice if you plot the series from Table 11–8 that the first approach appears to better capture the patterns of this particular data set.

INTEGRATED APPLICATION: MATRICES, MOVING AVERAGES, AND ENROLLMENTS

Enrollment forecasts are among the most critical elements of planning in education. Accurate enrollment forecasts are necessary from both an educational perspective and a budgetary planning perspective. Although various approaches to enrollment forecasting can be taken, the most common method involves considering students by grade level in schools or districts as a matrix of data, as seen in Tables 11–9 and 11–10. One simple method of forecasting enrollments might be to slide grade levels forward from the end of actual data. Presume that the data end in 1993. In this approach, 1993 kindergarten students become 1994 first graders, and so on. One problem with this method is that cohorts of students do not move 100% intact. Another problem is that as cohorts move forward, we eventually miss students entering the system in the early grades.

If we are to analyze in- and out-migration accurately, school districts must keep separate data on each. Otherwise, we can measure only the net change in a grade-level cohort from year to year. For example, what is the average change in number of students from 9th grade to 10th grade? This change might be an active transition as a result of dropout rates or private

TABLE 11-9
Static Multiplier

	Static Multiplier									Forecast Years				
	1985	1986	1987	1988	1989	1990	1991	1992	1993	1994	1995	1996	1997	Survival Rate (4 yr)
Birth–5 yr						2,119	2,100	2,120	2,140	2,318	2,240	2,283	2,283	–.3945
K	1,147	1,182	1,160	1,214	1,208	1,281	1,279	1,272	1,287	1,296	1,403	1,356	1,382	.0477
1	1,148	1,201	1,255	1,234	1,285	1,311	1,358	1,376	1,281	1,348	1,357	1,470	1,421	–.0022
2	1,113	1,114	1,173	1,219	1,223	1,319	1,305	1,387	1,344	1,278	1,345	1,355	1,467	–.0059
3	1,053	1,131	1,110	1,188	1,220	1,262	1,318	1,279	1,391	1,336	1,271	1,337	1,346	.0077
4	1,023	1,083	1,121	1,147	1,199	1,264	1,255	1,332	1,302	1,402	1,346	1,280	1,348	.0137
5	1,079	1,030	1,092	1,131	1,184	1,251	1,299	1,285	1,318	1,320	1,421	1,365	1,298	.0080
6	1,100	1,099	1,071	1,132	1,180	1,210	1,254	1,308	1,304	1,329	1,330	1,432	1,376	.0031
7	1,109	1,095	1,115	1,113	1,170	1,190	1,225	1,250	1,308	1,308	1,333	1,335	1,437	–.0027
8	1,197	1,131	1,090	1,159	1,124	1,176	1,189	1,224	1,242	1,304	1,304	1,329	1,331	.0448
9	1,351	1,270	1,190	1,131	1,212	1,140	1,232	1,262	1,255	1,298	1,363	1,363	1,389	–.0432
10	1,339	1,349	1,244	1,159	1,149	1,197	1,112	1,168	1,195	1,201	1,242	1,304	1,304	–.0270
11	1,256	1,307	1,319	1,153	1,122	1,109	1,172	1,085	1,126	1,163	1,168	1,208	1,269	–.0314
12	1,147	1,245	1,243	1,264	1,153	1,079	1,083	1,128	1,049	1,091	1,126	1,132	1,170	
Total	15,062	15,237	15,183	15,244	15,429	15,789	16,081	16,356	16,402	16,673	17,011	17,266	17,537	
Births	2,119	2,100	2,120	2,140	2,318	2,240	2,283	2,283	2,271					

TABLE 11–10
Dynamic Multiplier

	Dynamic Multiplier									Forecast Years				4-Year (Three-Period) Moving-Average Multipliers			
	1985	1986	1987	1988	1989	1990	1991	1992	1993	1994	1995	1996	1997	1993–1994 Multiplier	1994–1995 Multiplier	1995–1996 Multiplier	1996–1997 Multiplier
Birth–5 yr						2,119	2,100	2,120	2,140	2,318	2,240	2,283	2,283	−.3945	−.3939	−.3938	−.3941
K	1,147	1,182	1,160	1,214	1,208	1,281	1,279	1,272	1,287	1,296	1,405	1,358	1,383	.0477	.0435	.0328	.0413
1	1,148	1,201	1,255	1,234	1,285	1,311	1,358	1,376	1,281	1,348	1,352	1,451	1,414	−.0022	−.0014	−.0089	−.0041
2	1,113	1,114	1,173	1,219	1,223	1,319	1,305	1,387	1,344	1,278	1,347	1,340	1,445	−.0059	−.0077	−.0036	−.0057
3	1,053	1,131	1,110	1,188	1,220	1,262	1,318	1,279	1,391	1,336	1,268	1,342	1,332	.0077	.0121	.0126	.0108
4	1,023	1,083	1,121	1,147	1,199	1,264	1,255	1,332	1,302	1,402	1,352	1,284	1,356	.0137	.0090	.0041	.0089
5	1,079	1,030	1,092	1,131	1,184	1,251	1,299	1,285	1,318	1,320	1,414	1,358	1,296	.0080	.0099	.0109	.0096
6	1,100	1,099	1,071	1,132	1,180	1,210	1,254	1,308	1,304	1,329	1,333	1,430	1,371	.0031	.0000	.0010	.0013
7	1,109	1,095	1,115	1,113	1,170	1,190	1,225	1,250	1,308	1,308	1,329	1,334	1,432	−.0027	−.0033	−.0041	−.0034
8	1,197	1,131	1,090	1,159	1,124	1,176	1,189	1,224	1,242	1,304	1,304	1,323	1,330	.0448	.0438	.0380	.0422
9	1,351	1,270	1,190	1,131	1,212	1,140	1,232	1,262	1,255	1,298	1,362	1,353	1,379	−.0432	−.0494	−.0486	−.0471
10	1,339	1,349	1,244	1,159	1,149	1,197	1,112	1,168	1,195	1,201	1,233	1,296	1,290	−.0270	−.0291	−.0307	−.0289
11	1,256	1,307	1,319	1,153	1,122	1,109	1,172	1,085	1,126	1,163	1,166	1,196	1,258	−.0314	−.0340	−.0329	−.0328
12	1,147	1,245	1,243	1,264	1,153	1,079	1,083	1,128	1,049	1,091	1,123	1,128	1,156				
Total	15,062	15,237	15,183	15,244	15,429	15,789	16,081	16,356	16,402	16,673	16,988	17,192	17,442				

school transfers, which would negatively affect enrollments. At the same time, new students could be moving in as a result of new housing developments. Table 11–9 focuses on 4 years, or three periods. The attrition/growth fraction is determined by the following equation:

$$[(10\text{th Grade}_{1993} - 9\text{th Grade}_{1992})/9\text{th Grade}_{1992} + \cdots + (10\text{th Grade}_{1990} - 9\text{th Grade}_{1989})/9\text{th Grade}_{1989} \cdots]/4$$

Once you generate this formula for one grade shift in the matrix, drag and copy the formula down the column to generate a *static multiplier*. The static multiplier is used to generate the next year's enrollments by grade level. For example,

$$10\text{th Grade}_{1994} = 9\text{th Grade}_{1993} * 9\text{th}/10\text{th Fraction}$$

Again, once the formula is in one cell, drag and copy the formula down the column to generate forecast enrollments of other grade levels.

The fraction in Table 11–9 is called a *static multiplier* because it is used to forecast each year into the future. This forecast is the equivalent of a cohort linear forecast. You can also perform a cohort moving-average forecast. To do so, create several columns of multipliers that, with each additional year, include the newly generated cohort changes. This approach is displayed in Table 11–10. However, recall that moving-average approaches can exacerbate errors across time, especially because new forecasts rely on previously forecast data rather than on previous actual data.

One final issue is the question of students entering the system in the early grades. This issue can be dealt with in a number of ways, depending on the economic and demographic circumstances of the district. When a district's land area is almost fully developed, you might focus on childbirth rates among existing residents. Our sample models use this approach. In such cases, create a birth-to-kindergarten fraction the same way as you would other fractions. However, bear in mind that the span between birth and kindergarten is 5 years; because these children may not enter the system, the variance from birth cohort to kindergarten cohort can be large.

In districts experiencing high residential housing growth, try other approaches. You might retain the birth fraction component and add a migration fraction component. Determine the migration fraction by accessing data on new housing starts and zoning of residential land. These days, new suburban communities are carefully planned. Developers know exactly how many units of each type of housing will be constructed and who will typically inhabit each unit. Thus, you may be able to accurately determine the number of new families with 2.6 young children likely to enter your district during the next 5 years.

ASSESSMENT OF FORECAST ACCURACY AND MODEL TESTING

Given all the possibilities, how do you choose a method of forecasting to apply to a particular type of data? Also, how do you check your forecasting models for accuracy? Notice, in the previous example, that you used data through 1993 to forecast data from 1994 through 1997. Pretending to live in the past and practicing forecasting against the present is an effective way to test alternative forecasting techniques. Such practice prevents you from having to wait several years until you can check the accuracy of your forecasts.

TABLE 11–11

APE and MAPE Calculations for Static Multiplier Versus Dynamic Multiplier

Year	Actual Enrollment	Static Multiplier	APE	Dynamic Multiplier	APE
1994	16,406	16,673	1.6	16,673	1.6
1995	16,573	17,011	2.6	16,988	2.5
1996	16,686	17,266	3.5	17,192	3.0
1997	16,802	17,537	4.4	17,442	3.8
		MAPE	3.0	MAPE	2.7

Note: APE = absolute percent error; MAPE = mean absolute percent error.

The most common measure of forecast accuracy is mean absolute percent error (MAPE). In Table 11–11, we compare the enrollment forecasts generated by the static multiplier model and the dynamic multiplier model. Adjacent to the forecasts is the absolute value (=abs) of the percent error ([Predicted − Actual]/Actual) for that period (APE). To determine the MAPE for the forecasts, take the average of the APE. The absolute value is necessary to prevent positive and negative errors from canceling each other out.

For this enrollment model, the dynamic multiplier approach appears to slightly outperform the static multiplier approach.[2] However, such performance may not always be the case. Do not throw away the models that perform less well on practice tests. Rather, maintain a portfolio of forecasts for each critical indicator of your school or district. With time, you will be able to assign confidence ratings to various methods.

ADVANCED TOPIC: MULTIVARIATE FORECASTING

Technically, appropriate multivariate forecasting is a complex task that requires extensive study and training. To develop this skill, feel free to extend your learning beyond the scope of this book. Following is an introductory perspective on multivariate forecasting, given the tools you already acquired.

Multivariate forecasting is useful and generally more accurate than univariate forecasting because it takes into account contextual variables that affect the direction of the time series. However, multivariate forecasts rely on your ability either to create univariate forecasts of contextual variables or to determine that a given set of contextual variables at time T affects the dependent variable at a future point in time ($T + x$). That is, you must understand the lag structures of the system.

We return to the national average of per-pupil spending (CUREXP) example. Certainly, the amount that the U.S. public spends on schools depends on a number of contextual variables, such as economic conditions and the size of the student population. Consider the data in Table 11–12.

---

[2]If you wanted to test whether the difference in MAPEs was statistically significant, you could use a paired-group t test on the APE columns.

TABLE 11–12
Average PPE From 1981 Through 1995

Year	PCI	SGRNT	ADAPOP	CUREXP
1981	15,514	372	.166	4,226
1982	15,617	354	.161	4,236
1983	15,646	361	.158	4,405
1984	16,309	369	.155	4,561
1985	16,941	393	.154	4,800
1986	17,205	415	.153	5,047
1987	17,357	431	.153	5,219
1988	17,613	437	.153	5,352
1989	17,957	452	.152	5,606
1990	18,070	457	.153	5,715
1991	18,034	460	.154	5,741
1992	18,097	456	.154	5,737
1993	**18,419**	**456**	**.155**	**5,741**
1994	**18,621**	**468**	**.156**	**5,825**
1995	**19,167**	**473**	**.157**	**5,939**

Note: PPE = per-pupil expenditure; PCI = per capita income; SGRNT = state-level support to public education per pupil; ADAPOP = average daily attendance as a percentage of population; CUREXP = average per-pupil spending.

Table 11–12 lists average per-pupil spending from 1981 to 1995 (CUREXP) and three possible predictor variables: per capita income (PCI), state-level support to public education per pupil (SGRNT), and average daily attendance as a percentage of the population (ADAPOP). These three predictors are used by the National Center for Education Statistics in preparing their annual projection series. The prediction model used by the National Center for Education Statistics is a "contemporaneous" model. That is, the predictor variables at time T are related to the dependent variable at the same point in time. No lag occurs. Therefore, we will need forecasts of the predictor variables.

Multivariate forecasting begins by estimating a regression model to the data. The equation is as follows:

$$CUREXP = \beta_0 + \beta_1 PCI + \beta_2 SGRNT + \beta_3 ADAPOP + \epsilon$$

You can perform this regression analysis by using the same methods as discussed in chapter 8.[3] You must obtain an intercept value and coefficients (slopes) for the relationship of each predictor variable to the dependent variable. Also included in this equation is ϵ, which is the error term, or the portions of the dependent variable not explained by predictors. In

[3]Note that when you are dealing with economic data, you can often estimate better fitting models by log (ln) transforming the data. The Excel syntax is ln(cell).

TABLE 11-13

Coefficients and Forecasts of Predictors

Coefficients (Drag Copied)

Intercept	PCI	SGRNT	ADAPOP
467.15	0.11	6.41	-4,798.49
467.15	0.11	6.41	-4,798.49
467.15	0.11	6.41	-4,798.49
467.15	0.11	6.41	-4,798.49
467.15	0.11	6.41	-4,798.49
467.15	0.11	6.41	-4,798.49

Forecasts of Predictors

PCI	SGRNT	ADAPOP
18,042	313	.153
17,975	314	.154
18,029	311	.154
18,217	311	.155
18,317	311	.156
18,678	326	.156

Multiplied Values (b * x)

Intercept	PCI	SGRNT	ADAPOP
467.15	2,023.95	2,005.43	-733.31
467.15	2,016.40	2,017.25	-737.83
467.15	2,022.51	1,997.42	-740.06
467.15	2,043.57	1,997.29	-743.48
467.15	2,054.78	1,994.91	-746.29
467.15	2,095.36	2,087.98	-749.57

Summing and Accuracy Check

Year	Actual	Predicted	APE
1990	3,920	3763	4.0%
1991	3,923	3763	4.1%
1992	3,920	3747	4.4%
1993	3,916	3765	3.9%
1994	3,942	3771	4.3%
1995	3,979	3901	2.0%
		MAPE	3.8%

Note: PCI = per capita income; SGRNT = state-level support to public education per pupil; ADAPOP = average daily attendance as a percentage of population; APE = absolute percent error; MAPE = mean absolute percent error.

time-series data, the error term can take on interesting characteristics because the best predictor of the dependent variable at time T is usually the same variable at time $T - 1$.[4]

Once you perform regression analysis and obtain the slope and coefficients, obtain forecasts of your predictors. Often with general economic data like per capita income, you can obtain forecasts online from government agencies. If not, you can use the extrapolation techniques previously discussed, such as moving averages or linear extrapolation. You may also want to test alternative scenarios. That is, for one forecast, assume income growth to be 2.5% per year, and in another forecast, assume income growth to be 5% per year.

Once you have forecasts of predictor variables, enter these predictors in the equation to predict future values of the dependent variable. First, copy and paste (transpose) the coefficients into one block (Table 11–13, top left). Copy them into a matrix for easy multiplying. Second, place the future values of the predictors in a matrix adjacent to the coefficients (Table 11–13, top right). Third, multiply the coefficient matrix by the predictor matrix and add the intercept to create a new matrix (Table 11–13, bottom left). In the new matrix, each coefficient is multiplied by its respective predictor values. Finally, sum the multiplied values to determine the predicted values of the dependent variable (Table 11–13, bottom right).[5]

SUMMARY

In this chapter, you learned basic (and some advanced) tools for generating and checking forecasts. Remember that you cannot predict future events with complete accuracy. The best you can do is generate plausible scenarios that will help you develop reasonable policy options for the future. Thus, we encourage you to use the tools in this chapter not in an attempt to create the best possible forecast of the future, but to generate, test, and explain the multitude of possibilities that exist for any given situation. One way to think about alternative forecasts is in terms of probability. Each forecast predicts a range of changes. You might arrange your forecasts according to your expectations for the future. For example, if the birthrate increases by 1%, it will have x effect on the forecast; if housing starts slow by 5%, it will have y effect on the forecast; and so on.

PROBLEM I

Forecasting and Checking

Background: As in Problem H, the goal of this problem is to better prepare you for the part IV simulation, which combines a variety of issues related to time, change, and fore-

---

[4]For more details on this topic, see Vandaele (1983).

[5]Also try this forecasting model with the logarithmic, or natural logarithmic (ln), transformed data. Begin the process by logging all variables (independent and dependent). Then, estimate the regression equation and generate your forecasts. Next, un-log (=exp(cell)) your forecast values and compare them with actual values. Compare the MAPE for this forecast with the MAPE for the forecast performed in Table 11–12.

casting. This problem data set contains spending, income, and enrollment data on U.S. schools from 1959 to 1997.

Task 1: For each of the series, construct time-series plots to obtain a general picture of the trends and patterns. Apply linear trend lines to determine the average rate of change (entire period) for the plots.

Task 2: Difference the series (first = velocity; second = acceleration) to assess the rates of change, and plot the differenced series to find events that may appear more dramatic than originally perceived. Determine whether events in one series correspond to events in another. Do they seem to correspond at about the same time, or might there be lag effects? For example, does one series show a blip and another series show a blip a year or two later? Can you think of any reasons why the blips should be related?

Task 3: Try the exponential smoothing tool on each series and differenced series. When does "generalizing" the series seem useful and not so useful?

Task 4: Consider only 1959 through 1989 your training set. Use these data to construct linear trend lines and to determine moving averages. With your trend lines and moving averages, prepare forecasts for the years 1990 through 1997. Check them against the actual values to determine which method works better.

Task 5 (optional): Again, using only 1959 through 1989 data, run a regression analysis relating income (x) to spending (y). Separately, create a univariate forecast for income (either linear or moving average). You already did this in Task 4. Input your forecast values of income for 1991, 1992, and so forth into the regression equation (substitute x) to see what the predicted spending (y) will be for these years. Check this forecast to determine whether it works better than your univariate forecast of spending. Go back and try introducing more predictors.

PART IV SIMULATION

Feeling the Budget Crunch in Mission Valley Springs

You know it. You can feel it. You previously plotted the trends and can see that enrollments are creeping up in Mission Valley Springs. You have yet to determine exactly where the enrollments are headed, but you are concerned for various reasons. You perceive that less and less money is available to go around year after year. You are not sure where the pinch is. Your local tax base has remained strong, and local voters have (in your perception) been kind to the schools. State aid appears to still be coming in with fair allocations. Amidst your concerns, your district has tried to aggressively promote policies that you believe to be important to the long-run success of the schools. For instance, your district has tried continually, since the 1980s, to reduce class sizes to achieve more teacher contact for all students. In addition, your district has made its mission ensuring that these teachers are high quality and has tried to pay its staff appropriately and better each year. The time has come to assess what the future holds. You have called a strategic planning summit with your school board for next week. At that time, you hope to present the board with your analysis of the past and your view of the future.

Your initial goals are to determine (a) Are revenues growing, commensurate with internal needs? and (b) Are revenues growing, commensurate with the external, economic environment? What is the relative motion of revenues? Does the relative motion of local revenues differ from the relative motion of state revenues? Where is the pinch? What is the relative motion of pupil-to-teacher ratios, teacher salaries, and total staffing costs? What is the relative motion of staffing costs with respect to total revenues?

Once you exhaust the relative motion questions on the basis of historical data, determine some plausible scenarios for the next 3 to 5 years into the future. Begin by determining where your enrollments are headed. Try the cohort survival method referred to in chapter 11. From your enrollment forecasts, move on to staffing needs and staffing costs. Using historical data for pupil-to-teacher ratios, project where the ratios are headed, then determine staffing needs on the basis of your enrollment projections. Next, project where average salaries are headed (Univariate − Moving Average). Project your revenue future. Look at total revenue growth, then local and state revenue growth separately. Reassess this growth against inflation. Who is coming up short? Given your expected staffing needs and costs, and your policy objectives, will you be able to afford it all? Can you keep reducing pupil-to-teacher ratios? Are you eating up an increasing portion of revenues with salaries alone?

PART IV SUMMARY

For more than 30 years, the state of New Jersey has embarked on a much-publicized, court-ordered quest to close the gap in educational funding between its richest school districts and its poorest. Despite 30 years of litigation over school funding equity—from *Robinson v. Cahill* in 1973 to the sixth round of *Abbott v. Burke* in 2002—an equity gap remains. For which variable have New Jersey policy analysts been unable to account?

As you might recall from chapter 9, the answer is *time*. In Gary Paulsen's 1987 book *Hatchet*, a young man stranded on an island successfully spears fish only after he accounts for time. He must aim for the point where the fish will be by the time the spear moves through the air and into the water. By ignoring the effects of time on a system, decision makers are constantly trying to hit a moving target. Many still cannot understand why they are missing, even after decades of failure.

When it seems as though no innovation can positively affect your school, consider whether the seeds of change have had time to bear fruit. Has enough time elapsed to establish a level-shift change, a temporary change, or only a one-time response scenario? Which would you prefer as a response to a new bilingual program? as the response of your fourth-grade class to a first-year teacher?

Sometimes, the only factor holding certain institutions together is time. Remember Newton's laws of motion: A body at rest will remain at rest unless acted on by an outside force. A body in motion will remain in motion unless acted on by an outside force. These laws most decidedly apply to organizations. The "leaders" rest on their status quo, for whatever reason, and the institution survives—not thrives—solely because it was set into motion years ago and no one put forth the energy to stop or redirect it. Using the tools in chapters 10 and 11, you may be able to apply the laws of physics to influence the future state of such a system.

Forecasting, or extrapolation of a current system, enables you to see what history looks like when it repeats itself in the future. Certain techniques, such as linear extrapolation forecasting, moving-average forecasting, and exponential smoothing, will amplify or minimize the irregular turns of past data. Know when you want to amplify and when minimizing is best. This knowledge is best gained through practice. However, if your goal is to alter the direction of an organization, more is required. Remember, Archimedes said, "Give me a fulcrum point and a sufficiently long lever, and I can move the earth." It boils down to leverage.

Superintendents are often called on to act as fortune-tellers. When is the appropriate time to add on to an old school building or to build a new one? Are trailer classrooms a good interim solution to population swells, or will the influx continue? If I close a school this year, should I sell it to the town or will I need it 10 years later? To measure your accuracy, use the mean absolute percent error (MAPE) tool. Thorough, careful data analysis of future possibilities, and a method of determining your likelihood of accuracy, does not guarantee that the future will turn out as predicted. However, it does improve on reading tea leaves.

Part V
System Dynamics
of Schooling

The most dangerous, hideously misused and thought-annihilating piece of technology invented in the past 15 years has to be the electronic spreadsheet.

(Michael Schrage, 1991, *cited in Richmond & Peterson, 1996, p. vii*)

Schrage, a *Los Angeles Times* syndicated columnist, continued in a similar tone, leaving us to question the usefulness of parts II through IV of this book.

We acknowledge that spreadsheet analysis has its limitations. However, we do find it more useful than Schrage suggests. Whatever the kind of data or analyses—student achievement gains, financial data, statistical relationships between school performance and population demographics—each spreadsheet approach yields a limited set of information that focuses on symptomatic indicators of the system. We do not suggest that symptoms are unimportant. In fact, symptoms of schools and school systems, like symptoms of physical ailments, are important indicators that an organizational analyst can use to diagnose deeper causes. The spreadsheet is a tool in the same way that a medical record is a tool for organizing important indicators. Poor diagnosis is a problem of physician education. At the same time, perhaps the information on a medical record or a school report card could be better organized and more usefully presented so that important trends and patterns emerge more readily.

So, what is missing that is so important? As in treating ailments, trying to resolve problems in institutions leaves us with two choices: (a) treat the symptoms, or (b) treat the underlying process. The latter option is more effective for achieving long-term success (although it is sometimes slower to effect a "cure"). Unfortunately, the spreadsheet symptom-analysis tool kit does little to explain underlying processes and even less to explain the role of strategic management in affecting these processes.

Therefore, in this part, we introduce an alternative tool kit, a software package called *ithink*, developed by High Performance Systems, Inc., of Lebanon, New Hampshire. The developers of ithink began their software endeavors in the mid-1980s as developers of environmental modeling software known as *STELLA*. At that time, the field of systems thinking and dynamic systems modeling, founded in the 1960s by Jay W. Forrester of Massachusetts Institute of Technology, became popular for providing a way to study vastly interconnected, complex systems such as ecosystems. Some individuals began promoting the usefulness of this new paradigm in organizational management, and a few people even extended the paradigm to the management of educational institutions (Clauset & Gaynor, 1982). Since the popularization of Peter Senge's *The Fifth Discipline* (1990) and its accompanying field book, systems thinking as a mental discipline and as a theoretical framework for organizational management has made a comeback. We strongly recommend that you read *The Fifth Discipline* before you use ithink so that you may understand the mind-set behind the software.

The developers of STELLA, in response to renewed interest in systems thinking in management, developed software and demonstration models specifically for management decision making. The widespread availability of computers, coupled with the user-friendliness of STELLA and ithink, presents new possibilities for the growth of the systems thinking paradigm that did not exist when its popularity peaked in the early 1980s. Beyond broadening your conceptual understanding of complex systems, these applications allow you to develop simple, yet practical, process simulations for strategic analysis and planning.

Chapter 12 is an introduction to the tools of dynamic systems modeling from an operations research perspective. The objective in chapter 12 is to make you more comfortable with a pictorial approach to representing otherwise data-driven problems.

Chapter 13 contains ways that you can use process modeling to analyze your system. In chapter 14, you combine the tools and your new mind-set to address a series of case studies. The first is a single-feedback-loop systemic problem; the second, an analysis of years of dysfunction in New Jersey's school finance system; and the third, a study of root causes of the backlog of remedial training in New York's City University system. We encourage you to have patience as you learn not only the new tools, but also new ways of thinking about the ecology of school organizations. We are confident that with a modest effort you can acquire a new and powerful perspective on organizational dynamics.

12

From Data-Driven Analysis to Model-Driven Analysis

MODELING PROCESSES

Modeling dynamic systems merges the conceptual, technical, and analytic perspectives of multiple fields. Many systems modeling tools originate in the field of operations research (OR). Operations researchers study business operations processes and identify production and distribution problems or inefficiencies. Most OR involves the study of manufacturing processes, in which a series of raw materials must be purchased and moved through several steps by individuals and machines to create a product. Other OR studies focus on the management of inventories, purchases, and sales in an effort to determine optimal patterns of purchasing and financial management, under a given set of supply-and-demand conditions. What differentiates OR from the data analyses presented thus far in this book is that OR emphasizes the *process* and seeks to identify dysfunctional or especially functional processes. Operational researchers construct real and theoretical models of the process in an effort to identify problems and propose and test solutions. The process can be modeled, but outcomes or symptoms cannot. They are the result of modeling processes.

Consider a bicycle factory that consists of three departments, each of which is assigned one specific task. Imagine that the process of making bicycles consists of (a) making frames, (b) making wheels, and (c) assembling the bicycles, as illustrated in Figure 12–1.

Assume that Team 3 has become disgruntled because the team members are unable to assemble the required 20 bicycles per day. In addition, their work space is backlogged with spare parts. By analyzing the productivity rates of each team, you find that Team 1 produces 22 frames per day, and Team 2 produces 36 wheels per day.

Note the time dimension in this case. After 1 day, four frames are leftover and only 18 bicycles have been made. Team 1 makes two more frames per day than required, whereas Team 2 makes four fewer wheels per day than required. At two wheels per bicycle, Team 3 is two bicycles short and has four extra frames. The problem accumulates as the clock ticks forward. After 2 days, eight frames are leftover and 4 bikes are behind desired production. Testing policy options under these circumstances is simple. The goal is to produce the correct number of wheels to fit the correct number of frames per unit of time. The process must be synchronized. If the goal of 20 bikes is flexible, you could slow production of frames. If not, you must increase wheel production.

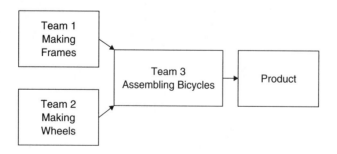

FIGURE 12–1
Bicycle-Making Process

This example should be kept in the back of your mind as you address the flow of students through the New York City schools in chapter 14. Also consider the following anecdote, overheard at an international education conference, where, on his way through an airport, a speaker read the following words on a sign:

120 arrivals per day. 103 departures.[1]

TWO VIEWS ON A CLASSIC EDUCATION OPERATIONS PROBLEM

How does all this relate to problem solving in schools? Dynamic systems modeling can be applied to schooling problems in two ways: (a) with hard data models and (b) with soft assumption models. The possibility of mixing these methods also exists. *Hard data models* deal with the flow of tangible, measurable objects, such as students flowing from grade to grade or teachers flowing up and along the salary step scale. *Soft assumption models* in education deal with less tangible items, such as knowledge accumulated and rate of learning. In this chapter, we introduce a hard data—OR—modeling approach to dealing with a classic school planning problem: linking enrollment and staffing demands and estimating costs.

Reviewing the Matrix Model

Recall the Integrated Application section in chapter 11, in which the matrix model of the flow of student enrollments was explained. First-grade students move to second grade and so on, with measurable rates of efficiency (proportions entering and leaving the system along the way or proportions being retained). A proportion of children, born within the school's attendance boundaries, eventually enters the system at kindergarten (or pre-K). Thus, the matrix of students flows diagonally. The number of students flowing through a system dictates the number of teachers required to teach them, if we assume a constant pupil-to-teacher ratio. Thus, the total volume of the matrix of students by grades, divided by the desired pupil-to-teacher ratio, yields the desired number of teachers (Figure 12–2).

FIGURE 12–2
Matrix Model

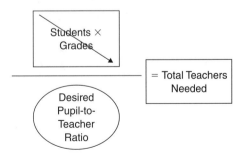

FIGURE 12–3
Multiplication of Two Matrices

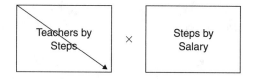

To estimate the cost of teachers, multiply the total number of teachers needed by the average salary. For a more accurate estimate, multiply the full-time-equivalent (FTE) distribution of teachers per step of the salary scale by the matrix of salaries at each step (Figure 12–3).

Remember that while the students flow forward from grade to grade, with some entering at the front end of the system and others graduating or dropping out, the teacher matrix also flows from step to step, which makes calculations increasingly complicated as the forecast extends into the future. Laying out matrices on a spreadsheet is useful for understanding the way in which the data interact. However, better ways for examining the flow processes exist.

Introducing a Systems Model of the Process

In this subsection, we orient you to the layout of ithink software. Rather than entering grids or matrices of data, you will draw pictures of the way the system works and how elements flow through it. As with Excel tools, all ithink tools are found on a toolbar across the top of the model window (go to http://www.hps-inc.com/ and download the free save-disabled demo, or download it from the Data and Models Web site that accompanies this book). Notice the up and down arrows, located in the upper left-hand corner of the model window. These arrows, like the tabs at the bottom of an Excel workbook, allow you to switch among the three layers of the model. The middle layer is the model layer, or the layer at which the pictorial version of the model is constructed. The top layer is a high-level map. This layer can present simplified representations (aggregations) of an underlying complex model or can create a user control panel for running the model. The bottom layer generates programming code for the pictorial model in the middle layer.

Three basic tools can be used to construct ithink models: stocks, flows, and converters. Adding tools to your model involves clicking them onto the toolbar, then clicking the pallet below. The stock tool (Figure 12–4) represents tangible, countable, physical accumulations. A *stock* is like a container—a box or a bucket. Stocks are the "nouns" in models. You can also use a stock to represent something less tangible, such as knowledge acquired.

Flows are like the pipes in a system and can be used to add to or take from a stock (Figure 12–5). Flows may be unidirectional, such as the inflow or outflow water pipe to a reservoir, or bidirectional, such as the changing prices of a good. A bidirectional flow can move in only one direction at a time but has the capacity to move in either direction. Flows are the "verbs" in models. They perform actions on stocks.

FIGURE 12–4
The Stock Tool

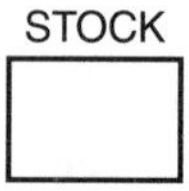

STOCK

FIGURE 12–5
The Flow Tool

FLOW

Converters add mathematical factors, like multipliers or divisors, to models. *Connectors* create linkages between the mathematically connected parts of models (Figure 12–6).

In our example, we aggregate students into four stocks instead of viewing each grade level as a stock (Figure 12–7). The model includes a stock of Preschool students (birth–5 yr; i.e., prior to schooling, not preschool), Elementary Students (K–Grade 4), Middle School Students (Grades 5–8), and High School Students (Grades 9–12). Students flow from each stock (school) to the next. Let us begin with stocks of 100 elementary students, 80 middle school students, and 80 high school students. Assume that elementary school takes 5 years to complete; middle school, 4 years; and high school, 4 years. Therefore, each year, one fifth of the elementary school students will pass to middle school, one fourth of the middle school students will pass to high school, and so on.

Let us use converters and connectors to define this feature of the flow. We add a converter and define it by double clicking it and entering the appropriate constant (unchanging number). For example, the flow of students from elementary school is mathematically defined as follows:

Flow Rate = Elementary Students/Years in Elementary School

If we draw connectors from the stock Elementary Students to the flow Entering Middle School and from the converter Years in Elementary School to the flow Entering Middle School, we can construct a formula using these two allowable inputs. *Remember:* Any feature of a model is ultimately defined by the items that connect to it.

A few variations on the model make running simulations more interesting. First, the initial inflow of the model (Birthing) is adjustable, so that you can run multiple possible scenarios. Second, there are two outflows from high school: Dropping Out and Graduating. Like the birthing rate, the dropout rate is adjustable. Different types of adjustment levers have been added to the top layer, or user control panel.

Not seen in Figure 12–7 are additional converters. They include the following: (a) Desired Pupil-to-Teacher Ratio (adjustable), (b) Average Teacher Salary, (c) Teachers Needed, and (d) Teacher Cost. The mathematical equations for the last two follow:

Teachers Needed = Total Pupils/Desired Pupil-to-Teacher Ratio

Total Pupils = Elementary Students + Middle School Students
+ High School Students

Teacher Cost = Teachers Needed × Average Teacher Salary

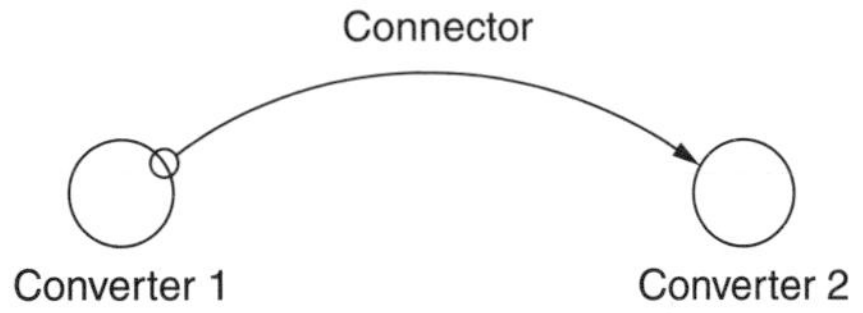

FIGURE 12–6
Converters and Connectors

Connector

Converter 1   Converter 2

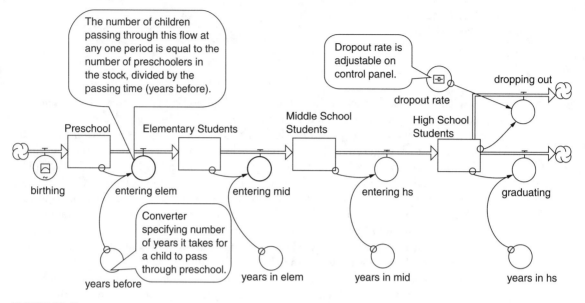

FIGURE 12–7

Sample School-Based Decision-Making Model: Enrollment/Staffing

Note: Framework developed by Chris Soderquist of High Performance Systems, Inc., Lebanon, New Hampshire. Modified by Bruce D. Baker.

Average Teacher Salary and Desired Pupil-to-Teacher Ratio are preset features of the model. Because they are determined external to the model, you might choose to refer to them as *exogenous*.

Introducing User Controls

Recall that by clicking the arrows in the upper left-hand corner of the model window, you may go to the top layer, or user interface layer, of the model (Figure 12–8). This interface provides both graphic output and tabular output. As in the model layer, in this layer features are added by dragging and dropping the feature from the toolbar to the pallet (Figure 12–9). Tables and graphs are defined by double clicking the table or graph and then selecting the variable to be graphed.

One useful type of graph is the comparative graph. You can graph only one variable, such as total enrollment, on a comparative graph. The comparative graph allows you to compare the given variable on many runs of the model while changing other model inputs.

Controls (sliding tabs, knobs, etc.) are added similarly. For example, to add the sliding bar adjuster to pupil-to-teacher ratio, (a) bring it down from the toolbar to the pallet and (b) double click the adjuster and assign it to the variable = pupil-to-teacher ratio.

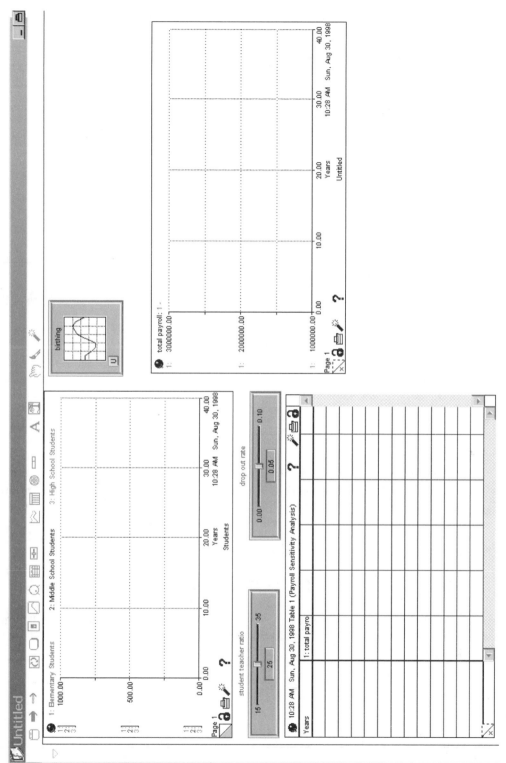

FIGURE 12–8
Sample User Interface for Enrollment/Staffing Model

209

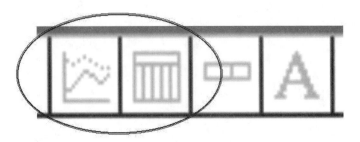

FIGURE 12–9
Graph and Table Output Tools

Running the Model, Testing Scenarios

Now that you have a pictorial representation with underlying mathematical definitions, what do you do with it? Run the model by clicking the small running figure in the lower left-hand corner of the model window. Doing so calls up a toolbar somewhat like the buttons on a cassette player. By going to the Time Specs drop-down menu, you can set the time period structure for running the model. The enrollment model is set to run forward 13 periods, where each period represents 1 year. When you click the forward arrow, the model plays forward through time, generating projections of enrollments, costs, and so forth.

Analyzing Sensitivity

In a sensitivity analysis, you can change one policy lever, or input to the model; run the model at different levels of the input; and study the effects on various outcomes. For instance, you might test the long-run costs of maintaining three pupil-to-teacher ratios (14:1, 16:1, 18:1). First, set the pupil-to-teacher ratio at 14:1 and run the model, then set the ratio to 16:1 and run the model, and so on. In such cases, comparative graphs and tables are handy.

A comparative sensitivity analysis can be run automatically by ithink. From the RUN toolbar, select "sensi-specs." Doing so brings up a window in which you can select the variable you want to incrementally adjust. Then, have ithink set a series of increments, either in standard increments or by spreading out the increments in a probability distribution. With the sensi-specs option ON, the model will run through each scenario after you select "run." Then, you can use your comparative output tables and graphs to determine the best policy options.

SUMMARY

Now you have a new set of tools at your disposal and the capacity to run multiple scenarios with a given model in a matter of minutes. Your objective with these models is to understand the behavior of a system under a variety of circumstances. Knowing that $x = 20$ at $T = 1$, or $y = 43.2$ at $T = 4$ is far less important than shifting your emphasis from outcomes and symptoms to processes. Vow to optimize the process, not the outcome. An optimized process will continually yield better outcomes, whereas optimizing outcomes may be effective only for the moment.

PROBLEM J

Experiments with the Enrollment Model

Getting Started: In this chapter, we provided you with a walk-through of the model structure and ithink software. Now, it is time to play. You may first need to install the ithink save-disabled demo, which can be obtained from the High Performance Systems, Inc., Web site at http://www.hps-inc.com. The ithink save-disabled demo installer may also be available on the Data and Models Web site. *Remember:* This version will let you manipulate and run models, but you will not be able to save any changes.

Once the save-disabled demo is installed, open your enrollment model from the Data and Models Web site. Orient yourself by clicking the up and down arrows in the upper left-hand corner of the model window.

Sensitivity Simulations: Your task is to run a series of sensitivity simulations with the model. First, address the question of changing policies for pupil-to-teacher ratios. Manually set the pupil-to-teacher ratio to 20:1 and run the model. Then, adjust the pupil-to-teacher ratio to 18:1, 16:1, and 14:1. Study the cost implications of these decisions.

Try performing the same analysis using the sensi-specs option. To do this, go to "sensi-specs." Select student-to-teacher ratio as your variable to adjust. Select "incremental distribution," from 14 to 20, for four increments. Click on the SET button. Click sensitivity ON. Click on OK, and run the model.

Altering Model Features: Following are specific directions for changing three major features of the ithink simulation.

Changing Feature Settings What if the birthing pattern were different? The birthing pattern flow can be changed by double clicking it, then redrawing the graph or reentering data. Typically, birthing data are based on historical information on the district. Try changing the birthing pattern and running the model. You may want to turn the sensitivity-analysis feature OFF for these runs.

Adding Stocks and Flows What if middle school dropouts were a factor? This option is not allowable in the current structure of the model, but with six simple additions, it becomes possible:

1. In the model layer, click the flow tool, then drag out a new flow from the top of the Middle School Students stock. You can bend the stock to the right or left by grabbing the spiral cloud, after you create the stock and move it to the desired position. Name the stock "MS Dropout."
2. Grab a converter from the toolbar and drop it near the new flow. Call it "MS Dropout Rate."
3. Grab a connector from the toolbar and drag it from the stock rectangle (Middle School Students) to the circle on the new dropout flow.

4. Grab another connector and connect the new converter to the flow (as in the HS Dropout Rate structure).

5. Double click the flow. Put your cursor in the formula box and click "Middle School Students," then "*," then "MS Dropout Rate." (This approach is similar to using the point-and-click method for constructing formulas in Excel.) Click on OK.

6. Double click the new converter and assign a default value of .05 (5% dropout rate).

Next, in the control panel layer, add a sliding adjuster. Bring one down from the tool-bar and double click it. Assign it to MS Dropout Rate (the converter, not the flow). Set the range from 0 to 1 (having more than 100% of students dropping out is impossible). Click on OK.

Adding Output Tables and Graphs Add an output table of the numbers of high school and middle school dropouts. Select a table from the toolbar, then drop it onto the pallet. Assign variables to the table by double clicking on the table then selecting the variables you want to display. Pin the table onto the pallet by clicking the small pin in the upper left-hand corner of the table.

Supplemental Model: See also Enrol2.ITM on the Data and Models Web site for an example of how to integrate staffing and financial information with the enrollment model.

13

Systems Thinking Applied

Systems thinking, like operations modeling, is about understanding processes. In chapter 12, you explored a system that flowed in only one direction. That is, students moved from preschool to elementary school, and so on. Systems become more complex when phenomena such as *feedback closed loops* are involved. Senge (1990) and Richardson (1992) classified and analyzed common feedback structures in social systems. In this chapter, you learn to understand feedback structures and to apply them to ithink modeling.

Unlike Excel, ithink allows you to study feedback structures, or closed-loop systems. *Feedback* exists when a measure *x* affects measure *y*, and *y* in turn affects *x*. Consider the reinforcing cycle shown in Figure 13–1. In biology, this cycle would be referred to as *positive feedback*. This cycle is an example of a competitive private school or college: The perceived quality of the school affects the applicant pool for the school positively. In turn, the improved quality of the applicant pool affects the quality of students at the school, which then affects the perceived quality of the school. Each effect is positive, which amplifies the level of each variable with each turn of the cycle (see the response curve in Figure 13–1).

Because of the relative complexity in the design of social or biological systems, growth patterns generated by this process do not continue forever unfettered. In general, constraints eventually temper, or balance, the growth of any particular system component. Consider the environmental constraint of food availability in the presence of a population boom of a particular species. An alternative systems archetype that is commonly used to explain such situations is the *balancing feedback cycle*. Its objective is to achieve equilibrium relative to internal or external constraints. This cycle occurs, for example, in the hormonal regulation of blood sugar levels. When we eat a food containing sugar or carbohydrates (which are broken down into sugars), the sugars are absorbed into the bloodstream through the intestines, and our blood sugar level increases. Assuming we are not quickly burning off these sugars (we are just lounging around), a hormone—insulin—is released into the bloodstream to stimulate the uptake of these sugars to the liver, where they are converted to glycogen and stored. Thus, insulin plays a balancing, or *negative feedback*, role. As the

FIGURE 13–1
Reinforcing Feedback Cycle

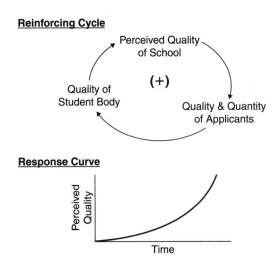

FIGURE 13–2
Balancing Feedback Cycle

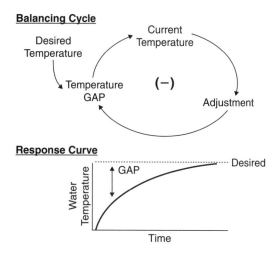

blood sugar level increases, insulin is produced, which decreases the blood sugar level and reduces the need to produce more insulin.

Adjusting your morning shower temperature is another example of negative feedback in daily life. Figure 13–2 displays a feedback loop representation of the shower temperature problem. The externally imposed constraint is the desired temperature. Current temperature is compared against desired temperature as a way to determine the temperature gap. Appropriate adjustments are made—if you are being scalded, you will either increase the cold water flow or decrease the hot, and vice versa. As discussed in the following sections, the balancing nature of these actions eventually guides you toward equilibrium.

ithink MODELS OF FEEDBACK STRUCTURES

How can you model the shower example by using ithink tools? The condition of interest is the current water temperature, the only stock in the model. Because the water can be made hotter or colder, you must attach a bidirectional flow to this stock (Figure 13–3).

FIGURE 13–3
ithink Model of Shower
Temperature Example

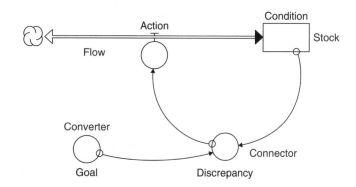

FIGURE 13–4
Oscillating Overcompensation

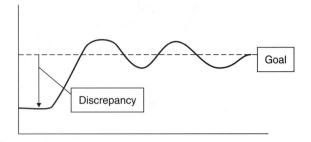

Recall that the temperature is adjusted against an externally imposed constraint, the desired temperature. You can represent this constraint as an exogenous converter (Goal). The gap between the desired temperature (Goal) converter and the current temperature stock is represented as the Discrepancy converter, with appropriate connectors applied.

Ideally, the action taken is to close the current gap. The change cannot be instantaneous; it must occur with time. In fact, if our system did function as graphed, establishing the ideal shower temperature would be easy. Unfortunately, a delay usually occurs between action taken and desired change (closing of the gap). You could introduce this delay by adding another converter called Time Delay and attaching it to the flow. This converter could simply be a divisor to the rate of flow, slowing the actual change in temperature.

Meanwhile, you, in the shower, are still measuring current condition against desired condition. Although you just adjusted the knob, the water remains too cold. You ignore that warmer water is on its way but has not arrived yet. Thus, perceiving the gap to be larger than it is, you overcompensate and adjust the knob for even warmer water. Figure 13–4 shows the graphic representation of your oscillating overcompensation. Eventually, after several adjustments, you converge on your goal.

OUT OF THE SHOWER AND INTO THE SCHOOL

Consider this educational feedback loop: How does a person make hiring decisions for a dynamic organization that is changing in size and does not necessarily have a stable workforce? The goal, as with the perfect shower temperature, is a form of equilibrium, which is managed by hiring for growth. Our case involves a midsize New Jersey city in the early 1990s, where enrollment growth necessitated increasing the total staff of the district while employee attrition rates were increasing.

Figure 13–5 depicts one cycle of the hiring/attrition feedback loop that was developed in the district at the time. Total staff vacancies of 125 were posted in 1992–1993. By interviewing and hiring time, vacancies had increased to 731. Given the pool of applicants, 233 offers were made, and 197 individuals were hired, which left a new deficit of 534, or nearly 25% of the total staff. Continuation of such a cycle would no doubt create significant problems for a district already experiencing various other problems.

In this case, the personnel department was guilty of short-term planning. Planning for the future requires an understanding of the time dimension, so that you can anticipate future needs, rather than responding to current needs as if they were future needs. Modeling systems

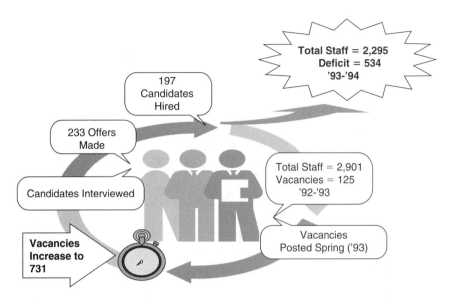

FIGURE 13–5
Hiring/Attrition Feedback Loop

processes in ithink gives you the opportunity to test changing scenarios and to learn from mistakes made without facing real-world ramifications. Using ithink will enhance your intuitive understanding of the role of time in systems problems.

Figure 13–6 displays a basic human resource model (a standard ithink infrastructure) that can anticipate personnel needs in a changing organization.[1] In this case, the number of teachers leaving the system (attrition) is proportional, not absolute. This assumption is important because as the organization grows, the same teacher quitting rate will necessitate a greater number of absolute hires for the system to hold at equilibrium. That is, if in 1997 you have 1,000 teachers and a 10% rate of quitting teachers, you will expect to need 100 new teachers for the following year. If the organization is growing at a rate of 10% per year, your total number of quitting teachers the next year (at 10%) will be 110, not 100. Typically, such values are based on historical patterns in the district and are used to test plausible alternative scenarios. However, history is not always the best indicator of the future.

To set the attrition fraction, or teacher quitting rate, double click the Teacher Quitting Rate converter and enter a value (see Figure 13–7, bottom right). Initially, this factor should be based on historical knowledge of organizational attrition. Once you have a current total number of teachers and the teacher quitting rate, you can define the Quitting Teachers flow.

When you double click the flow, you will see a window on the upper right on the following page (Figure 13–8). The window, Required Inputs, tells you the various model components that are connected to the Quitting Teachers flow. We use these components

---

[1]The ithink software comes with a series of infrastructure models that represent common business archetypes. These models can be directly adapted to specific problems and provide excellent examples from which you may construct personalized models.

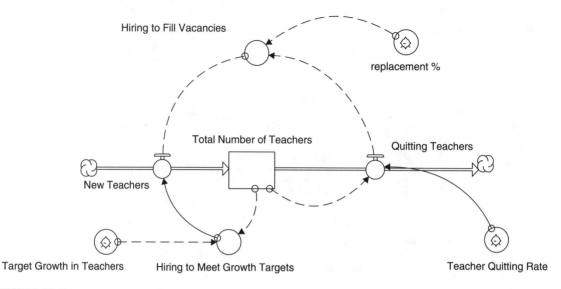

FIGURE 13–6

Human Resources Infrastructure (New Teachers/Quitting Teachers)

Note: Adapted from *STELLA: An Introduction to Systems Thinking,* by B. Richmond and S. Peterson, 1996, Hanover, NH: High Performance Systems.

to specify the Quitting Teachers flow, which in this case equals the total number of teachers times (*) the teacher quitting rate. You need not write out the equations entirely. Click on an input, and it will appear in the equation window. Your role is to specify the mathematical nature of the relationship.

A key exogenous factor, or imposed constraint, is the growth rate of your organization. Exogenous factors are external to the system and preset at the arbitrary boundaries of the model. For example, the desired temperature in the shower model is an exogenous factor. If you were working in a private corporation (and most ithink examples were constructed for such purposes), you would likely establish a desired growth rate, just as you established a desired shower temperature. Like the quitting teachers rate, the growth rate would probably be proportional. In public education, the growth rate is still exogenous—imposed from the outside—and you cannot usually pick and choose the growth rate. Rather, the environment imposes a growth rate on you. As with quitting teachers rates, you can use historical information to set growth rates and test alternative scenarios. The ithink software allows either numerical or graphic input. In Figure 13–7 (bottom right), the graphical user interface maps the target growth in teachers of the organization. The Hiring to Meet Growth Targets converter is a function of target growth in teachers and total number of teachers (see upper left window of Figure 13–7).

The variable of interest in the New Jersey example is the necessary new teachers rate, or the New Teachers flow. The New Teachers flow is a function of two other factors: the hiring to fill vacancies rate and additional hiring to meet growth target rates. Hiring to fill vacancies and hiring to meet growth targets cumulatively affect new teachers. The mathematical definition of the flow (Hiring to Meet Growth Targets + Hiring to Fill Vacancies) can be seen in Figure 13–8 (top left). Figure 13–9 shows how to create a graphical user interface for this example.

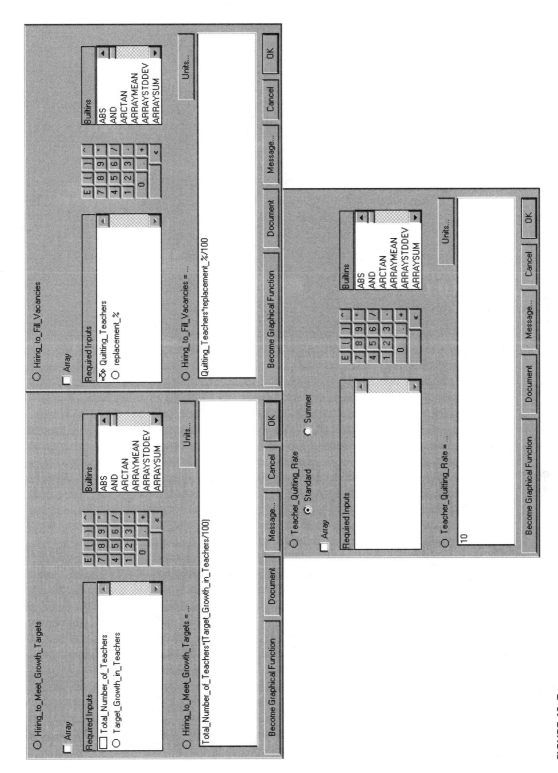

FIGURE 13-7
Defining Converters

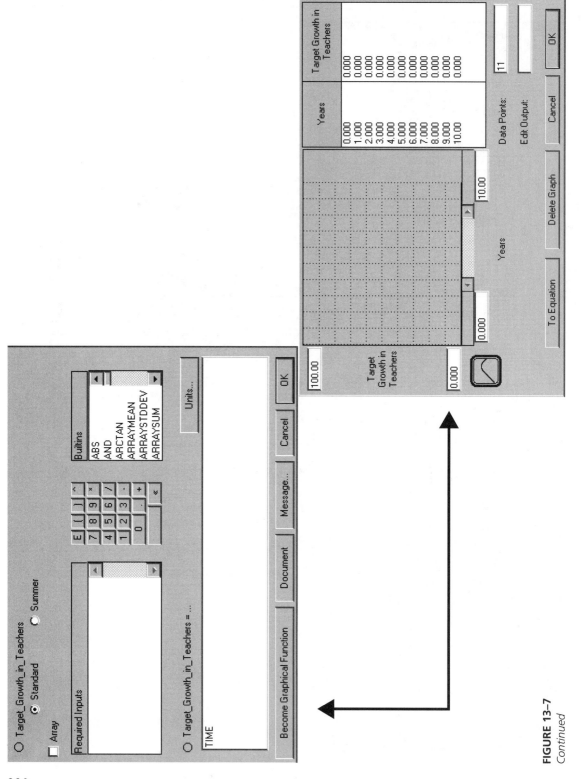

FIGURE 13-7
Continued

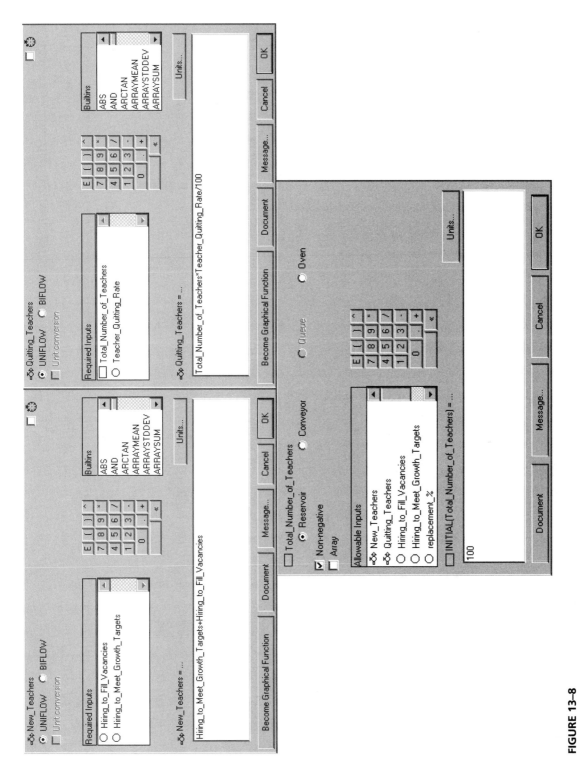

FIGURE 13-8
Defining Stocks and Flows

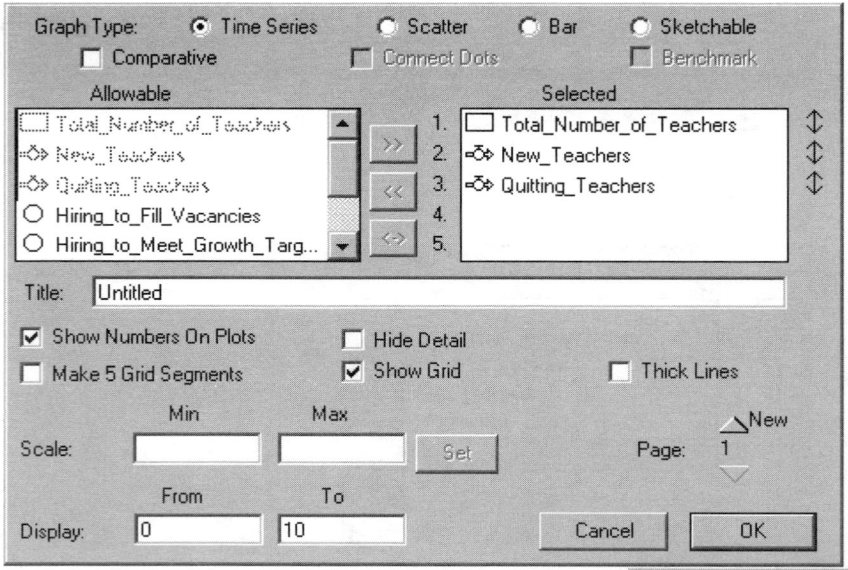

FIGURE 13-9
Creating a Graphical User Interface

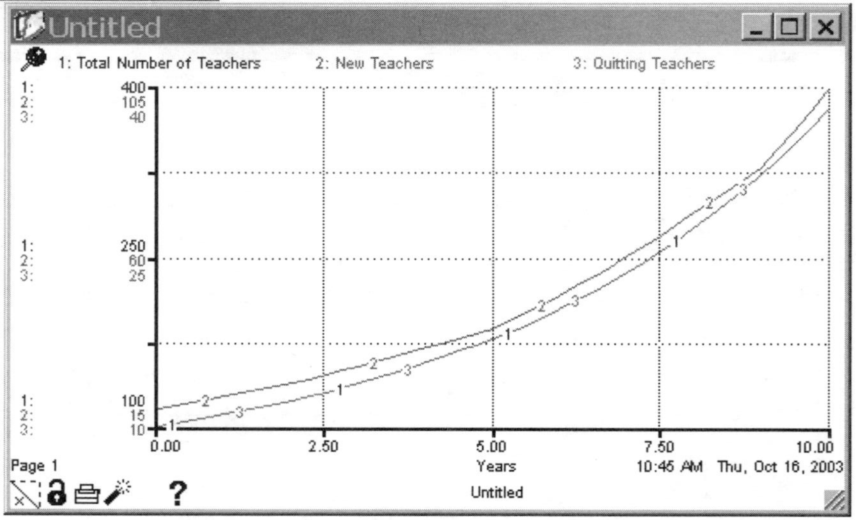

222

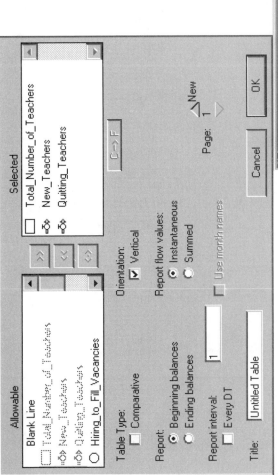

(b)

(d)

FIGURE 13–9
Continued

223

SAMPLE SYSTEMS ARCHETYPES[2]

In this section, we discuss four systems archetypes: limits to success, shifting the burden, escalation, and tragedy of the commons.

Limits to Success

A Limits to Success structure is characterized by a reinforcing loop which is offset by a balancing loop. The reinforcing loop initially shows added performance for additional effort, which in turn feeds additional effort. This continues until some constraint produces a limiting action, and additional effort does not produce additional results. (Bellinger, n.d.)

The example in Figure 13–10 models the struggle and resulting balance between school discipline policies and student behavior. To a point, behavioral guidelines must be specified and policies carried out to maintain order in schools. Yet, increasingly restrictive policies elicit resistance from students, which results in the leveling off or decline of control that administrators exercise over the school environment (Figure 13–11).

Shifting the Burden

A Shifting the Burden structure is characterized by two balancing loops, each of which moves toward the desired direction. One of these loops provides a better long-term solution to the situation, yet has an associated time delay. The other balancing loop, the one most often chosen, has a short term result, but does not actually resolve the fundamental difficulty, and the perceived problem returns. (Bellinger, n.d.)

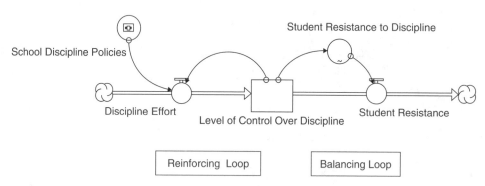

FIGURE 13–10
Limits to Success Archetype

---

[2]The following examples are drawn from a Web site called *Mental Model Musings*, a collection of extremely useful descriptions and sample applications of system dynamics modeling authored by Gene Bellinger: http://www.outsights.com/systems/welcome.htm.

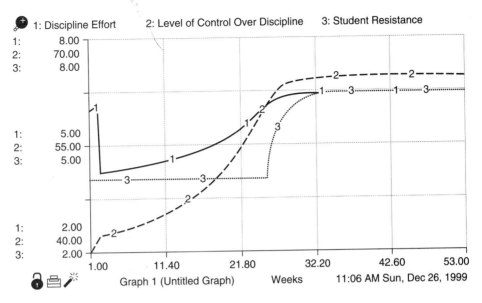

FIGURE 13–11
Limits to Success Model Output

We need new teachers each year because of attrition. There has been high attrition for the past several years because of a decline in work environment quality. To balance the system, we could either continue to hire more teachers or improve the environment (Figure 13–12). Hiring more teachers is a more tangible solution and therefore the more popular choice. However, this option guarantees that more teachers will be needed each year (Figure 13–13).

Escalation

An Escalation structure is characterized by two balancing loops which interact in a single reinforcing structure which may be either virtuous or vicious. [A virtuous cycle is self-healing. Each

FIGURE 13–12
Shifting the Burden Archetype

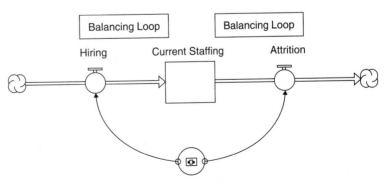

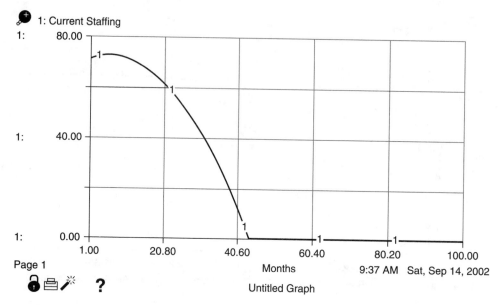

FIGURE 13–13
Shifting the Burden Model Output

time the cycle repeats, it draws closer to the goal of the system. A vicious cycle does the oppo-site.] This structure is stable until a fluctuation is introduced. When this happens, A and B may each rise or decline, depending on the initial fluctuation. (Bellinger, n.d.)

School A and School B are prestigious high schools competing to get their students into the same prestigious colleges. As one school works harder to help its students get better grades, the other school is pushed to work harder, which is to the students' ultimate learn-ing advantage (Figure 13–14). A more negative interpretation would be that the schools

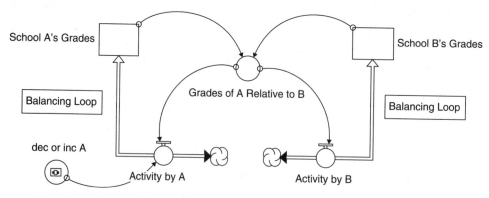

FIGURE 13–14
Escalation Archetype

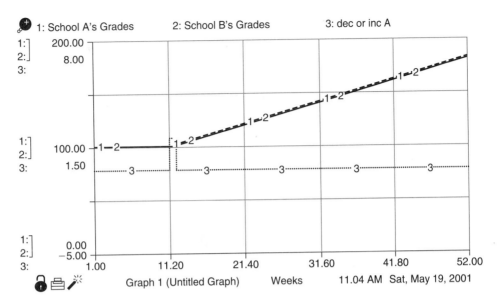

FIGURE 13-15
Escalation Model Output

are engaging in *escalating*—in this case, competitive grade inflation—to make their students look better to admissions officers (Figure 13–15).

Tragedy of the Commons

A Tragedy of the Commons structure is characterized by two reinforcing loops which are offset by two balancing loops. In this example, A and B rely on a common resource for their gains. As each gains, it increases use of the common resource, until the resource is depleted. When this happens the Gain of both A and B is limited. (Bellinger, n.d.)

As public schools are deprived of public funds, many of these schools attempt fund-raising efforts similar to those used by private schools. Yet, each community has a finite set of available contribution resources. Increasing public school fund-raising may strain this finite pool (Figure 13–16). For example, Catholic schools are subsidized by contributions to the Catholic diocese. Contributors include all parishioners, not just parents of children in the Catholic schools. That is, some parishioners' children attend public schools. These parents must now divide their contributions between the church and the public schools.

As public schools step up their efforts to draw resources from the pool, private schools respond by stepping up their efforts in a positive feedback loop. Eventually, the combined drain of public schools and private schools on the resource pool exceeds the growth of the resource pool (community income; Figure 13–17).

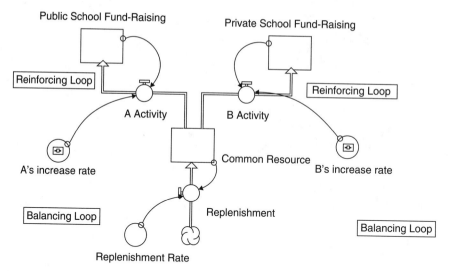

FIGURE 13–16
Tragedy of the Commons Archetype

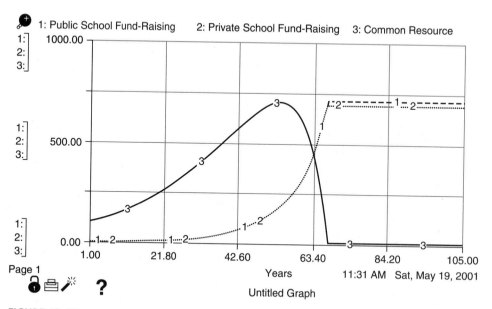

FIGURE 13–17
Tragedy of the Commons Model Output

SUMMARY

In this chapter, you learned how to understand feedback structures and to apply them to ithink modeling. We investigated the hiring/attrition feedback loop in a school district in a midsize New Jersey city in the early 1990s and examined a basic human resource infrastructure. The chapter ended with a discussion of four sample systems archetypes: limits to success, shifting the burden, escalation, and tragedy of the commons.

PROBLEM K

Reversing Reinforcing Feedback: A Policy Example

Background: In 1993–1994, the Connecticut legislature attempted to solve the problem of poor standardized test performance. The state had recently implemented a statewide mastery test across content areas and had begun tracking mastery failure percentages for school districts. Connecticut decided to provide an additional 25% of base aid to school districts for each child who failed the state mastery test. Mastery failure rates for school districts would be determined by a 3-year running average. Legislators perceived that, with this new policy in place, the districts that desperately needed resources the most would have more resources available.

In 1997–1998, data were collected to determine the progress and effectiveness of the mastery aid program. Table 13–K–1 lists the 10 districts with the highest mastery failure rates in 1993–1994. To the legislators' surprise, only 2 districts among the 10 worst had improved their performance, and that of many of the poor-performing districts had dramatically worsened despite the boost in state aid.

TABLE 13–K–1
Highest 10 District Failure Rates in 1993–1994

District Name	Failure Rate in 1993–1994 (%)	Failure Rate in 1997–1998 (%)	Change (%)
Hartford	46.63	57.14	10.50
New Haven	44.46	53.05	8.60
Bridgeport	39.10	43.28	4.19
Waterbury	36.46	42.89	6.44
New Britain	36.36	40.69	4.33
New London	34.41	43.08	8.66
Windham	30.89	38.48	7.59
Norwalk	30.23	28.39	−1.84
Stamford	29.09	32.43	3.34
Middletown	25.72	22.40	−3.32

TABLE 13–K–2

Highest Rates of Increase in Mastery Failure From 1993–1994 to 1997–1998

District Name	Failure Rate in 1993–1994 (%)	Failure Rate in 1997–1998 (%)	Change (%)
Hartford	46.63	57.14	10.50
New London	34.41	43.08	8.66
New Haven	44.46	53.05	8.60
Windham	30.89	38.48	7.59
Meriden	23.15	29.95	6.80
Waterbury	36.46	42.89	6.44
Bloomfield	20.25	26.51	6.27
Morris	8.96	14.83	5.87
Thompson	13.04	18.11	5.06
Windsor	16.93	21.86	4.92

Bridgeport—#16

Could it be that most districts in the state had depreciated throughout the period in question? Table 13–K–2 displays the 10 districts that declined most rapidly through the period. Five of the 10 were among the initial group of 10. Despite the funding boost, the performance at these schools not only appeared to be worsening, but was doing so at the fastest rate.

A Simple Explanation? In a recent meeting of the state department of education, a copy of the positive feedback loop (Figure 13–K–1) was distributed to legislators. The legislature learned that the 1993 plan created a reinforcing feedback loop of increased dependence on new funding, and that each increase in funding drove the desire to attain even more funding from the state. The best route toward more funding was increased failure rates.

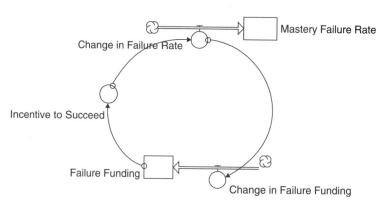

FIGURE 13–K–1

Positive Feedback Loop

Disgruntled, and somewhat insulted by this representation of its policy, the state board of education responded by putting a footnote in the annual report on school funding: "While in some ways this policy may seem illogical—rewarding failure—we must emphasize that these schools really do need additional support, and with time, things will get better." The policy remains in place.

Your Task: Your task is to develop an alternative to the existing policy structure that will promote reinforcing feedback toward a uniform goal of excellence (with respect to mastery test success). First, review the existing policy and its root dysfunction. Second, describe your new policies (you should have two or three options) and design corresponding ithink diagrams. Third, if possible, construct, test, and demonstrate your models in the ithink save-disabled demo.

14

Dynamic Models
of Schooling

In this chapter, we present three cases, accompanied by ithink simulations. Each case focuses on a particular issue facing a school district or state department of education. The first, Simultaneity of Language and Knowledge Acquisition, is based on a study in New York City. In this study, researchers discovered that thousands of students in the city's public schools fail to acquire language skills by graduation and fail to acquire the knowledge prerequisite to taking full advantage of opportunities at City University. The second case is Chasing the Moving Target. For years, the state supreme court encouraged the New Jersey legislature to moderate spending discrepancies between the state's poor "special needs districts" and the state's wealthy suburban districts. This model allows you to test policy options for spending equity under a series of alternative economic scenarios. The third model addresses the complexity of implementing large-scale class size reduction and the potential unintended consequences.

You may choose to write policy briefs on any of or all these models. You are also encouraged to take the models to task, question their design, and propose alternatives and extensions. If you have the full version of ithink, be sure to make and test these modifications.

CASE 1: SIMULTANEITY OF LANGUAGE AND KNOWLEDGE ACQUISITION

Background

For students to acquire knowledge, they must speak the language in which the knowledge is conveyed. The results of a study of New York's K–16 school system suggest that its managers may be overlooking this fact. The system is referred to as K–16 to address the continuity between New York City (NYC) K–12 public schools and the City University of New York (CUNY) system. For the past several years, a number of students reaching the CUNY system have required substantial remediation across the curriculum. This fact is disturbing for a number of reasons. For instance, the same city that supports CUNY has been paying $8,000 to $10,000 a year for 12 to 13 years to educate students prior to their arrival at CUNY.

View the system for a moment as a garden, where the ground is prepared by one team; seeded, weeded, and watered by the second; and harvested for consumers by the last. In the case of the NYC K–16 system, the harvesting team has to go back and reseed, weed, and water—that is, perform each prerequisite step that should have long been accomplished by the time the students reach this team's department—all at great delay and cost to the college system.

Another disturbing outcome of the study was that researchers could predict, with significant accuracy, which students would require remediation by the time they were in the 8th grade. One key predictive factor in 8th, 10th, and 12th grades appeared to be the language proficiency level of the children in the study. What is so interesting is that these children retained their label of *limited English proficient* (LEP) through 8th, 10th, and 12th grades, which created a situation analogous to that of the bicycle factory example. For these children, learning consists of two simultaneous tasks, knowledge acquisition and language acquisition, in which language acquisition is prerequisite to (but in a continuous loop with) knowledge acquisition.

The Model—NYC.ITM

The model for this case addresses the issue of simultaneity of language and knowledge acquisition. Other systemic issues and problems beyond this simple model contribute to the dysfunction of the NYC public schools, but even in the simplified version of the simulation, its power will become evident.

Figure 14–1 is a representation of the ithink model. The teaching of knowledge and knowledge acquisition is a simultaneous, interlocked, positive feedback loop with the teaching of language and language acquisition. The rate of knowledge acquisition or language acquisition depends on the exogenous characteristics of the incoming student population, which defines an average rate of learning efficiency in this model.

One idea driving the structure of the model is that the total amount of teaching that can be applied to a child or a group of children is finite. That is,

$$\text{Teaching Knowledge} + \text{Teaching Language} = 1 \text{ (arbitrary finite value)}$$

The implication is that we cannot simply add more language instruction while retaining the current amount of knowledge instruction.

For example, if we teach all knowledge and no language, we may find that the students acquire less knowledge than they should because they lack the language skills to acquire the knowledge we are trying to teach. Similarly, we could teach all language, which would increase their proficiency in language but not teach them any knowledge. Which is better? If we consider each type of teaching to be an input effort or an input cost, our objective would be to find the appropriate combination of teaching knowledge and teaching language to yield the best outcome for the least input effort. Finding this combination is the basic objective of the simulation as it is designed.

Unfortunately, because the simulation is designed primarily for demonstrative purposes, it will not allow you to generate the definitive answer to the best combination. Because the model is built on soft assumptions, an arbitrary answer is built into the model. Thus, the key is not to identify the arbitrary optimum but to study the behavior of the system on

FIGURE 14–1
Knowledge Acquisition Model

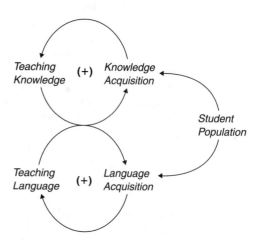

either side of the optimum. For example, how does overteaching for language or knowledge affect the relative efficiency of our efforts?

Within the simulation are two versions of the model. The first is a simple, feed-forward representation, in which language acquisition aids knowledge acquisition as a multiplier. In the second, feedback loops are included whereby knowledge acquisition aids further knowledge acquisition, and language acquisition aids further language acquisition, which creates a learning acceleration effect. The extent to which learning supports further learning should reduce input effort, or improve efficiency.

Suggested Simulations

Begin by opening the model NYC.ITM. From the main menu window, you can modify the characteristics of the incoming student population in terms of average language proficiency and average socioeconomic status. These two factors combined affect the average learning efficiency of the student population.

Basic Simulation

Upon clicking on the Simulation button, you will see the manual simulation control panel. You can adjust the rate at which you are teaching for language by default by adjusting the rate at which you are teaching for knowledge. As you make adjustments, you can study the effects on knowledge acquired and language proficiency on the top level of the graph, and the effects on total teaching for language and total teaching for knowledge on the second level of the graph. You can alternate between levels on the graph by clicking on the lower left-hand corner of the graph. Try to find the option that produces the overall highest level of knowledge acquired.

Sensitivity Simulation

The first thing you need to do in the sensitivity analysis is to set the sensi-specs. With this model, you can perform a series of repeated runs at different levels of teaching for language (much as you did manually in the previous simulation). Clicking on the Sensitivity Analysis button brings you to the dialog box for the sensi-specs. Click Sensitivity ON, then click on OK.

When you click on RUN, the model will run five times, presenting, on the top layer, a comparison of Knowledge Acquired, and on the second layer, a comparison of the Knowledge efficiency ratios. Find the run that provides the best combination of knowledge acquired and efficiency in teaching.

Feedback Model

Teaching for knowledge or language is like pushing a ball up a hill. If you want the ball to continue uphill, you must continue to push it, providing more and more input effort. What if your input efforts could stimulate a reinforcing feedback loop, so that teaching language yields language proficiency, which enables students to learn more language, and so on? This scenario would be analogous to pushing the ball downhill and thus reducing your input effort. If you achieve greater gains with less effort, your system should be much more efficient. Note that the feedback archetype is more effective with substantial and substantive peer interaction than with teacher-directed language instruction.

On this control panel, adjust Teaching Language Rate 2, the language rate for the feedback model. All your runs of the feedback model will be compared against the performance of the original model. However, note that the original model will be running at whatever teaching language rate was most recently set for that model. We suggest leaving it at 0.5. Also, you should remember to turn off the sensi-specs before running the feedback model. Your goal is to observe how much more knowledge can be acquired when learning feedback is involved, and the change in teaching-process efficiency.

Modification and Extension

What happens when the population is 50, 60, or 80% LEP? Research has shown that we tackle language training by similar methods under these circumstances—adding English as a second language (ESL) staff, classroom support, and special pullout activities. However, when the population who is LEP is in the majority, these methods are cost inefficient. The principle of diminishing returns is at work. Is there an alternative way to structure the model, or an alternative model for the system, when the population reaches such a breaking point?

CASE 2: CHASING THE MOVING TARGET—MEETING EQUITY DEMANDS IN NEW JERSEY

Background

Since the early 1970s and the case of *Robinson v. Cahill*, the New Jersey state legislature has been under the gun to remedy inequities in school spending between poor urban districts and wealthy suburban districts. Court decisions (*Abbott v. Burke*, rounds 1, 2, and 3) have centered on the goal of achieving 100% parity between the state's urban special needs districts (SNDs) and mean spending of a cluster of districts known as the *I&J districts*.[1] The New Jersey legislature has developed and implemented various formulas for the redistribution of aid to school districts. Regardless of the formula structure, the chronic pattern of legislative behavior has been to underestimate future need and underfund the formula with respect to the court mandate.

At least one part of the continued dysfunction has been the combination of Chasing a Moving Target, where the target is the continually increasing I&J district spending, and a Planning for Now strategy. The objective is to close the gap between SND per-pupil expenditure (PPE) and I&J spending during the next 3 years.

$$I\&J\ PPE - SND\ PPE = Gap$$

$$Goal: Gap = 0$$

---

[1]New Jersey created a banding system of district factor groups that, in particular, focused on the relative wealth of the districts. There are 10 bands, from A through J, where the A districts are the poorest (and include the SNDs) and the J districts are predominantly small, wealthy suburban districts.

The goal is to converge on the moving target. You must know where the target is now and where it will be at the time you want to reach it.

This task would be simple if resources were infinite. Given the large number of pupils in the SND schools and the high spending level of the I&J districts, achieving 100% parity is, to say the least, an expensive endeavor, and not the only responsibility of the state. What if achieving convergence requires spending an additional 10% per year on SND schools, but the state budget grows by only 1 or 2%? What if the tax base in SNDs grows poorer, which reduces their ability to provide a local share? In addition, what if the student population in these districts continues to grow, which adds to the total budget required to achieve parity in per-pupil spending? With all these rates of change intertwined, this model becomes difficult to ponder intuitively.

Model Structure

The model includes the opportunity to test and compare Planning for Now with Planning for Then. Two alternative model structures exist in which the gap is defined as follows:

Option I: Planning for Now

$$\text{Gap} = \text{I\&J PPE} - \text{SND PPE}$$

Option II: Planning for Then

$$\text{Gap} = \text{I\&J PPE}\,(t + 3) - \text{SND PPE}\,(t)$$

The bottom line, as you will see when you run the simulations, is that you cannot catch up if you plan for now.

The first sector of the model centers on policy goal setting, addressing the following two basic sets of questions:

1. How much parity is sufficient? Can we achieve 90% parity instead of 100%? Is this more affordable?
2. What if we slow the moving target? Can we achieve greater parity against a slower moving target at a more reasonable cost?

Again, each policy decision must be made in a context of finite resources. We delineate the resource bases into two other sectors of our model. The first is the local sector. The local sector includes the population growth rate factor, which drives the rate at which both local and state resources are consumed. Local, fiscal resources are derived from tax rates applied to a tax base. Local citizens have a limited capacity to pay the taxes. Thus, we assign a critical threshold of 50 mills (5% of property wealth), at which the voters become disgruntled with their politicians and revolt. Tax revenues, although limited by voter behavior, are also limited by the wealth of the tax base. If we hold the tax rates constant and the tax base recedes, the revenues decrease. Holding the revenues constant would require increasing the rates.

The state sector is also limited in capacity and inextricably linked to limits placed on local capacity. Any money the state spends on SND schools is money that it cannot spend elsewhere. The state cannot continually allocate a larger and larger share of its budget to

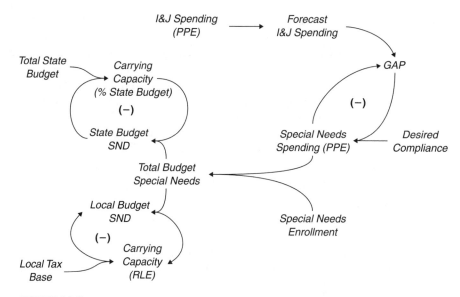

FIGURE 14–2
Equalizing Per-Pupil Spending in New Jersey

Note: PPE = per-pupil expenditure; SND = special needs district; RLE = required local effort.

these schools. The share of funds to SND schools must ultimately stabilize, or reach equilibrium. We set a critical threshold of 20% of the total state budget to be allocated to reaching parity. Note that reducing the state's role in spending, by necessity, causes local taxpayers to pick up the slack. Thus, reducing state responsibility is simply shifting the burden (Figure 14–2).

Suggested Simulations

Each simulation consists of exogenous conditions (economic and demographic factors) and endogenous levers, or variables, that you can manipulate. (Remember: Process models are intended not to generate exact estimates of solutions or forecasts but to study system behavior under different conditions.) Therefore, run each simulation under several sets of exogenous conditions. We have created plausible scenarios for you, but you may think of more.

Exogenous Conditions and Scenarios

Scenario 1: Let the Good Times Roll

- ◆ Urban Renewal With Moderate Tax Base Increases = 3.5% Annual Growth (reduced slightly as a result of tax breaks to stimulate renewal)
- ◆ Booming Urban Enrollments = 8.5% Annual Growth
- ◆ Increased State Receipts (Income Growth; Table 14–1)

TABLE 14–1
Projected State Budget Growth:
Scenario 1

Year	Forecast
1995	.048
1996	.050
1997	.054
1998	.057
1999	.064
2000	.075
2001	.089
2002	.099
2003	.103
2004	.100

♦ Moderate Tax Base Growth—Other Districts (Balance of Booming Suburbs and Lagging Rural Economies) = 3.5% Annually
♦ Moderate Enrollment Growth—Other Districts = 3.5% Annual Growth

Scenario 2: A Slippery Slope
♦ Declining Urban Tax Base = −1.5% Annual Decline
♦ Stable Urban Enrollment = 0% Annual Growth
♦ Moderate Growth—Other Enrollment = 3.5% Annual Growth
♦ Stable Other Tax Base = 2% Annual Growth
♦ Frozen State Budget = 0% Growth Next 3 Years, 2% Thereafter

Scenario 3: Centripetal Forces
♦ Declining Urban Enrollments = −5% Annual Decline
♦ Declining Urban Tax Base = −2.5% Annual Decline
♦ Moderate State Budget Growth (mainly shifting of patterns; Table 14–2)

TABLE 14–2
Projected State Budget Growth:
Scenario 3

Year	Forecast
1995	.035
1996	.037
1997	.039
1998	.041
1999	.045
2000	.050
2001	.045
2002	.043
2003	.041
2004	.041

TABLE 14–3
Policy Levers: Simulation 1

Lever	Suggested Range (%)
Allowable target change	0–5
Compliance goal	85–100
State share	50–80

♦ Rapid Growth of Middle Wealth District Enrollment = 8.5% Annual Growth
♦ Moderate Growth of Middle Wealth District Tax Base = 5% Annual Growth

Simulation 1: Planning for Now

In the Planning for Now scenario, the model is designed to close the gap between current SND spending and current I&J spending. The intent is to close this gap during a 3-year convergence period. Thus, the model is designed so that in 3 years SNDs will spend what I&J districts are spending now. Your task is to study the results of this approach, which even on the surface appears to be dysfunctional (Tables 14–3 and 14–4).

Simulation 2: General Model

Now that you tested and determined the expected outcomes of a dysfunctional approach, design a set of feasible solutions—solutions that yield dynamic equilibrium in terms of state and local resource use. Test different sets of exogenous conditions by using the preceding scenarios. These conditions include expected state revenues, enrollment growth rates for SNDs, and tax base changes in SNDs. For some exogenous conditions, you will be able to enter a constant growth rate to be carried through the forecast period; for others, such as state revenues, you will be able to forecast expected rates of change for each period.

Next, adjust a series of policy levers (Table 14–5). Your policy levers include the compliance rate, a lever that allows you to adjust the system to achieve 85, 90, or 100% parity between SNDs and I&J districts. Your next policy lever is the growth rate of I&J district spending. Slow the moving target to see the effects on state and local taxpayers. Finally, shift the average state share between the state and local communities. This lever determines the share of special needs spending the state is willing to put forth. However, what the state fails to supply, the local community must provide for the compliance goal to be achieved (Table 14–6).

TABLE 14–4
Systems Monitoring: Simulation 1

Indicator	Threshold	Goal
Range ratio		Stated objective
Percent compliance		Stated objective
SND share	20%	Seeking leveling (dynamic equilibrium)
RLE	50 mills	Seeking leveling (dynamic equilibrium)

Note: SND = special needs district; RLE = required local effort.

TABLE 14–5
Policy Levers: Simulation 2

Lever	Suggested Range (%)
Allowable target change	0–5
Compliance goal	85–100
State share	50–80

Simulation 3: Unintended Consequences

The Unintended Consequences model includes the nonlitigant districts in the state as well as the wealthy I&J districts and the litigant SNDs. The way the court mandate was imposed, the legislature is responsible only for bringing the SNDs to parity with the I&J districts. We designed the model such that total education equalization aid receives a finite share of the finite pool of state resources. Distribution of this aid is prioritized so that the litigants meet parity objectives. Whatever is leftover becomes the pool of state aid for nonlitigant districts. Unlike the litigants, the nonlitigants will not be required to replace reductions in state aid with increased local revenues. We hold these districts to a maximum local tax threshold (Tables 14–7 and 14–8).

Flight Simulator

We also included an interactive version of the *Abbott v. Burke* model on the Data and Models Web site. In this case, the exogenous economic and demographic conditions are randomized in the underlying model structure. You may observe different versions of the randomized exogenous variables by running the model on the Exogenous Conditions screen. Then, go to the Simulation Controls screen to manipulate policy levers without throwing either the legislature or local communities into political upheaval.

CASE 3: UNINTENDED CONSEQUENCES OF CLASS SIZE REDUCTION

Background

The final model integrates educational research from various sources to construct a dynamic representation of the interplay among class size policies, teacher labor market conditions, effects of teachers on students, and the costs and cost-effectiveness of alternative policies. Alternative policies include not only targeted versus statewide class size reduction, but also wage premiums as incentives to keep high-quality teachers in low-income

TABLE 14–6
Systems Monitoring: Simulation 2

Indicator	Threshold	Goal
Range ratio		Stated objective
Percent compliance		Stated objective
SND share	20%	Seeking leveling (dynamic equilibrium)
RLE	50 mills	Seeking leveling (dynamic equilibrium)

Note: SND = special needs district; RLE = required local effort.

TABLE 14–7
Policy Levers: Simulation 3

Lever	Suggested Range (%)
Average state share	50–80
Maximum state education share	20–50
Target change	0–5
Compliance goal	85–100

schools. In the wake of the Tennessee STAR (Standardized Testing and Reporting) Study and the Wisconsin SAGE (Student Achievement Guarantee in Education) Study—two detailed reductionist accounts of the effects of a single input, class size reduction,[2] on a narrow set of student achievement outcomes—states are increasingly considering policies and allocating resources to reduce class sizes in public schools. Yet, researchers of California's class size reduction policy are already beginning to question the wisdom of such policies. Unfortunately, the research on class size reduction policies, and other similar policies such as standards-based reforms and whole-school reform models, remains largely disconnected and "unsynthesized." As a result, substantial effort is required on the part of decision makers desiring to use research to guide their understanding of a necessarily complex system.

Currently, four major findings on class size reduction and class size reduction policies are as follows:

1. Kindergarten through third-grade students in classes with 13 to 17 pupils perform slightly better than similar students in classes with 22 to 26 pupils; greater differences are seen among minority students (Finn & Achilles, 1999).

TABLE 14–8
Systems Monitoring: Simulation 3

Indicator	Threshold	Pattern/Goal
SND compliance		Stated objective
SND range ratio		Stated objective
Others compliance		Stated objective
Others range ratio		Stated objective
SND education share	Relative	Stabilizing—not increasing
Others % of state budget	Relative	Stabilizing—not declining

Note: SND = special needs district.

---

[2]A more appropriate term is *different class sizes* because neither study involved changing class size through time.

2. Under California's class size reduction policy, schools serving students most in need (low income or at risk) experienced a decline in numbers of certified teachers and an increase in numbers of emergency certified teachers (CSR Research Consortium, 2000; WestEd, 1999).

3. Findings are mixed as to whether or not teacher certification or emergency certification affects student performance (Darling-Hammond, 2000; Goldhaber & Brewer, 2000).

4. Class size reduction is a costly endeavor (Brewer, Krop, Gill, & Reichardt, 1999) and may not be a cost-effective endeavor (Levin & McEwan, 2001).

The systems model presented in this case was originally guided by the CSR Research Consortium's finding that California's class size reduction policy was resulting in a reduction in qualified teachers, as measured by certification status, in schools serving higher numbers of students from low-income families. This finding posed an initially intriguing question: What are the costs and benefits of having more students in smaller classes, but with uncertified teachers? Would money be better spent on certified teachers than on smaller classes? Unfortunately, this particular link—the effect of teacher certification on student performance—is uncertain (at best) in existing literature. Further, our opinion is that when certification standards vary widely from state to state, teacher preparation programs that comply with these standards vary widely within states, and the academic ability of students entering teacher preparation programs also varies widely, such credentials are unlikely to ever be an effective indicator of teacher quality.

Nevertheless, related research does indicate that some teachers can consistently outperform others in producing student achievement gains and that these teachers can be identified through statistical methods. Research on the Tennessee Value-Added Assessment System (TVAAS) indicates that students with the highest performing quintile of teachers achieve substantially greater annual achievement gains than those of students with the lowest performing quintile of teachers, and that positive effects are greater for students who are lower achieving (Sanders & Rivers, 1996). We might presume that under a system like the TVAAS, in which individual teachers can be assigned average student gain scores, teachers could leverage the scores toward desirable teaching jobs. We might further presume that ultimately higher wealth schools providing desirable working conditions could recruit and hire high value-added teachers, which would make teacher recruitment and retention substantially more important to student achievement. The model that follows integrates this view of teacher quality, teacher quality effects on student performance, and the perception that such quality measures may be used in labor market sorting of teachers. Needless to say, the ability of high wealth districts with better working conditions, easier students to teach, and more resources to recruit more talented teachers even more effectively than they do now might be an unintended and negative outcome of such a model.

Model Structure and Assumptions

The basic structure of the teacher labor market sector of the class size reduction ithink simulation model is shown in Figure 14–3. For simplicity, two stocks of schools were created: Low-Wealth Schools (LWS) and High-Wealth Schools (HWS), each with a stock of 1,000

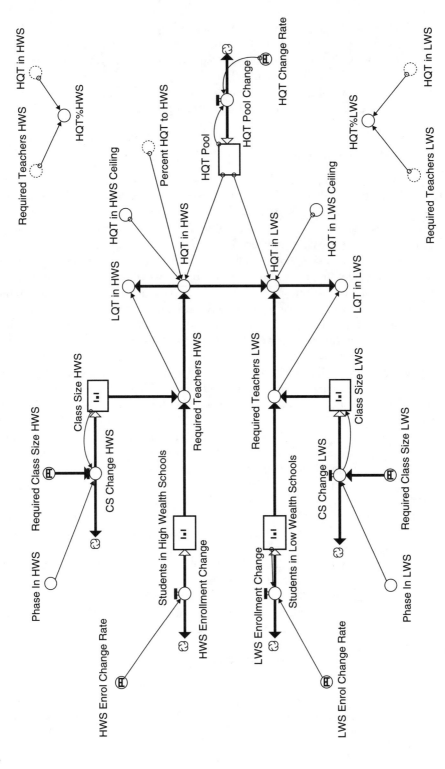

FIGURE 14–3

Linking Class Size Reduction Policy With the Teacher Labor Market Context (General Model)

Note: HWS = high-wealth schools; HQT = high-quality teachers; CS = class size; LWS = low-wealth schools; LQT = low-quality teachers.

students and an initial enrollment change rate set to zero. HWS are assigned an initial Class Size stock of 20, and LWS an initial Class Size stock of 25, from which required numbers of teachers are generated (Enrollment/Class Size). On the right-hand side of the diagram, a stock of High-Quality Teachers (HQT) is created, with a change-rate converter designed to allow entry of time-varying data.

The most important feature of this sector is the definition of the process that sorts HQT into HWS or LWS. One defining factor is the converter Percent HQT to HWS, which defines the percentage of the HQT pool that would go to HWS if positions were available. This value is initially assigned at 95% but can be manipulated on the interface and could be changed, for example, by policies that pay wage premiums to teachers to teach in LWS. In addition to the constraint that not all HQT will go to HWS, the HQT in HWS Ceiling converter defines that a HWS will never have only HQT. This value is also set at 95%, which indicates that 5% of low-quality teachers (LQT) will typically "slip through the cracks" into HWS for any number of reasons. This value is also adjustable. As a result, the HQT in HWS pool is defined as follows:

HQT in HWS = IF (Percent_HQT_to_HWS*HQT_Pool < HQT_in_HWS_Ceiling* Required_Teachers_HWS) THEN ROUND (Percent_HQT_to_HWS*HQT_Pool) else ROUND (HQT_in_HWS_Ceiling*Required_Teachers_HWS)

That is, if 95% of the available pool is more than is needed for HWS, such schools function at their ceiling. If fewer HQT are available than the ceiling, 95% of these available teachers will be accepted into HWS. "ROUND" values are used to ensure that only whole teachers are assigned to either LWS or HWS.

Numerous oversimplifications to this labor market mechanism exist, but, in short, the mechanism allows higher wealth schools to gain access to greater portions of HQT when they are available and, when excess HQT are available, LWS may gain greater access. If all change rates—HQT pool and enrollments—are set to zero and no class size changes are implemented, the distribution of the 60 HQT remains at 12 of 40 (30%) in LWS and 40 of 50 (80%) in HWS.

The Required Class Size converters are the levers for applying class size mandates to both sets or either set of schools. The Phase-In converter simply spreads the period of the reduction across 3 years but is adjustable.

Student performance effects are generated by the model sector displayed in Figure 14–4. The central stock of this sector is LWS Achievement, which can be either increased or decreased (bidirectional flow). Two major factors affect achievement in the model: class size reduction and teacher quality. Interactions between the two are not considered for the time being, thus only additive, not multiplicative, effects are modeled. Both effects are treated in terms of "change in x with respect to change in y during a 1-year period." That is, class size changes per year are calculated by subtracting previous class size from current year class size, where a reduction is represented as a positive value so as to affect the bidirectional flow on achievement in the correct direction.[3]

---

[3]Actually, this is accomplished by simply reversing the equation so that this year's class size is subtracted from last year's class size and so on.

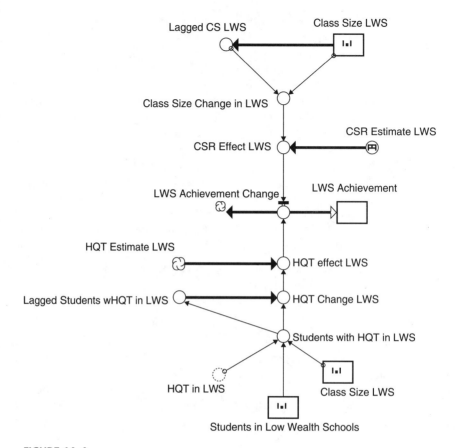

FIGURE 14–4

Class Size Reduction Model Student Performance Sector

Note: CS = class size; LWS = Low-Wealth Schools; CSR = class size reduction; HQT = High-Quality Teachers.

The change in class size is then multiplied by the estimate of the achievement effects of a unit (pupil) change in class size. The default value for the class size reduction effect is 0.35 point (100-point scale) for each unit reduction in class size for HWS, and 1.19 points (100-point scale) for each unit reduction in class size for LWS. These estimates are loosely based on Finn and Achilles' (1999) findings on the differential effects of class size reduction on White and minority students on "basic skills test" performance (Table 14–9). The mean basic skills performance of minority students in reduced class sizes was 10.75% (Grades 1–3) higher than that of minority students in larger classes, and the mean basic skills performance of White students in reduced class sizes was 3.18% higher. Because class size was reduced by approximately 9 students (from 24 to 15), presuming (most likely falsely) that the performance differences are linearly related to pupil reductions in class

TABLE 14–9

Class Size Reduction Effects

	% Change	
Test	White	Minority
BSF Reading		
Grade 1	4.8	17.3
Grade 2	1.6	12.7
Grade 3	4.0	9.3
BSF Math		
Grade 1	3.1	7.0
Grade 2	1.2	9.9
Grade 3	4.4	8.3
Average	3.18	10.75
Unit effect	0.35	1.19

Note: BSF = Basic Skills First (Test). Adapted from "Tennessee's Class Size Study: Findings, Implications, Misconceptions," by J. D. Finn and C. M. Achilles, 1999, *Educational Evaluation and Policy Analysis, 21*(2), p. 99.

size, the unit change for minority students was 1.19 (10.75/9) and for White students was 0.35 (3.18/9).[4]

Determining HQT effects is similarly speculative. This process begins with estimating the number and then the proportion of students in low-wealth (or high-wealth) schools in classes with HQT. In the model, student performance changes are related to changes in the proportions of students in classes with HQT, or the difference between current numbers of students in classes with HQT and previous numbers of students in classes with HQT. As noted previously, the HQT estimates are derived from Sanders and Rivers's (1996) work on teacher evaluation with the TVAAS. Table 14–10 displays the gain scores for fifth-grade math for students across the four achievement groups taught by teachers in the lowest and highest two performance quintiles. Comparable first- through third-grade reading scores were unavailable. Although third-grade math scores were available, sample sizes were substantially smaller than those for fifth grade.

Effect magnitudes for the simulation are derived by comparing performance differences between the lowest and highest two quintiles of teachers for both low- and high-performing students. Simulation estimates are based on differences in gains between the lowest and highest two quintiles of teachers, as a percentage of the possible range of scores, which in

---

[4]We recognize the potentially inflammatory response to linking minority student performance with LWS in this model: the implication that minority students are by definition low wealth or attend LWS. We do not argue the appropriateness of this linkage but suggest that the problem may lie in the work of Finn and Achilles, who chose to compare minority and White students under the contention that minority students are uniformly disadvantaged learners. A more appropriate approach would have been for Finn and Achilles to have addressed both additional issues, such as family income, and more educationally relevant measures of student "risk" status. Baker, Keller-Wolff, and Wolf-Wendel (2000) have provided statistical evidence of using more comprehensive measures than student race to address achievement differences.

TABLE 14–10

Teacher Quality Effects From the TVAAS

	Achievement Group 1 (Lowest)		Achievement Group 2		Achievement Group 3		Achievement Group 4 (Highest)	
	Mean	N	Mean	N	Mean	N	Mean	N
Quintile 1	13.8	109.0	4.3	277.0	4.8	83.0	2.2	9.0
	20.0	343.0	4.7	317.0	6.2	40.0	(33.3)	4.0
Average/N	18.5	452.0	4.5	594.0	5.3	123.0	(8.7)	13.0
Quintile 2	23.5	95.0	0.9	347.0	18.5	122.0	13.4	9.0
	25.9	242.0	9.6	383.0	10.8	82.0	(36.0)	3.0
Average/N	25.2	337.0	0.2	730.0	15.4	204.0	1.1	12.0
			Mean	19.0			Mean	10.5
Quintile 4	29.1	46.0	9.5	272.0	23.7	245.0	10.5	38.0
	37.9	171.0	7.6	399.0	23.1	73.0	18.0	5.0
Average/N	36.0	217.0	8.4	671.0	23.6	318.0	11.4	43.0
Quintile 5	53.0	47.0	7.9	220.0	33.3	247.0	25.0	89.0
	46.1	113.0	2.9	425.0	31.1	268.0	14.9	52.0
Average/N	48.1	160.0	4.6	645.0	32.2	515.0	21.3	141.0
			Mean	33.6			Mean	27.1
		Difference		14.6		Difference		16.6
		Possible range		100 pt[a]		Possible range		100 pt[b]
		Percentage		14.6		Percentage		16.6

Note: TVAAS = Tennessee's Value-Added Assessment System. Data from *Cumulative and Residual Effects of Teachers on Future Student Academic Achievement* (p. 9), by W. L. Sanders and J. C. Rivers, 1996, Knoxville, TN: University of Tennessee Value-Added Research and Assessment Center. [a]650–750. [b]750–850.

each case is 100. Although low-performing students generally gained more than high-performing students did, the difference between low-performing students with low- and high-quality teachers (14.6%) was slightly less than the difference between high-performing students with low- and high-quality teachers (16.6%). As with the race–income linkage between research and model on class size effects, the prior student performance–wealth linkage is not clean. That is, we cannot assume that prior low-performing students necessarily exclusively attend LWS.

Remaining sectors of the class size reduction model are displayed in Figure 14–5. First, the total demand for teachers is the sum of required teachers in high- and low-wealth schools. A quality gap is specified as the gap between the number of teachers required and the number of available HQT. Second, the cost of class size reduction is estimated as a function of teachers required to accomplish specified class sizes, given enrollments, times the average teacher salary, which may be time variant. Third, the

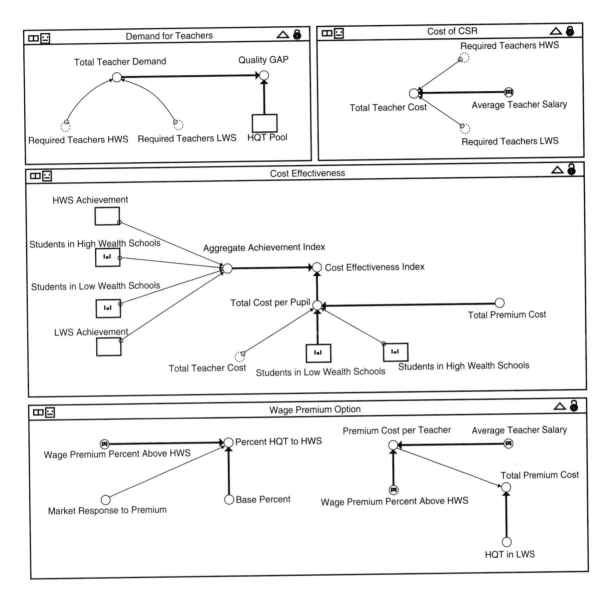

FIGURE 14–5

Class Size Reduction Cost and Cost-Effectiveness Sector

Note: HWS = high-wealth schools; LWS = low-wealth schools; HQT = high-quality teachers; CSR = class size reduction.

wage premium sector is shown at the bottom of Figure 14–5. The change in distribution of HQT between high- and low-wealth schools is a function of the percentage of above average salaries offered as a premium and a predetermined market response to the premium. The initial value is that each additional 10% in wages will stimulate the movement of an additional 5% of HQT to LWS instead of HWS. The cost of the wage premium is estimated only as the premium above average salaries times all (rather than just those who move) HQT in LWS. Finally, cost-effectiveness (middle of Figure 14–5) is determined as a ratio of the total costs of all policies applied divided by the average achievement of all students.

Suggested Activities with the Class Size Reduction Model

Numerous possible experiments can be run with the model as we chose to design it. We encourage you to take a systematic approach to testing the effects of individual policy levers. For example, set wage premiums to zero throughout the simulation and focus only on adjustments to class size. Then, set class sizes constant and focus only on adjustments to wage premiums.

Perhaps the more valuable exercise to perform with this model is to dissect the structure of the model as we proposed it and present potential alternative structures or modifications to the structure. The model we proposed makes numerous simplifying assumptions. Further, we recognize that the model is a representation of our interpretation of how this particular mechanism might work, and embedded within the underlying assumptions of this model are a plethora of our professional biases.

Technical Note on the Class Size Reduction Model

Underlying the class size reduction model is a special type of *input generator*. When you are developing models of this type, you can either use actual time-series data on teacher labor market changes and student population dynamics in an attempt to model the system as it exists, or existed, or produce simulated time-series data as inputs to the model. John Sterman, of the Sloan School of Business at Massachusetts Institute of Technology (MIT), in his book *Business Dynamics* (2000) and accompanying simulations, developed a standard input generator for testing model behavior. Sterman's input generator produces a *pink noise* input. The pink noise process around which the generator is built produces time series that are partly random (white noise) and partly deterministic. The class size reduction model allows you to adjust the amount of variation that may occur in teacher labor markets during the period studied.

NOTES ON APPROACHES TO SYSTEMS MODELING IN EDUCATION

As mentioned previously in this book, systems models and modeling exercises may be delineated as hard or soft data models. Hard data models are based on stocks and flows of tangible, measurable objects, and converters or coefficients are relatively easily defined. Soft data models rely heavily on assumptions imposed by the modeler. Many of these assumptions may appear to be arbitrary, but they should at least be driven by a logical understanding of how the system works, usually derived through a process of group consensus (Richardson & Andersen, 1995). Note that the delineation between hard and soft data models is not absolute. For instance, many uncertainties may exist in processes that involve apparently tangible objects. Further, almost any comprehensive model of a system will contain a collection of both easily measurable stocks and well-understood flows and converters, and others that are predominantly hypothetical.

An approach for classifying systems modeling exercises in education policy is to view the modeling process as (a) physical or mechanical systems modeling, (b) hypothetical modeling, (c) research synthesis modeling, and (d) combinations of all three in varying degrees.

Physical Systems Modeling

Physical or mechanical systems models of schools and schooling are the nearest equivalent of hard data operations research models. In education policy, a number of interconnected hard data elements may be physically represented with dynamic systems models. For instance, in the standard structure of schooling, discrete quantities of students pass through grade levels, in classrooms, in contact with discrete quantities of teachers. Further, teachers gain experience, and, in general, move up pay scales structured in step increments. The demand for teachers is dictated primarily by changes in enrollments. The cost of teachers is dictated by the numbers of teachers placed at various positions on a step scale. Simultaneously, payment for teachers is typically drawn from a resource pool that consists primarily of state aid and local tax revenues, each of which can also be estimated with some certainty and precision.

Hypothetical Systems Modeling

Systems models may also be used to generate hypotheses of systems behavior for which little or no empirical evidence currently exists. Such models are almost entirely soft data models and by necessity include numerous debatable assumptions. Yet, such models may be informative to the extent that they force modeling participants to construct function simulations as representations of theoretical systems. Such a process is far more powerful than simply debating how the system might work on preconceived but less well defined notions. Further, the hypothetical model-building process may lead to specific hypotheses to test and aid researchers in prioritizing the empirical evidence needed to explore the validity of the hypothesis presented.

Research Synthesis Modeling

Most educational research deconstructs education systems into single causal hypothesis tests, and most of the time these tests rely on data that represent symptoms of an underlying process. One example is the Tennessee STAR Study, which involved testing the effects of a randomized class size reduction experiment on student achievement measures. The simple causal policy adjustment that follows from this study is to impose class size reduction to 17 pupils for all K–3 classrooms. Yet, the results of research suggest that the reductionist research-oriented approach to deriving policy recommendations, or conventional data-driven decision making, may not be as effective or efficient as policy makers might desire.[5]

Researchers have begun to place more emphasis on inductive exploration of schooling processes through qualitative research frameworks. Although a valuable complement to quantitative hypothesis tests, maintaining inductive and deductive, and quantitative and qualitative approaches at arm's length still provides a limited perspective on education systems as a whole. Research synthesis modeling involves gathering the evidence provided in quantitative reductions of system features and qualitative explorations of system processes, and combining this evidence with soft assumptions and hard data to synthesize and simulate the behavior of the system as a whole.

NOTES ON MODEL DEVELOPMENT

The Systems Dynamics in Education Project at MIT has been instrumental in gathering and organizing existing resources and creating new resources to provide a basic education in systems thinking and systems modeling. In fact, the goal of the project is to create and disseminate teaching materials as a way to infuse systems thinking and systems dynamics activities into K–12 education. Albin (1997) outlined a model development framework proposed by Randers (1980) that consists of four stages: (a) conceptualization, (b) formulation, (c) testing, and (d) implementation. (Refer to http://sysdyn.clexchange.org/sdep/Roadmaps/RM8/D-4597.pdf.)

The basic objective of conceptualization is to render a causal loop diagram of the system to be modeled and to identify important stocks, flows, and converters. This diagram ultimately guides the simulation construction. In the conceptualization phase, you must begin with a broad perception of the system to be modeled, but not necessarily a specific hypothesis to be addressed or variables to be manipulated. For example, you might decide to model the financial interaction between special education funds and general education funds given other contextual variables including costs, demographics, policy changes, and so forth.

The next step is to determine how inclusive the model must be. Systems models can expand until they duplicate the original system, but this defeats the purpose of a model. The real art of modeling is to create a model that captures the essential features of a dynamic system in such a way that we can improve the sustainability and effectiveness of the system. For example, in a model of school funding, a logical approach might be to create a Local Property Wealth stock, which changes with time, and a Local Tax Rates converter to be used in conjunction with the property wealth stock to determine local district revenues. However, it might also be interesting to identify the factors that affect local property wealth, including migration patterns and housing development, as well as the extent to which differential tax burdens and service quality across districts might influence migration and

[5]See, for example, Brewer et al.'s (1999) critique of the costs of class size reduction policies, Levin and McEwan's (2001) critique of the cost-effectiveness of class size reduction policies, and the CSR Research Consortium's (2000) analysis of teacher labor market effects of California's class size reduction policy.

development. You might also expand on the state revenue flow, looking at state revenues as a whole, and the state's economic context. Each change adds information but also deepens the complexity of the model. Determining model boundaries is a critical step in the modeling process.

Delineation of model variable types begins in the conceptualization phase and involves identifying endogenous variables, or variables involved in the feedback loops of the system, and exogenous variables, or components whose values are not directly affected by the system (Albin, 1997). It is also important to identify which features of a system can be directly manipulated as policy levers, which features are beyond the direct control of policy makers, and which outputs are critical to understanding the condition and behavior of the system. These delineations guide the formulation of the model. They also become particularly relevant as the model is implemented and tests are run to determine the effects of alternative policies and combinations of policy leverage on critical outputs. For example, in school funding decisions, legislators must be able to directly adjust state aid, but not the economic context that generates state aid. Likewise, local administrators must *not* be able to directly adjust their state aid, but may be able to apply political influence that may lead to state aid adjustment.

Formulation of the model involves translating systems diagrams to a computer simulation using Stock, Flow, and Converter tools and specifying the mathematical relationships among model elements. Note that when policy levers are concerned, mathematical specifications involve default values but allow the user to manipulate these values during the simulation. For example, this might be the case with local tax rates or foundation levels in a school finance model. Similarly, when exogenous conditions are uncertain, you can choose to randomize exogenous variables or allow alternative scenarios to be constructed.

Model validation or testing is critical to the acceptance of model findings generated under the implementation step. That is, a well-defined method must be prescribed for validating that the model behaves similar to the way that the system might be expected to behave. For purely hypothetical models, validation comes after the fact. Shreckengost (1985) outlined a series of tests for model validity (see http://sysdyn.clexchange.org/sdep/Roadmaps/RM5/D-4463.pdf). In brief, Shreckengost addressed *model structure tests*, which compare model features, including parameters, with the structure and empirical evidence regarding relationships in the system being modeled, and *model behavior tests*, which involve assessments of the extent to which model output, given varied conditions, is consistent with the expected or documented behavior of the system being modeled.

SUMMARY

Remember that embarking on dynamic systems modeling and using systems modeling software often requires a new problem-solving mind-set and a new set of computer skills. Therefore, we highly recommend the following two books as a starting point:

1. Richardson, G. P. (1992). *Feedback thought in social science and systems theory.* Philadelphia: University of Pennsylvania Press.
2. Senge, P. (1990). *The fifth discipline: The art and practice of the learning organization.* New York: Doubleday.

If you choose to go beyond this part of this book in your systems modeling endeavors, your next step will be to choose your software. One advantage of ithink is the quality of instructional resources that accompany the software. Alternatively, George P. Richardson of the State University of New York, Albany, suggested a software package called Vensim, which may be obtained from http://www.vensim.com, where you can download a free demo version. Richardson's work with Vensim includes models of foster care caseloads in New York State and Medicaid reform in Vermont (Richardson & Andersen, 1995).

Bromley and Jacobson (1998) wrote, "There is a pervasive concern that computers tend to isolate learners and therefore are antithetical to collaborative learning" (p. 144). Other educators have voiced similar concerns about the uses to which computers are put in educational settings. However, perhaps the greatest value of the systems thinking paradigm and dynamic systems modeling can be derived from group interaction during the model development process. Richardson focused on the group process of model building in the public policy setting (Andersen & Richardson, 1994; Richardson & Andersen, 1995). Given the proliferation of site teams in school-based decision making, ithink or other systems modeling software provides a novel opportunity for creative, strategic problem solving that unites rather than isolates constituents.[6]

---

[6]Bromley and Jacobson's (1998) point was to also suggest that even spreadsheet problem-solving activities, as presented in Richards (1987), need not isolate learners but can unite groups by means of case-based analyses.

PART V SUMMARY

This part required a difficult mind shift. For the entirety of this book, you collected tools for monitoring symptoms. In part V, you learned to diagnose disease. Doctors do the same thing. Their stethoscopes, thermometers, blood pressure gauges, scales for height and weight, flashlights, and rubber hammers (to name only the most basic accoutrements) are symptom monitors. Years of medical training, internships, and residencies, and years of experience enable them to synthesize information about your body and determine a possible ailment. However, despite doctors' expertise, patients often request second opinions and alternative treatments. The field of educational systems analysis is in the toddler stage compared with the field of medicine. Do not be disappointed if your early attempts at understanding systems processes are crude. You are in training. So are we, for that matter. Our models in this chapter are admittedly underdeveloped.

The mayor of New York City, Michael R. Bloomberg, currently faces a decision that many leaders face at one point or another: whether to do right by the budget or to do good for the city's long-term benefit. The crux of his dilemma: the cost-effectiveness of metal and plastic recycling versus the environmental repercussions of increased landfill use. Some people might be appalled at the idea that the future of waste management can be reduced to a bottom line. Yet, the same decisions are frequently made in opposition to children's well-being.

The structural elements of ithink software are stocks, flows, and converters. Conduct a sensitivity analysis on your first model and adjust the receptivity of your model to fluctuations in data. Use comparative output tables and graphs to compare options. Think about feedback structures and the many places in your daily life where they occur. Two examples are the ebb and flow of the stock market and the supply and demand principle, and the use of heart rate monitoring during aerobic exercise. Know that your basic systems archetypes are of two fundamental types: dynamic equilibrium models or growth models. Senge (1990) described several of each type well in *The Fifth Discipline*; for example, he described limits-to-success, shifting-the-burden, escalation, and tragedy-of-the-commons archetypes. We summarized some of these in chapter 13 and modeled others more extensively in chapter 14.

Take advantage of the opportunity to work collaboratively with other educational leaders. Two or more minds are better than one, and with the combined faculties and backgrounds of several educators, you will greatly increase your chances of recognizing systems processes, archetypes, and functions. In part VI, we give you several problems to work with, as well as suggestions for improving teamwork.

Part VI

Pulling It All Together

15   A Guide to Structured Improvisation

In part VI, we help you apply the analytic tools and models to an ecological analysis of real-world situations. This part includes no contrived cases. In chapter 15, we provide you with a framework for performing ecological analysis of your organization.

A Guide to Structured Improvisation

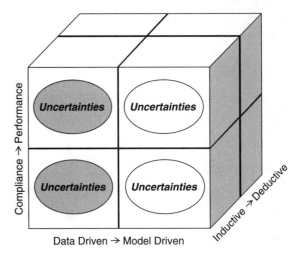

FIGURE 15–1
Analytic Framework

In this chapter, we guide you through the practice of analyzing your chosen organization. Take the perspective of a school leader (or the leader of another organization at the appropriate site level), but assume that many of the goals and objectives herein are applicable to the district (regional), state, or even national level of a system. This chapter contains a framework for beginning a comprehensive, open-ended, ecological analysis of your organization. With time, you will develop your own framework for organizing the project.

The following approach is a structured improvisation. The goal is to systematically conduct a series of data-driven analyses and a series of model-driven analyses and to finish with an ecological assimilation of the knowledge gained along the way. Each step contains elements of inductive exploration and deductive hypothesis testing. You will identify both the predictable features and the uncertain features of your system. A schematic of this model is shown in Figure 15–1.

Throughout the analytic process, try to recognize when individual work or collaboration is preferable. The process of ecological analysis requires collaboration so that you can generate a complete, minimally biased understanding of your organization. Recall that no researcher or analyst is outside the system. However, sometimes a team member must take his or her turn individually exploring and becoming acquainted with the data, without other team members present.

In structured improvisation, you use the analytic tools acquired in the earlier parts of this book and spend time experimenting with the appropriate tools within each quadrant shown in Figure 15–1. We begin with data-driven analyses.

DATA-DRIVEN ANALYSES

The first task in a data-driven analysis is to organize data into a format suitable for Excel analysis. Recall from chapter 3 the types of data you might gather. Consider, but do not limit yourself to, Table 15–1 to guide you. Ultimately, you should gather data of various types, at various levels, from your organization.

TABLE 15–1
Data-Gathering Matrix or Checklist

	Performance	Demographic	Financial
Students			
Classrooms			
Schools			
Districts			
State			

Gathering and organizing data is most efficient as a team effort. Various constituents will likely have access to different data. This process might begin with a team meeting in which five objectives are as follows:

1. Generate a list of known available data.
2. Generate a list of desired data and the likelihood of their availability.
3. Identify potential data sources.
4. Decide on the basic organization of the database, where it will be housed, and how it will be accessed.
5. Assign group members to acquire, clean, and organize the data.

During data collection and organization, the team members should periodically reconvene to update one another and to divide the preliminary tasks of data exploration. Keep in mind that data gathering will never be complete. Thus, data gathering is not Phase I and analysis, Phase II. You will often find that certain data analysis causes you to think, "What if I had . . . ?" Thus, a reinforcing feedback loop takes hold, whereby the more you learn from your data, the more you want to find out with new data. Eventually, you will decide where to cut off this feedback loop, for initial reporting purposes, but the feedback loop should continue as part of an ongoing ecological analysis. Do not forget the value of historical or trend data in drawing conclusions. For this exercise, 5 years' worth of such data should be sufficient.

Compliance Analysis

The first level of data-driven analysis to perform is compliance analysis. Compliance analyses provide the basis for all subsequent analyses, answering questions such as "Is the organization staying afloat?" Every organization needs to comply with local, state, and federal regulations and laws. In the first level of compliance analysis, you try to determine how well your organization is thriving in the regulatory web in which it is embedded. In the second level of compliance analysis, you consider which, if any, such regulations, rules, or laws are dysfunctional or have unintended negative effects on the vision and mission of the organization. (For schools, some of these might be Carnegie units, special education regulations, union contracts, and so forth.)

The next step is to perform both inductive and deductive analyses, but the emphasis is on inductive data exploration. Create a summary table of means, medians, and standard deviations for all variables (descriptive statistics). Sort and plot the variables, and aggregate and disaggregate the data in various ways (class averages, school averages, district averages, etc.). Prepare PivotTables of the data. In an effort to assess the basal compliance of your organization, compare your data with established benchmarks. At this stage, you are not assessing performance (how the school compares with regard to student achievement outcomes). Rather, you are comparing the school against the standard or regulation. Does the school have certified teachers if it is required to do so by state law? Do the students spend the required minutes, hours, and days of instruction at school? What proportion of children are classified? Do students have individual education plans if they are classified? Has the state monitored your organization? What are the results? What are the results of the last school accrediting agency evaluations (e.g., middle states)?

Because of the substantial volume of material and data, you may want to assign individuals to particular areas of study. Avoid the temptation to assign one person "compliance," another "demographics," and so on because doing so limits individuals' perspectives. A more useful method is to have one individual construct a series of PivotTables across all data, while another performs the descriptive statistics, and another prepares the graphics (Table 15–2).

As your team describes the data, questions that warrant further exploration will emerge. In addition, numerous questions will no doubt already be in team members' minds, emerging from innate curiosity or from the most recent board or Parent–Teacher Association (PTA) meeting. Such questions may include "How are minority students performing in advanced math and science classes?" or "How has the percentage of money going to extracurricular programs changed with time?" Some of these questions may stimulate the need to acquire new data, whereas others may be addressed with available data. With the team, brainstorm these questions and identify the data (and source) required to address them. Again, team members can be assigned specific questions to pursue. As you understand the compliance web more fully, you will see how it naturally leads to questions of organizational performance and the emerging tensions between a leadership agenda focused on mere compliance and one focused on performance.

At some point, summarize your group's progress on compliance analyses and begin to raise questions for performance analyses. You might list all major findings, remaining compliance questions, and pressing performance questions. The difficult part of this stage is sifting through redundancies in the analyses to identify those that best present the compliance condition of the organization.

TABLE 15–2
Compliance Analysis: Inductive Framework

Available Data	Potential Analyses	Tools	Knowledge Gained/ Questions Raised
		PivotTables	
		Charts and graphs	
		Shares and ratios	
		Descriptive statistics	

TABLE 15–3

Performance Analysis: Inductive Framework

Available Data	Potential Analyses	Tools	Knowledge Gained/ Questions Raised
		Correlations	
		Scatterplots	

Performance Analysis

Like compliance analysis, performance analysis consists of both open-ended exploration and question-guided analysis. The primary goal is to identify and characterize linkages (part III) in the data. One useful exploratory step is to perform correlation analyses and scatterplots (Table 15–3). Recall that the goal of correlation analysis is to raise questions. After team members individually prepare data correlation analyses, reconvene the team to identify the following three types of correlations:

1. High correlations that raise interesting questions (e.g., a high correlation between the number of available computers and student math performance)
2. High correlations that represent obvious issues (e.g., a strong inverse relationship between per capita income and percentage of students participating in free and reduced-price lunch programs)
3. Low correlations when you would expect high correlations (e.g., a low correlation between family income and student performance)

At this point, the team should identify and assign key questions to be pursued in the deductive analyses.

Your deductive analyses of linkages should begin with studies of linkages between two variables at a time. You may want to address several questions with scatterplots, using trend lines, R^2 values, and linear and nonlinear equations to characterize linkages. You may also want to perform several group comparisons, t tests, and analyses of variance (ANOVAs) in an effort to discern statistically significant differences in the characteristics of groups (Table 15–4). Recall that group comparisons take the place of scatterplots when one variable is nominal, or categorical. An obvious choice might be a comparison of male and female test scores; a less obvious, but potentially meaningful, comparison

TABLE 15–4

Performance Analysis: Deductive Framework

Questions	Required Data	Analyses/Tools	Knowledge Gained
		Group comparisons	
		Scatterplots	
		Regression analyses	

might be the average family income levels of schools with Internet access and those without Internet access.[1]

You may also construct multiple regression analyses at this stage. Constructing the questions for these analyses should be conducted as a team exercise. Recall that a multiple regression analysis tests the relationship of an independent variable with a dependent variable, given the presence of (or controlling for) other independent variables. One critical task is to organize your equations to avoid redundancy of variables; however, be sure to include all necessary controls. This "specification" problem is why, with time, some regression equations, such as the education production function, have become highly defined. For example, we now know that if we want to study the relationship of fiscal inputs and student outcomes, we must have some measures that use student background characteristics as controls.

Recall that each analysis thus far reveals symptoms of your system that are ultimately related to underlying processes. Now, lay the analyses out on a large table or on the floor and search for story lines, connections, or patterns among the various symptoms you revealed. For example, you can list $x \rightarrow y$ relationships and the strength (R^2) and characteristics (slope, etc.) of these relationships.

Next, consider whether some of your ys (outputs) from one linkage are the xs (inputs) of another. Doing so is the first step of modeling organizational processes. (Refer to chapter 8.) Once you identify several critical paths in your data, begin identifying unknowns. These unknowns may include unmeasurable or unmeasured xs, or "missing links." At this stage, you will hypothesize underlying characteristics of your system on the basis of evidence gathered to this point, using measures of outcomes or symptoms. The next step is to hypothesize a model of the processes themselves.

Dynamics Mapping

Whenever possible, you should map the dynamics of your organization. That is, make use of the tools presented in part IV. All too easily, we can get caught up in the group comparisons and relationship analysis tools discussed primarily in part III. Ultimately, however, you must know not only where your organization is, but also where it is headed.

MODEL-DRIVEN ANALYSES

Organization

In discussing the organization stage, we draw heavily from the work of Andersen and Richardson, who discussed teamwork in *Scripts for Group Model Building* (see Andersen & Richardson, 1994, and Richardson & Andersen, 1995). These authors have experience working with client groups on public policy analyses. In Richardson and Andersen's work,

---

[1]Note that these analyses can be performed by using regression analysis as well by coding binary categorical variables with 1s and 0s such that 1 = yes and 0 = no.

the assumption is that a client group has identified a problem in its organization. A team is convened, including experienced system modeling consultants. We summarize team member roles as described by Richardson and Andersen (1995) as follows:

Facilitator: This person functions as group facilitator and knowledge elicitor. He or she pays constant attention to group process and individual and group roles and elicits knowledge and insights from team members. The person in the facilitator role constantly works with the group to advance the development of the model.

Modeler/Reflector: The person in this role ignores group process and attends to model development. He or she seeks to represent the model graphically, feeds information back to the team, modifies feedback loops, clarifies implicit assumptions that need to be explicit, and seeks to manifest important features of structure and behavior. (Both the facilitator and the modeler/reflector in Richardson and Andersen's experiments were experienced system dynamics modelers, but the person in this role must make do with his or her available skills.)

Process Coach: The person in this role focuses exclusively on group process and need not be a systems modeler. The process coach is largely invisible to the clients but serves to help the facilitator remain sensitive to potentially dysfunctional members and facility behavior.

Recorder: The person in this role documents the progress of the group. With the notes of the modeler/reflector and the notes of the facilitator, the notes and sketches made by the recorder provide a history of the thinking of the group. The recorder does a better job if he or she has prior experience as a modeler.

Gatekeeper: The gatekeeper role represents the client group and carries corporate responsibility for the project. He or she has often initiated it, framed the problem, identified the appropriate participants, and worked with the modeling support team to structure the session. The gatekeeper wears two hats: He or she defends the modeling process to the wider organization, and within the modeling support team he or she keeps the modeling process focused on the organization's problem. The gatekeeper will significantly influence the process and the outcome.

If your team is working on its first school- or district-based analysis, chances are that you lack both the diversity and the depth of team model-building experiences described by Richardson and Andersen. We recommend that you practice these roles to acquire an understanding of how they aid organizational learning. Some suggestions for organizing in-class activities follow.

Modifications for Class Activities and Practice Exercises

We recommend as an in-class exercise that the course instructor assume the role of the gatekeeper, framing the general problem for teams of students. For example, the problem might be finding ways to achieve optimal class size for improving educational productivity in a sustainable and ecologically sound way, as discussed in chapter 14. The course instructor may also assume the role of process coach. Our experience has been that students' early role-playing with group system dynamics modeling should get them directly involved in the modeling process. More distant, process analysis and observational roles are better suited to individuals with more experience with the process. For example, advanced doctoral students could play these roles in support of master's students' work.

Each consulting team of students will then have three role-players: (a) a facilitator, (b) a modeler, and (c) a recorder. The facilitator on each team must keep the team on track in terms of the modeling process. The modeler should posit potential model structures for the problem at hand and respond to feedback from other group participants with appropriate modifications and adaptations. That is, as the conversation among the participants progresses, the modeler is concerned primarily with sketching systems model diagrams that represent group members' ideas about how the system works.

The recorder should diligently take notes on the evolution of ideas but not on the model structure. For example, when, why, and how were specific modifications added to the model? Without this role formalized, a team might be able to trace through their various systems diagrams to find when certain changes were made. However, the team might be at a loss to explain why such changes were made, the original intent of the changes, and whether the rationale for the changes still applies later in the process. The client group can include 3 to 5 students.

Recall from chapter 14 that the modeling process typically consists of four stages: (a) conceptualization, (b) formulation, (c) testing, and (d) implementation. Most in-class modeling activities progress to only the first and second stages. Previously, we discussed some of the details of the first and second stages. Students must gain in-depth experience with the second stage of the process. That is, students must learn to express mathematically both hard and soft modeling concepts generated in in-class activities. Jay W. Forrester, founder of systems dynamics modeling, went to great lengths to emphasize that mental models alone are not sufficient, and we agree with his assessment. As such, the instructor should plan for a modeling process that allows enough time for at least the first two stages. Small groups should present their model conceptualizations to the larger group for feedback. Small groups should also propose a formulation for at least one submodel or feedback loop within their larger model. Ideally, students will be able to use system dynamics software to display the behavior of their submodel (part of the testing phase).

Problem Definition

Your team modeling session should begin with a discussion of key issues raised by your data-driven analyses. When possible, focus on issues for which time-series data are available. Time-series data are important because you ultimately want to model the dynamic behavior (change across time) of your system. Actual measures of the system's behavior across time serve as a guide to the accuracy of your models. Deriving assumptions of the dynamic behavior of a system from cross-sectional data is more speculative.

Andersen and Richardson (1994) recommended spending time up front "defining a reference mode, probing system boundaries, and clarifying purpose, audience, and possible policy levers for solving a possible problem" (p. 8). Team members might engage in a complete-the-graph activity. In this activity, the behavior of a system feature is plotted across time for a defined period. Team members then speculate the continued time path of the measure. For example, you might discuss the expected path of total enrollments in the enrollment model, or the paths of student grade point averages in the escalation archetype described in chapter 13. One team member might suggest that grades will continue escalating until all students receive a perfect average, whereas another member might suggest a rationale for a leveling off in grade inflation. Andersen and Richardson (1994) noted that "discussion of discrepancies over how the time path was completed often yields rich insights into the problem under study" (p. 8).

Conceptualization of the Model Structure

In your "modeling conference," you will likely spend a great deal of time sketching (and erasing) pictures of how your system works. In part V, we presented two approaches to sketching systems models: causal loop diagrams (arrows and signs) and ithink icons. We recommend that in your modeling conference, to avoid confusion and to reduce the number of steps in the process, you sketch your preliminary ideas using ithink icons. Andersen and Richardson (1994) recommended a top-down, model-by-sector approach to conceptualizing the general model structure.

Top-Down Approach

The top-down approach identifies the general model sectors, such as finance and operations, or student learning. Among the initial tasks is to determine the sector boundaries. Once the major sectors and their boundaries are identified, the team, or subgroups within the team, may develop a structure of how a particular sector functions.

Within a sector, the first step is to identify the major stocks and flows. Initially, the team should avoid becoming deeply involved in the full complexity of feedback structures. For example, consider the enrollment model in chapter 14. This model was a simple, unidirectional flow model of students passing through a public school system. An expanded model might infer that increasing dropout rates lead to an overall negative perception of the public schools, which further increases dropout rates in a reinforcing feedback cycle.

Feedback Structures

Andersen and Richardson (1994) pointed out that identifying feedback structures is the "last and most difficult task in conceptualizing model structure" (p. 9). Refer to the system archetype ithink diagrams at the end of chapter 13 for assistance. With the team, walk your way through each template (and others included in Senge's [1990] *The Fifth Discipline*) and discuss how they may or may not be related to behavioral patterns in your organization. You are not likely to find examples of each archetype, but you should find that at least one archetype characterizes a scenario in your organization.

After identifying and sketching feedback cycles, you must consider how these archetypes may be integrated into your larger systems model. Which sectors do they affect? Is the feedback entirely within a sector, or does it involve overlap between sectors? For example, in chapter 14, our New York City model of knowledge and language acquisition included two "within-sector" feedback loops, in which increasing knowledge led to acceleration of further increased knowledge, with an identical reinforcing feedback loop for language acquisition. Similarly, we could include the previous example of reinforcing feedback on dropouts in the enrollment model by making dropouts a separate stock, rather than a converter, with a flow out of the high school population and into the dropout pool that is positively affected by increasing numbers of dropouts. An example of a feedback loop between sectors might be when demographic changes in the community affect public perception of the community, which thus affects property values and ultimately affects school revenues.

Equations and Parameters

Parameter estimation and equation definition takes the most "tweaking" and requires that you move from the drawing board to the modeling environment. Ideally, this stage is performed in a conference room with computer projection as well as workstations, though you can crowd your team members around a single computer monitor if necessary. Andersen and Richardson (1994) suggested a Data Estimation Script:

> Using a marker pen, we code the major stocks, flows, and parameters on the structure diagram(s) with which the group has been working. We then type up a list of all of these key variables and hand it out to the whole team. Using a nominal group technique, we ask the participants to fill in the numerical values for each major variable that they have been discussing for the day. Then all of the estimates from all of the participants are collected and shown. (p. 10)

When quantifying hard data models, you have data with defined scale units. Estimating soft data models requires determining arbitrary scales to apply to specific variables. Recall how we assigned arbitrary whole number values to the Academic Knowledge Acquired stock and the Language Proficiency stock in the New York model. You can, given student assessment data and linkage analyses, quantify these terms with grade-level assessment.

In addition to quantifying the initial values and scales of terms, you must consider the time units of the model. Typically, as used throughout part V, school changes occur during 1-year cycles, though the shifting-the-burden archetype for discipline policies may escalate during a period of weeks or months instead. Use the most appropriate units for your situation.

Preliminary models of individual archetypes should be constructed first. Then, following the data estimation exercise, assign values to model components and test the archetypes individually. You may want to break the team into subgroups to test particular model components. Be sure that the subgroups use compatible scales when the models are merged.

Finally, the team must integrate the model sectors and archetypes and include additional between-sector feedback loops. The model should be tested at each step along the way. Creating multiple versions of the model at varying levels of complexity may be reasonable at times. We recommend doing these as separate model files, unlike in our examples.

ECOLOGICAL ANALYSES

We now move to the final stage of our organizational analysis—ecological analysis. Prior to running simulations, but following basic testing of model behavior, the team must refer to the models and list (a) the exogenous conditions that affect the behavior of the model, and (b) the policy levers that may be manipulated to affect model behavior and outcomes. The *Abbott v. Burke* models in chapter 14 provide a clear example of this approach.

Exogenous Conditions

By this point, you have specified a variety of exogenous conditions in your models. Assigning values to these conditions has required assumptions on your part. In some cases, arbitrary values were assigned so that you could assess whether the model would behave as expected. Now, study the system's behavior under a variety of exogenous conditions. Following is a systematic method for testing scenarios.

First, team members might construct plausible scenarios, or story lines, about the exogenous conditions. We used this approach in the original version of the *Abbott v. Burke* model, in which we described one scenario as Let the Good Times Roll and another as A Slippery Slope. Each refers to a plausible combination of economic and demographic change events that the state legislature could face. Specific parameters are assigned to exogenous conditions that describe each scenario.

A second approach is to let the model choose scenarios for you and to try to manage the system in flight simulator mode. Assign a random number selection to your least certain exogenous conditions, perhaps as converters, that randomly multiply the economy into a period of growth or recession.

Policy Levers

Finally, you must better understand your role as part of the system. You know that some system features are within your control and others are beyond your control. To this point, you focused on the elements beyond your control—the exogenous conditions. Now, identify elements of the system that are within your control—policy levers.

In the real world, adjusting a policy lever is not as simple as tweaking a virtual knob slightly to the left or right. After determining the effects of various leverage applications on the system, team members should address the realities associated with each policy lever. For example, consider the policy levers associated with the *Abbott v. Burke* model: (a) target district (I&J) spending increases, (b) compliance goal, and (c) average state share. Recall that changing the state share affects both the burden on the state budget and the local tax rates required to make up for state shortfalls. Therefore, decreasing the state share as leverage may be economically appealing to the legislature (internal constituents) but not to local taxpayers (external constituents). Because of the external backlash against such an approach, negative political ramifications may occur both internally and externally. You can use a framework, as discussed in chapter 2, to assess your leverage points as policy options (Table 15–5). Similarly, we can identify the costs, utility, benefits, effectiveness, and feasibility (Table 15–6).

TABLE 15–5
Consideration of Policy Option Levers

Policy Lever	Internal			External		
	Economic Feasibility	Political Support	Technical Capacity	Economic Feasibility	Political Support	Technical Capacity
Reduce state share	High	Medium	High	Low	Low	Unknown

TABLE 15–6
Further Parameters to Consider

Policy Lever	Costs	Utility	Benefits	Effectiveness	Feasibility

You may find that evaluating your leverage points leads to extensions of the model that include additional system responses. For example, you may decide that the *Abbott v. Burke* model requires an additional, political dynamics component, whereby policy decisions require consensus building to take root. Or, you may decide to allow the outcomes of some policy decisions. For example, the dramatic increase in local property taxes would result in a dramatic change in the political makeup of the legislature, which would make subsequent decisions to shift the burden to local taxpayers more difficult. The modeling and scenario testing process is an endless game if you allow it to be. Thus, as with each stage of your organizational analysis, you must know when to stop and summarize your findings.

Reconciliation of Discrepancies

One critical step in the summative phase of your organizational analysis is to reflect on the findings from the model-driven analyses and the data-driven analyses. Through the model-driven analyses, you will no doubt reach new levels of speculation about the behavior of your organization, some more realistic than others. You may find patterns of output from your models that support the data-driven analyses, or you may have contradictory findings. Any contradictions should be the basis for in-depth team discussion so that you can determine why the data produced by the organization do not coincide with the theoretical model.

Feedback and Follow-Up

The ecological policy brief is more formative than summative. The first time through an analysis of this type is laborious but worthwhile. You have accumulated a wealth of knowledge about your organization. Subsequent analyses are much easier. First, you and your team are familiar with the process and develop and refine methods that work best in your environmental context. Second, you have developed extensive analytic skills and tools by carrying out the process. Third, you have created organized data structures that can be expanded and modified for subsequent analysis. Fourth, you have acquired baseline data for comparison in subsequent analysis. Finally, you have developed archetypical models of the behavior of your organization that may be extended and reused in future analyses.

The ongoing development of organizational analyses and organizational learning are themselves reinforcing feedback loops. The more you know, the more you need and want to know.

SUMMARY

In this chapter, you learned how to analyze your organization by conducting a series of data-driven, model-driven, and ecological analyses, then assimilating the knowledge you gained. You also learned to be alert for times when collaboration is useful to the analysis and how to assign individuals on your team to particular areas of study. The value of role-playing was discussed, and Andersen and Richardson's (1994) top-down approach to conceptualizing the model structure was reviewed. You learned not only how to incorporate both inductive exploration and deductive hypothesis into your analysis, but also how to identify predictable and uncertain features of the system. In this chapter, you were able to pull together all the tools you developed to this point and use them in analysis of real-world situations. We hope the concepts, tools and models you have learned will lead you to many fruitful hours of your own structured improvisations.

References

Abbott v. Burke, 798 A.2d 602 (N.J. 2002).

Albin, S. (1997). *Building a system dynamics model. Part I: Conceptualization.* Cambridge: Massachusetts Institute of Technology. Retrieved from http://sysdyn.clexchange.org/sdep/Roadmaps/RM8/D-4597.pdf

Andersen, D. F., & Richardson, G. P. (1994). Scripts for group model building. *Proceedings of the 1994 Conference of the System Dynamics Society,* Stirling, Scotland, July 1994.

Argyris, C. (1990). *Overcoming organizational defenses: Facilitating organizational learning.* Boston: Allyn & Bacon.

Baker, B. D., Keller-Wolff, C., & Wolf-Wendel, L. (2000). Two steps forward, one step back: Race/ethnicity and student achievement in education policy research. *Educational Policy, 14*(4), 511–530.

Bankes, S. (1993). Exploratory modeling for policy analysis. *Operations Research, 41*(3), 435–449.

Bateson, G. (1991). *Sacred unity: Further steps to an ecology of mind* (R. E. Donaldson, A. Cornelia, & M. B. Book, Eds.). New York: Harper Collins.

Beer, M. (1980). A social systems model for organizational development. In T. G. Cummings (Ed.), *Systems theory for organization development* (pp. 73–114). New York: Wiley.

Bellinger, G. (n.d.). Archetypes: Interaction structures of the universe. *Mental model musings.* Retrieved September 14, 2002, from http://www.outsights.com/systems/arch/arch.htm

Betts, J. (1996). Is there a link between school inputs and earnings? Fresh scrutiny of an old literature. In G. Burtless (Ed.), *Does money matter?* (pp. 141–191). Washington, DC: Brookings Institution.

Bliss, J. R., Firestone, W. A., & Richards, C. E. (1991). *Rethinking effective schools: Research and practice.* Upper Saddle River, NJ: Prentice Hall.

Bratton, S. E., Jr., Horn, S. P., & Wright, S. P. (1996). *Using and interpreting Tennessee's Value-Added Assessment System: A primer for teachers and principals.* Knoxville, TN: Value-Added Research and Assessment Center, University of Tennessee.

Brewer, D. J., Krop, C., Gill, B. P., & Reichardt, R. (1999). Estimating the cost of national class size reductions under different policy alternatives. *Educational Evaluation and Policy Analysis, 21*(2), 179–192.

Brigham v. State of Vermont. 692 A.2d 384 (1997).

Bromley, H., & Jacobson, S. (1998). Technology and change in school administrator preparation. In K. Westbrook (Ed.), *Technology and the educational workplace* (pp. 127–149). Newbury Park, CA: Corwin Press.

Bryk, A. S., & Raudenbush, S. (1992). *Hierarchical linear models.* Newbury Park, CA: Sage.

Clauset, K. H., & Gaynor, A. K. (1982). A systems perspective on effective schools. *Educational Leadership, 40*(3), 54–59.

Coleman, J. S., Campbell, E. Q., Hobson, C. J., McPartland, J., Mood, A. M., Weinfeld, F. D., et al. (1966). *Equality of educational opportunity.* Washington, DC: U.S. Government Printing Office.

Cronbach, L. J. (1982). *Designing evaluations of educational and social programs.* San Francisco: Jossey-Bass.

CSR Research Consortium. (2000). *Class size reduction in California: The 1998–99 evaluation findings.* Palo Alto, CA: Author.

Cuban, L., & Tyack, D. (1993). *Tinkering toward utopia: A century of public school reform.* Cambridge, MA: Harvard University Press.

Culbertson, J. A. (1988). A century's quest for a knowledge base. In N. J. Boyan (Ed.), *Handbook of research on educational administration* (pp. 3–26). New York: Longman.

Darling-Hammond, L. (2000). Teacher quality and student achievement: A review of state policy evidence. *Education Policy Analysis Archives, 8*(1). Available at http://epaa.asu.edu/epaa/v8n1/

Deming, E. (1993). *The new economics.* Cambridge, MA: MIT Press.

Edgewood Independent School District v. Kirby, 777 S.W.2d 391 (1989).

Eisner, E. W. (1991). *The enlightened eye: Qualitative inquiry and the enhancement of educational practice.* New York: Macmillan.

Figlio, D. N. (1999). Functional form and the estimated effects of school resources. *Economics of Education Review, 18*(1), 241–252.

Finn, J. D., & Achilles, C. M. (1999). Tennessee's Class Size Study: Findings, implications, misconceptions. *Educational Evaluation and Policy Analysis, 21*(2), 97–109.

Gerald, D., & Hussar, W. (1996). *Projections of education statistics to 2006* (Publication No. NCES 96661). Washington, DC: National Center for Education Statistics, U.S. Department of Education.

Goldberg, B., & Sifonis, J. G. (1994). *Dynamic planning: The art of managing beyond tomorrow*. New York: Oxford University Press.

Goldhaber, D., & Brewer, D. (1996). Evaluating the effect of teacher degree level on educational performance. In W. Fowler (Ed.), *Developments in school finance* (pp. 197–210). Washington, DC: National Center for Education Statistics.

Goldhaber, D. D., & Brewer, D. J. (2000). Does teacher certification matter? High school teacher certification status and student achievement. *Educational Evaluation and Policy Analysis, 22*(2), 129–146.

Goodwin, B. (1994). *How the leopard got its spots: The evolution of complexity*. New York: Scribner's.

Griffiths, D. (1988). Administrative theory. In N. J. Boyan (Ed.), *Handbook of research on educational administration* (pp. 27–52). New York: Longman.

Hanushek, E. A. (1996). School resources and student performance. In G. Burtless (Ed.), *Does money matter?* (pp. 43–73). Washington, DC: Brookings Institution.

Hanushek, E. A. (1999). Some findings from an independent investigation of the Tennessee STAR experiment and from other investigations of class size effects. *Educational Evaluation and Policy Analysis, 21*(2), 143–163.

Harvey, G. (2003). *Excel 2003 for Dummies*. New York: Wiley.

Hedges, L., & Greenwald, R. (1996). Have times changed? The relation between school resources and student performance. In G. Burtless (Ed.), *Does money matter?* (pp. 74–92). Washington, DC: Brookings Institution.

Holland, J. (1995). *Hidden order: How adaptation builds complexity*. Reading, MA: Addison-Wesley.

Kofman, F., & Senge, P. (1993, Autumn). Communities of commitment: The heart of learning organizations. *Organizational Dynamics, 22*(2), 5–23.

Leakey, R., & Lewin, R. (1995). *The sixth extinction*. New York: Doubleday.

Lempert, R., Schlesinger, M., & Bankes, S. (1996). *When we don't know the costs and benefits: Adaptive strategies for abating climate change* (Document No. RAND/RP-557). Santa Monica, CA: RAND.

Levin, H. M. (1983). *Cost effectiveness: A primer*. Thousand Oaks, CA: Sage.

Levin, H. M., & McEwan, P. J. (2001). *Cost-effectiveness analysis* (2nd ed.). Thousand Oaks, CA: Sage.

Lewin, R. (1992). *Complexity: Life at the edge of chaos*. New York: Macmillan.

Makridakis, S. G. (1990). *Forecasting, planning & strategy for the 21st century*. New York: Free Press.

Marsick, V., & Watkins, K. (1999). *Facilitating learning organizations: Making learning count*. Brookfield, VT: Gower.

Mock v. State of Kansas, 91CV1009 (Shawnee County District Court, slip. op. Oct. 14, 1991).

Naess, A. (1989). *Ecology, community and lifestyle* (D. Rothenberg, Trans.). Cambridge, UK: Cambridge University Press.

National Policy Board for Educational Administration. (1993). *Principles for our changing schools: The knowledge and skill base*. Fairfax, VA: Author.

Nye, B., Hedges, L., & Konstantopoulos, S. (1999). The long-term effects of small classes: A five-year follow-up of the Tennessee Class Size Experiment. *Educational Evaluation and Policy Analysis, 21*(2), 127–142.

Organization for Economic Cooperation and Development. (1999). *Education at a glance*. Paris: Author.

Paulsen, G. (1987). *Hatchet*. New York: Simon & Schuster.

Penrose, R. (1994). *Shadows of the mind*. London: Oxford University Press.

Popper, C. (1959). *The logic of scientific discovery*. New York: Basic Books.

Randers, J. (Ed.). (1980). *Elements of the system dynamics method*. Cambridge: Massachusetts Institute of Technology Press.

Richards, C. (1987). *Microcomputer applications for strategic management in education: A case study approach*. New York: Longman.

Richards, C. E., & Sheu, T. M. (1992). South Carolina's school incentive program: A policy analysis. *Economics of Education Review, 11*(1), 71–86.

Richardson, G. P. (1992). *Feedback thought in social science and systems theory*. Philadelphia: University of Pennsylvania Press.

Richardson, G. P., & Andersen, D. F. (1995). Teamwork in group model building. *Systems Dynamics Review, 11*(2), 113–137.

Richmond, B., & Peterson, S. (1996). *STELLA: An introduction to systems thinking*. Hanover, NH: High Performance Systems. (Accompanies computer software ithink, Version 4.0)

Robinson v. Cahill, 303 A.2d 273 (N.J. 1973).

Russell, P. (1995). *The global brain awakens: Our next evolutionary leap*. Palo Alto, CA: Global Brain.

Ryan, F. (2002). *Darwin's blind spot*. Boston: Houghton Mifflin.

Sanders, W. L., & Rivers, J. C. (1996). *Cumulative and residual effects of teachers on future student academic achievement*. Knoxville, TN: University of Tennessee Value-Added Research and Assessment Center.

Sarason, S. (1996). *Revisiting the culture of the school and the problem of change*. New York: Teachers College Press.

Schein, E. (1992). *Organizational culture and leadership*. San Francisco: Jossey-Bass.

Schreckengost, R. C. (1985). *Dynamic simulation models: How valid are they?* (DHHS Publication No. 85-1402). Washington, DC: U.S. Government Printing Office. Retrieved from http://sysdyn.clexchange.org/sdep/Roadmaps/RM5/D-4463.pdf

Scott, R. W. (1981). *Organizations: Rational, natural, and open systems*. Upper Saddle River, NJ: Prentice Hall.

Senge, P. (1990). *The fifth discipline: The art and practice of the learning organization*. New York: Doubleday.

Sheldrake, R. (1995). *Seven experiments that could change the world*. New York: Riverhead Books.

Simon, H. (1957). *Models of man: Social and rational*. New York: Wiley.

Sterman, J. (2000). *Business dynamics: Systems thinking and modeling for a complex world*. Boston: Irwin/McGraw-Hill.

Thompson, D., Honeyman, D., & Wood, R. C. (1994). The Kansas School District Equalization Act: A study of fiscal equity of funding categories. *Journal of Education Finance, 19*(1), 36–68.

Vandaele, W. G. (1983). *Applied time series and Box–Jenkins models*. New York: Academic Press.

WestEd. (1999). *Class size reduction: Great hopes, great challenges* (Policy Brief). San Francisco: Author.

Wilson, E. O. (1971). *The social insects*. Cambridge, MA: Harvard University Press.

Zohar, D., & Marshall, I. (1994). *The quantum society: Mind, physics, and a new social vision*. New York: Quill/Morrow.

Name Index

Subject Index